THE ULTIMATE FAMILY QUIZ BOOK

First published in 2005 by Miles Kelly Publishing Ltd
Bardfield Centre, Great Bardfield, Essex, CM7 4SL

Copyright © Miles Kelly Publishing Ltd 2005

Some material in *The Ultimate Family Quiz Book* was first published
by Miles Kelly Publishing © 2003

2 4 6 8 10 9 7 5 3 1

Publishing Director: Anne Marshall
Editorial Director: Belinda Gallagher
Project Editor: Amanda Learmonth
Assistant Editor: Nicola Sail
Editorial Assistants: Lisa Clayden, Amanda Askew
Picture Research Manager: Liberty Newton
Designers: Debbie Meekcoms, Tom Slemmings
Proofreader: Ann Kay

ISBN 1-84236-639-4

Printed in China

British Library Cataloguing-in-Publication Data
A catalogue record for this book is available from the British Library

www.mileskelly.net

info@mileskelly.net

The publishers would like to thank the following sources for the use of their photographs:
Page 32 (B/C) Twentieth Century Fox/Pictorial Press; 52 (B/R) Sony Computer Entertainment;
61 (T/R) Sony Computer Entertainment; (B/L) Entertainment/Cinergi/Robert Stigwood/Dirty
Hands/Pictorial Press; 69 (T/R) Universal/DreamWorks/Scott Free/Pictorial Press;
72 (B/C) TCF/Icon/Ladd/Pictorial Press; 80 (R/C) UIP/Paramount/LucasFilm/Pictorial Press;
82 (B/R) Rank/Parkfield/Pictorial Press; 88 (B/R) Warner Bros/J.K.R/Pictorial Press;
96 (T/R) Buena Vista/Walt Disney/Pictorial Press; 102 (B/C) Sony Computer Entertainment;
109 (T/R) Pictorial Press; 114 (B/C) Buena Vista/Walt Disney/Jim Henson;
138 (B/L) Twentieth Century Fox/Pictorial Press; 139 Pictorial Press;
170 (B/R) Universal/Pictorial Press; 181 (B/R) Warner/Castle Rock/Pictorial Press;
195 (B/C) Pictorial Press

All other pictures from: CASE, Castrol, Corel, Digital Vision, digitalSTOCK,
FlatEarth; Hemera, ILN, PhotoAlto, PhotoDisc, Stockbyte

The publishers would like to thank the following artists for contributing to this book:
Syd Brak, John Butler, Steve Caldwell, Martin Camm, Vanessa Card, Jim Channel, Peter Dennis,
Richard Draper, Wayne Ford, Nicholas Forder, Chris Forsey, Mike Foster/Maltings Partnership,
Terry Gabbey, Luigi Galante, Terry Grose, Alan Harris, Sally Holmes, Richard Hook, Ian Jackson,
Rob Jakeway, John James, Mick Loates, Janos Marffy, Andrea Morandi, Helen Parsley, Roger Payne,
Gill Platt, Terry Riley, Steve Roberts, Martin Sanders, Peter Sarson, Mike Saunders, Susan Scott,
Rob Sheffield, Ted Smart, Guy Smith, Sarah Smith, Gwen Touret, Rudi Vizi, Mike White

Introduction

Why do people enjoy quizzes so much? Is it because there's something quite special about answering a really tough question correctly, especially if there are lots of people there to witness it? Is it because quizzes make us more competitive, bringing out that burning desire to win? Or is it because they can help improve our mental agility? Whatever the reason, people love to take part in quizzes.

Which tree provided the main wood for English naval ships in the 18th century?

See page 251 for the answer

The Ultimate Family Quiz Book has something for everyone. There are more than 4000 questions covering ten subject areas. The book is divided into five levels of difficulty. Level 1 is perfect for children as the picture clues and background images will help them to answer correctly, or keep them, and you, guessing. Level 5 is not for the faint-hearted!

You can play in pairs, in teams, or individually. Pick a topic to concentrate on, or choose subjects that people are good at (or pick those they know little about!). However you use your book, have fun. The answers at the back will solve any disputes, and remember this isn't just a quiz book, it's an amazing source of knowledge.

The tubing of which brass instrument is curved into circles?

See page 235 for the answer

Contents

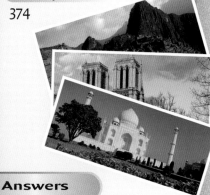

How to use

Your book is split into five levels that become progressively more difficult. Each level is in turn divided into nine sessions. The quiz panels contain questions from different subject areas listed below. Whether music is your thing, or you're a natural movie buff, *The Ultimate Family Quiz Book* has something for everyone. Answers to all of the quizzes can be found at the back of the book.

Questions
Ten questions appear within each quiz.

Subject Areas
Your book is divided into ten subject areas from which you can select the quizzes that you are most interested in. Each subject is represented by its own tint.

Quiz Numbers
Each quiz is clearly numbered. There are 438 quizzes in total.

Global Matters

Great and Famous

Lights, Camera, Action!

Making History

Music Mania

Natural Selection

Scientifically Speaking

Sporting Chance

Total Trivia

Written Word

THE FAMILY QUIZ BOOK

52

83 Natural Selection

1 Which birds have strong talons and hook-shaped beaks: waders or birds of prey?
2 Which lays its eggs in water: the newt or the lizard?
3 What is a scorpion: an insect or arachnid?
4 Which small rodent famously has a weakness for cheese?
5 Is ebony wood very light or very heavy?
6 What sort of yellow bird is the cartoon character Tweetie Pie?
7 Did plant-eating dinosaurs walk mainly on two or four legs?
8 Which are larger: stag beetles or rhinoceros beetles?
9 Do clams live in sandy seabeds or attached to seaweed?
10 Does the marine otter live on land or at sea?

Question 4

★ BACKGROUND BONUS ★
Which plant is thought to bring good luck if you find one with four leaves?

84 Total Trivia

1 Which island is at the southern tip of Italy?
2 Who are the infantry?
3 The Chinese were making ice cream some 5,000 years ago: true or false?
4 What people wrote in hieroglyphics?
5 Which creature did St. George slay?
6 What is the capital of Germany?
7 What is another word for unite?
8 In The Simpsons, what is the name of Mr. Burns' aide?
9 What shape is a cylinder?
10 What is marine algae?

Question 5

Picture Clues
Each quiz has one picture clue. The question number to which it relates appears beside it.

Levels and Sessions
The book runs from Level 1 to Level 5. Each right-hand page tells you exactly which level and session you are in.

51 Written Word

1 Is the word fish a noun, a verb or both?
2 What is the silent letter in the word psychiatrist?
3 The cunning fox escaped from the hounds by hiding up a tree. Which word is the adjective?
4 How many vowels does the word vowels have?
5 What is the past tense of the word shoot?
6 Which three-letter word can precede ring, stone and hole?
7 Which Shakespeare play is commonly referred to as the Scottish play?
8 In the Roald Dahl story, which giant fruit did James sail in?
9 Which five-letter M word is given to the grinding teeth at the back of your mouth?
10 What term is used for setting fire to property on purpose?

Question 8

52 Natural Selection

1 Which has the keenest eyesight: eagle, duck or ostrich?
2 Which species of snake shares its name with a Cuban dance?
3 Does the sea anemone catch food with jaws or tentacles?
4 Is an albino animal white, black or brown?
5 Do vultures hover or soar in circles?
6 Which are taller: foxgloves or bluebells?
7 Leech, scorpion, chameleon: which is the reptile?
8 Which appeared first on Earth: spiders or dinosaurs?
9 Elephant, hippo, camel: which usually lives longest?
10 Are baby dolphins born on beaches or underwater?

Question 1

★ BACKGROUND BONUS ★
What birds are pink due to the shrimps and algae that they eat?

53 Scientifically Speaking

1 What kind of clock measures time by the Sun?
2 What is another name for perspiration?
3 What is the name for pieces of ice falling from clouds?
4 On a 24-hour digital clock, what numbers are displayed at 11:45 pm?
5 What is the name of our galaxy?
6 Which invention was first called a phonograph?
7 What part of your body works like a pump?
8 Which word describes how loud a sound is?
9 How many degrees is half a turn?
10 How many sides has an octagon?

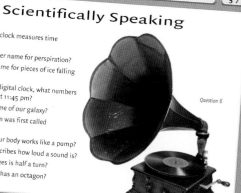
Question 6

54 Total Trivia

1 *Vespa* is the Italian word for which insect?
2 What grew in length when the puppet boy Pinocchio told lies?
3 What is apiphobia a fear of?
4 What is the more common name for the capsicum?
5 Which shark is named after the shape of its head and is also the name of a tool?
6 What is the only dog breed to have a blue-black tongue?
7 Which is the lightest planet in our Solar System?
8 What is known as the Red Planet?
9 Who was the first woman mentioned in the Bible?
10 What kind of reptile is a basilisk?

Question 4

Background Bonus
There is a background bonus question on each spread. The large background image behind the panels gives you a clue to the answer.

Tinted Panels
The tinted panels relate to the subject areas. For example, pink panels hold Total Trivia quizzes. See left for the list of subject areas and their tints.

Picture Quizzes
Look out for the picture quizzes. These are pages dedicated to photographic quizzes. The answers are at the back of the book.

1 Total Trivia

1 What work did the Seven Dwarfs do?

2 What is mutton: calf meat, sheep meat or lamb meat?

3 In which country is the city of Bombay situated?

4 Are modern British fire engines green, red or black?

5 Which magical character emerged from Aladdin's lamp?

6 Cirrus and cumulus are examples of what kind of natural feature?

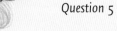

Question 5

7 What natural substance is chocolate made from?

8 What does a thermometer measure?

9 What is the modern name of the Roman port of *Londinium*?

10 Is a cello a stringed or a wind instrument?

2 Natural Selection

1 Which moth has a skull-like shape on its back?

2 Do albatrosses spend most time in the air or on land?

3 Which has bigger leaves: a banana tree or a horse chestnut tree?

4 Jaguar, cheetah, lion, tiger: which cools off in rivers?

5 Is a yak a hairy ape or an ox-like animal?

6 Is the world's smallest bird a wren or a hummingbird?

7 What animal is the longest-living of all vertebrates?

8 When birds preen are they feeding, feather-cleaning or singing?

9 Which snake's head can be as big as a human's: the king cobra or vine snake?

10 What do you call a baby goose?

Question 7

★ **BACKGROUND BONUS** ★
What kind of animal is a gannet?

3   Sporting Chance

1   In boxing, what does TKO stand for?

2   How many lanes are there in an Olympic-sized swimming pool?

3   What baseball team plays at Wrigley Field?

4   What sport features a quarterback?

5   In which sport can you throw a curve ball?

6   How many events make up a biathlon?

7   What animal print is on the shorts worn by boxer Prince Naseem?

8   In which sport do England and Australia compete to win the Ashes?

9   Ralf and Michael Schumacher are famous names in which sport?

10 What is the first shot in a tennis rally called?

Question 5

4   Making History

1   What was the Colosseum in Rome used for?

2   Which World War II German general was nicknamed The Desert Fox?

3   This country was once called Siam: what is its modern name?

4   Explorers in South America caught and ate cavies: what are cavies?

5   What is an ammonite: a metal, a fossil or a kind of tree?

6   What were U-boats?

7   What were pieces of eight?

8   Which country used Zero fighters during World War II?

9   Who is the odd one out of these three leaders: Truman, Macmillan, Bush?

10 Against whom did Richard the Lionheart fight in the Crusades?

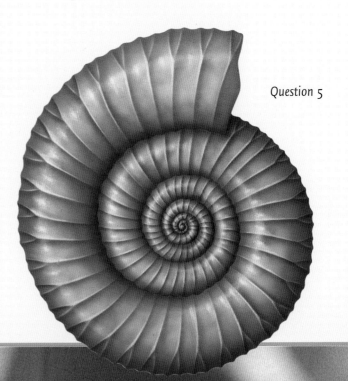

Question 5

5 Making History

1. Which queen of England ruled from 1837 to 1901?

2. If sailors suffered from the disease scurvy, what vitamin did they lack?

3. Which country celebrates its independence on 4th July?

4. Of which country was Helmut Kohl leader until 1998?

5. What was the first living creature sent into space in 1957: a dog or a monkey?

6. What did Caligula, Augustus and Titus all have in common?

7. Was Columbus born in Spain or Italy?

8. Was a pike a long, spearlike weapon or a helmet with a spike on top?

9. In 1642, Abel Tasman landed on a new island that he called Van Diemen's Land. What is it called now?

10. Which Indian leader was known as the Mahatma or "Great Soul"?

Question 8

★ **BACKGROUND BONUS** ★
What kind of places of worship were built by some ancient American civilizations?

6 Sporting Chance

1. On what surface is the Wimbledon Tennis Championship played?

2. What does a boxing referee count to, to signify a knockout?

3. Which sport is sometimes called ping-pong?

4. What is Canada's national sport?

5. In which sport do you wear either quad or in-line skates?

6. What kind of race is the Tour de France?

7. What shape is a boxing ring?

8. In which sport do you putt the ball?

9. On a chessboard, what piece is also a member of the clergy?

10. In tennis, what is the score when an umpire calls deuce?

Question 5

7   Natural Selection

1. Rockhopper, macaroni and emperor are all types of which bird?
2. What is a squirrel's nest called?
3. Bactrian and dromedary are types of what?
4. Which dog is known as a sausage dog?
5. Sponge, coral, kelp: which is the plant?
6. What is a group of leopards called: a pod or a leap?
7. Tent-building, vampire and hog-nosed are all types of which animal?
8. Which large bird builds an eyrie as a nest?
9. What do you call a female goat?
10. Do herons nest in trees or in floating plants?

Question 4

8   Scientifically Speaking

1. What is the name for the curved glass in spectacles?
2. What black powder did the Chinese invent to make fireworks?
3. What is 50 percent of 80?
4. Which G word describes the force that pulls objects to the middle of the Earth?
5. Which of these numbers is not exactly divisible by 7: 7, 17, 21, 14, 28?
6. What would you lose if you had laryngitis?
7. What in space is an enormous collection of stars?
8. Is crimson deep red or light blue?
9. Is a bathyscaphe used to explore underground, under the sea or outer space?
10. What is the remainder when 26 is divided by 3?

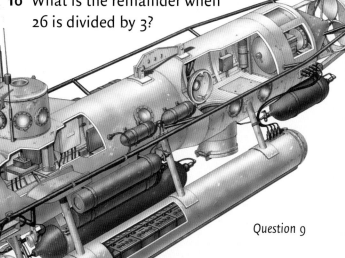

Question 9

9   Scientifically Speaking

1   What do vaccinations protect you from?

2   Does electricity flow through metal or rubber?

3   Which children's toy uses a spring to make it jump out of its box?

4   What is 532 + 629 + 423?

5   Are the letters on a computer keyboard lower case or upper case?

6   What do we call the imaginary points at either end of the Earth?

7   Which part of your body has a palm?

8   In which continent would you find zebras and elephants?

9   What is 0.25 as a fraction?

10 What is the name of the unit used for measuring the loudness or intensity of sound?

Question 3

★ **BACKGROUND BONUS** ★
What natural occurrence is called a tsunami?

10   Total Trivia

1   What does Popeye eat for strength?

2   Which part of an aircraft is the fuselage?

3   How many blackbirds were baked in a pie?

4   Which limbs of the *Venus de Milo* sculpture are missing?

5   Which animal is usually ridden in the desert?

6   What is agoraphobia a fear of?

7   Which of these numbers can be divided by both 3 and 4: 9, 12, 15, 16?

8   Joseph Barbera and William Hannah created which cat and mouse duo?

9   What is the missing number: 18 x ? = 180

10 Is Robin Hood associated with blue or green?

Question 5

Spot the Sport

11

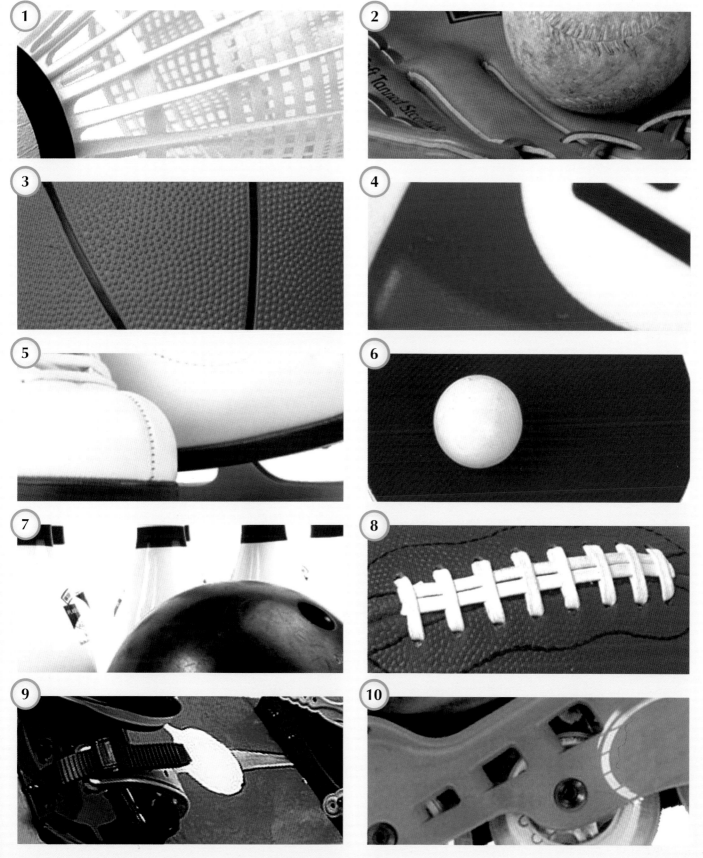

Can you identify the sports that these objects relate to?

12 Total Trivia

1. What is the opposite of the word brave?
2. The date is 10 May. What will the date be in two weeks' time?
3. What does the French word *légume* mean in English?
4. What is one-quarter of a half?
5. What does a biologist study?
6. What is the plural of sheep?
7. Frog spawn, tadpole. What comes next?
8. By what title is the Bishop of Rome also known?
9. What does the Roman numeral V equal?
10. Which sport would you learn on nursery slopes?

Question 3

> **★ BACKGROUND BONUS ★**
> Grevy's and Burchell's are two species
> of what kind of animal?

13 Written Word: The Bible

1. What creature tempted Eve to disobey God?
2. What did God ask Abraham to do to his son Isaac?
3. What were the Ten Commandments written on?
4. Which special food did the Israelites eat in the desert after they had escaped from Egypt?
5. What did Jesus do with five loaves and two small fishes?
6. What is the name of the town where Jesus grew up?
7. Who climbed a tree so that he could get a better view of Jesus?
8. What was King Solomon famous for?
9. Who ruled Palestine at the time of Jesus?
10. How many Gospels are there?

Question 1

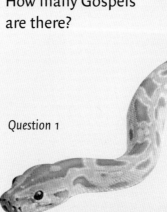

14   Great and Famous

1   Was the composer Frédéric Chopin English, French, Italian or Polish?

2   For which sport did Michael Jordan become famous?

3   Thor Heyerdahl sailed on a raft from Polynesia to which country: Peru, Australia or the United States?

4   By what nickname is Emma Bunton better known?

5   Who wrote the music for *The Lion King*: George Michael, Sheryl Crow, Andrew Lloyd-Webber or Elton John?

6   Which Italian dictator was known as *Il Duce*?

7   Jacques Cousteau is associated with what sort of exploration: undersea or rainforest?

8   Stanley Gibbons was a dealer in which collectable item?

9   Which Judy played Dorothy in the movie version of *The Wizard of Oz*?

10 Annie Mae Bullock is the real name of which hugely successful U.S. singer?

Question 8

15   Scientifically Speaking

1   What does not have a tail: a kite, a boat or a jet?

2   What instrument is used for drawing circles?

3   Does a meteorologist study meteorites, the ocean or the weather?

4   Which planet is nearest the Sun?

5   How many seconds in three minutes?

6   What is the joint that lets you bend your arm?

7   What part of your body wrinkles when you frown?

8   In which direction does a compass needle point?

9   If you had hayfever, what would you be allergic to?

10 Where would you find your calf muscle?

Question 9

16 Global Matters

1 What is the alternative name for the Netherlands?

2 In which continent does the country of Croatia lie?

3 What is the capital city of Peru: Bogotá, Lima or Quito?

4 AK is the abbreviation for which U.S. state?

5 What does the D stand for in Washington D.C.?

6 What is the highest mountain in the United Kingdom?

7 What is the world's largest island?

8 In which country are the cities Seville and Madrid?

9 Which gemstone provides part of Ireland's nickname?

10 Is Greenland north or south of the Equator?

Question 7

> ★ **BACKGROUND BONUS** ★
> What is the name of the steplike terrain on which rice is grown?

17 Natural Selection

1 Was the dodo a bird or a kind of deer?

2 Do snakes have two teeth or many teeth?

3 Is ivy a tree, a climber or a bush?

4 Do leopards store prey in trees or underground?

5 What common natural event can cause forest fires?

6 Does the praying mantis chase its prey or ambush it?

7 Which tree-living rodent with a fluffy tail mainly eats conifer seeds?

8 With which part of their body do anteaters collect termites?

9 Does the European wildcat live in thick woodlands or open meadows?

10 Which of these is the largest cat: bobcat, cougar or tiger?

Question 6

18 Scientifically Speaking

1 What has hands, a face and wheels?

2 What did Clarence Birdseye invent in 1924?

3 What is the name of a giant block of ice floating in the sea?

4 Why is blinking good for your eyes?

5 What are the two passages in your nose called?

6 What is the layer of air around the Earth called?

7 On a compass, which direction is opposite east?

8 What is the name for walls of rock that go down to the sea?

9 How many seconds are there in one and a half minutes?

10 What is the total of three 3s and seven 4s?

Question 3

19 Sporting Chance: Soccer

1 Which Scottish soccer club does Rangers play in the Old Firm derby?

2 In which country does the soccer team Bordeaux play its home matches?

3 Which Paulo pushed a soccer referee over: Di Canio, Maldini or Wanchope?

4 What is the name of the only Scottish soccer league team beginning with K?

5 In a soccer penalty shoot-out, how many penalties does each side take before sudden death begins?

6 In which English city does the soccer team Aston Villa play its home matches?

7 In which European country are the headquarters of FIFA?

8 What country, which shares its name with a bird, was knocked out of the 2002 World Cup semi-finals?

9 In which Scottish city does Celtic play its home matches?

10 Royal and Woolwich were formerly part of the name of which London soccer club?

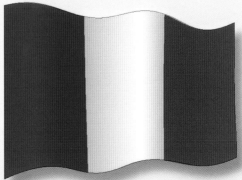

Question 2

20 Natural Selection

1. Which of these fish is striped: herring, mackerel or trout?
2. Do grasshoppers jump and fly, or only jump?
3. Shark, dolphin, salmon: which breathes in air using lungs?
4. Cookie-cutter and basking are types of which animal?
5. Which part of a tree dies in winter?
6. The blue poison-dart is what kind of animal?
7. Thrush, pheasant, goose: which is the smallest?
8. What creature sat down beside Little Miss Muffet?
9. Do dogs keep cool by panting or sweating?
10. Where do giant squid live?

Question 6

21 Making History

1. The people of which ancient classical civilization wore togas?
2. Which composer went deaf in his later years?
3. Which ancient peoples devised the 365-day calendar?
4. How many voyages did Columbus make to the Americas: one, two, three or four?
5. What country did Napoleon invade in 1812?
6. When did Euclid write *Elements of Geometry*, one of the most influential mathematics books ever: 1300BC, 300BC or AD12?
7. What was the nickname of the U.S. Confederate General, Thomas Jackson?
8. When was gunpowder first used in battle in Europe: 1346, 1446 or 1546?
9. Which Scottish king killed King Duncan, but was himself killed by Duncan's son, Malcolm III?
10. Which king ordered the Domesday Book to be made in England?

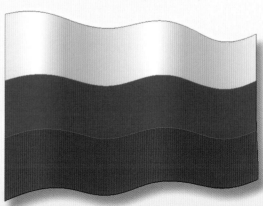

Question 5

22 Lights, Camera, Action!

1 Which sport featured in the movie *The Natural*?

2 What was the title of the 1990 movie sequel to *Three Men and a Baby*?

3 Who plays the central character in the TV show *Malcolm in the Middle*?

4 According to Mary Poppins, how much did it cost to feed the birds?

5 Name Mickey Mouse's pet dog.

6 In the *Bugs Bunny* cartoons, is Yosemite Sam's beard black, red or white?

7 What type of creature is Willy in the *Free Willy* movies?

8 Which edible onions are also the name of the central family in *Rugrats*?

9 Who played Cruella de Vil in the 1996 movie *One Hundred and One Dalmatians*?

10 In the movie *Jimmy Neutron*, what piece of kitchen equipment is made into a satellite?

Question 7

★ **BACKGROUND BONUS** ★
Which Los Angeles district is central to the TV and movie industries?

23 Total Trivia

1 Is a mandolin a stringed instrument or a keyboard instrument?

2 How many fiddlers had Old King Cole?

3 What is claustrophobia a fear of?

4 In 1993 who became the 42nd president of the United States?

5 Where is the bow of a ship?

6 Which bird lays the largest egg?

7 *Costa* is the Spanish word for what?

8 What is Holland's national flower?

9 In which African country is Tripoli?

10 Where is the city of Turin?

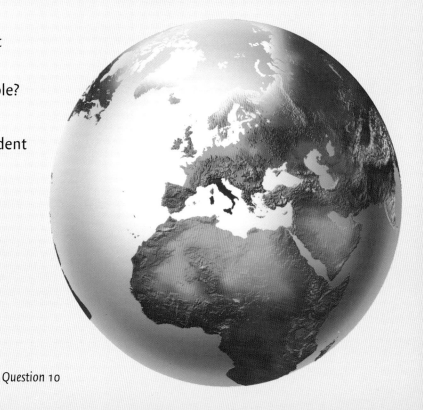

Question 10

24 Total Trivia

1 What currency is used in France?

2 Which tree does an acorn come from?

3 What are forget-me-nots and marigolds examples of?

4 What is another name for a microprocessor in a computer?

5 What is 7 less than 3,000?

6 What is an ingot?

7 Which dinosaur had large, upright plates on its back?

8 Which games, held every four years, first took place in ancient Greece?

9 What are winkle-pickers: farmers, a type of shoe or a type of food?

10 Handel, Mozart and Brahms were all what?

Question 7

25 Music Mania

1 A fanfare is a short piece of ceremonial music played on which instrument?

2 What instrument is often called a squeeze box?

3 What is the title of the Spice Girls' first U.K. No. 1 hit?

4 What is the last name of the singing sisters Dannii and Kylie?

5 Which singer and actress sometimes abbreviates her name to J-Lo?

6 In the video for the Robbie Williams hit "Angels", does he ride a horse or a motorbike?

7 Which hip-gyrating singer appears as himself in the movie *Mars Attacks*?

8 Which animated movie about a green ogre climaxes with a karaoke session?

9 What is the first name of John Travolta's character in the movie *Grease*?

10 Are cymbals a percussion or brass instrument?

Question 2

★ BACKGROUND BONUS ★
In the 1970s and 1980s, which kind of music sparked up a fashion for crazy spiked hair?

26 Sporting Chance

1 How many minutes long is a round in boxing?

2 In which sport do athletes throw a spearlike object?

3 Which watersport was originally called soccer-in-water?

4 Which fruit is traditionally eaten with cream at the Wimbledon Tennis Championships?

5 In which of the following sports is a volley not allowed: tennis, table tennis or badminton?

6 In what park does the New York Marathon finish?

7 From where does kendo originate?

8 In which sport do competitors travel on a skeleton?

9 In baseball, what is a "dinger"?

10 Describe the flag that is waved in Formula One racing when a driver crosses the finishing line.

Question 10

27 Making History

1 Which country built the *Nautilus*, the world's first nuclear submarine?

2 When was the first microscope invented: 1230, 1590 or 1750?

3 Which Italian artist painted the roof of the Sistine Chapel in Italy?

4 In which year was the first pistol made: 1540, 1680 or 1810?

5 The mythical monster, the minotaur, is a man with the head of what: a lion, a bull or an eagle?

6 What weapon did jousting knights use when on horseback?

7 For what did the ancient Egyptians use a *shaduf*: moving stones or raising water?

8 What was a dragoon: a foot-soldier or a horse-soldier?

9 Which Greek conqueror founded the Egyptian city of Alexandria?

10 What was the name of the winged horse in Greek legend?

Question 7

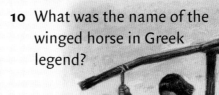

28 Natural Selection

1 What is the name given to a female pig?

2 Which big cat lives the longest: the lion, the panther or the tiger?

3 What do we call the claw of a bird of prey?

4 In which part of its body does a koala keep its young?

5 What body part does a fish breathe through?

6 What is a great bustard: a bird or a fish?

7 Which creature has the largest eye in the animal kingdom?

8 What is a lacewing: a bird or an insect?

9 Which horse-like animal has a reputation for being stubborn?

10 Do sand vipers live on beaches or in deserts?

Question 8

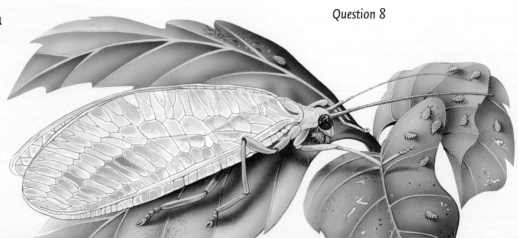

29 Total Trivia

1 Which fleet of ships tried to invade England in 1588?

2 What is the name of Donald Duck's girlfriend?

3 The tubing of which brass instrument is curved into circles?

4 In a desert, what is an area where water is found and plants grow called?

5 What is a thatched roof made from?

6 What shape is the base of a pyramid?

7 Which country has the largest population in the world?

8 What kind of bird is Captain Flint in *Treasure Island*?

9 Is a chameleon a mammal, marsupial or reptile?

10 What is a group of lions called?

Question 3

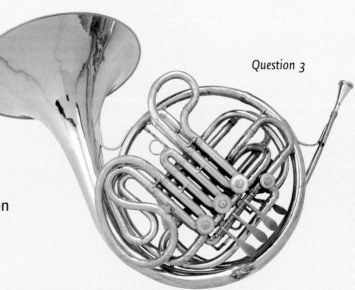

30   Making History

1   Where was the empire ruled by Akbar the Great?

2   Which planet, also the Roman god of the sea, was first seen in 1846?

3   On which river was Rome built?

4   What was a penny farthing?

5   Was a Tin Lizzie an early car or an early washing machine?

6   Which ocean did explorers cross to reach India from East Africa?

7   What was a Roman soldier in charge of 100 men called?

8   In 1868, which European country held the first cycle race?

9   In World War I, what was a Sopwith Camel?

10   Who was the king of the Roman gods?

Question 4

31   Sporting Chance

1   How many players are in a beach volleyball team?

2   At which horse and ball sport have British princes, William and Harry, been team mates of their father Prince Charles?

3   What do the letters PB next to an athlete's time indicate?

4   Which medal is awarded for third place in an Olympic final?

5   What name is given to a golfer's assistant who carries the clubs?

6   What is passed from runner to runner in a relay race?

7   In tennis, what is the line at the back of the court called?

8   On a yacht, what are sheets?

9   What is the duration of a basketball match?

10   What is worn in the mouth by boxers to protect their teeth?

Question 6

★ BACKGROUND BONUS ★
In which popular British game must players first pot 15 red balls?

32 Total Trivia

1 What three-word motto is used by the SAS?

2 What kind of flowers do we associate with the Impressionist painter Claude Monet?

3 Ciabatta, pitta, soda and naan are all types of what?

4 What is sometimes referred to as Adam's ale?

5 Closely associated with Count Dracula, in which country is Transylvania?

6 Was *Indiana Jones and the Temple of Doom* the first or second movie in the series?

7 Judogi is the cotton outfit worn by competitors in which martial art?

8 A seal is a pinniped. What does this mean?

9 The Caspian Sea is the world's largest what?

10 What insects are kept in an apiary?

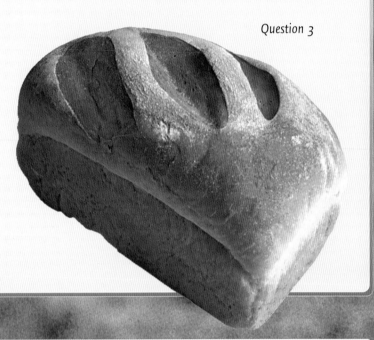

Question 3

33 Natural Selection

1 Seagull, kingfisher: which can swim best?

2 Do crocodiles hold their mouths open to cool off or to trap insects?

3 Which grasshopper relative feeds in enormous swarms?

4 Do male deer shed their antlers every year or every five years?

5 Red admiral and cabbage white are types of what?

6 What type of creature is a redback?

7 What is the name used for a male swan?

8 Do scorpions lay eggs or give birth to live young?

9 Which animal has the biggest ears?

10 Which North American animal is the largest member of the deer family?

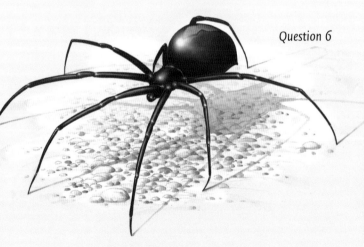

Question 6

> ★ **BACKGROUND BONUS** ★
> The okapi is related to which African animal?

Flower Power

34

Can you give the common name for each of these flowers?

35   Total Trivia

1 In which country is the Costa del Sol?

2 In which game is a shuttlecock used?

3 What is the plural of mouse?

4 In which century was 1314?

5 Where is Uluru (formerly Ayers Rock)?

6 What do you call a barrier that holds back water?

7 Which aircraft carries the most passengers?

8 Where are your incisors?

9 How many wives did King Henry VIII have?

10 What is the past tense of eat?

Question 7

36   Lights, Camera, Action!

1 Which Hollywood actress starred in the movie *Notting Hill*?

2 Which brick road did the characters follow in *The Wizard of Oz*?

3 Where does Bart Simpson live?

4 Which cartoon movie tells the story of a lost Russian princess?

5 What U.S. state shares its name with Dr. Jones' first name?

6 Which cartoon duck was 65 years old in 1999?

7 What is the profession of the main characters in the movie *Top Gun*?

8 Which capital city did the Rugrats venture to in the 2000 movie?

9 What does the A stand for in the Steven Spielberg movie *AI*?

10 What kind of animal is Maid Marian in the Disney cartoon version of Robin Hood?

Question 7

★ **BACKGROUND BONUS** ★
In which Italian city is a world famous movie festival held every year?

37   Natural Selection

1   What do you call a baby eagle: an eagling or an eaglet?

2   Which is the smallest of these dinosaurs: *Triceratops*, *Compsognathus*, *Tyrannosaurus*?

3   What is the name given to a male giraffe?

4   How many arms does a starfish usually have?

5   Which is the biggest fish: the sea horse, whale shark or squirrelfish?

6   Do parrots live in tropical forest or coastal sand dunes?

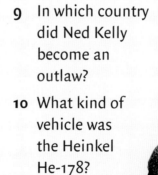

Question 5

7   Fish, snake, toad: which does not have scales?

8   Can a sea urchin move along the seabed?

9   Is the peacock's cry very loud or very quiet?

10 Do grapes grow on trees or vines?

38   Making History

1   Which ancient peoples first brought the cat to Europe?

2   In which war were the battles of Bull Run and Gettysburg fought?

3   Which British queen married a German prince called Albert?

4   In which World War did poet Wilfred Owen fight?

5   Which Disney movie is based on a novel by French writer Victor Hugo?

6   Which device, invented in Asia 5,000 years ago, is used for doing sums?

7   Roughly how many stone slabs are there in the Great Pyramid: 2,000, 20,000 or 2,000,000?

8   What is the arrow of a crossbow called: a shot, a bolt or a spear?

9   In which country did Ned Kelly become an outlaw?

10 What kind of vehicle was the Heinkel He-178?

Question 3

39 Lights, Camera, Action!

1 The wrestler called The Rock played which king in the movie *The Mummy Returns*?

2 In which movie was Samuel L. Jackson devoured by a super-intelligent shark?

3 What type of creatures are Sam, Merry and Pippin in *The Lord of the Rings*?

4 What is the name of the evil lord in the movie *Shrek*?

5 The movie character Austin Powers featured in the video for which Madonna song?

6 Is the hero of the movie *Chicken Run* called Ricky, Stocky or Rocky?

7 What natural disaster did Pierce Brosnan combat in the movie *Dante's Peak*?

8 In which city is the movie *Moulin Rouge* set?

9 Which part of the body is the scarecrow searching for in *The Wizard of Oz*?

10 In which movie did Robin Williams dress up as a nanny?

Question 8

40 Natural Selection

1 Which weasel-like animal can be tamed as a pet: the ferret or pine martin?

2 What is a male bee without a sting called?

3 Is the dung beetle so-called because it smells of dung or because it collects it?

4 What does the swallow build its nest from: twigs, mud or flowers?

5 Does rhubarb taste sweet or sour?

6 Which creature can contain a natural pearl inside its shell?

7 How long does a honey bee live for: six weeks, six months or six years?

8 Do bees swarm to find new nesting sites or to feed on nectar?

9 Which great ape beats its chest to scare enemies?

10 Are camels' feet best suited to sand, rock or marsh?

Question 9

41 Scientifically Speaking

1   When a dentist extracts teeth, what do they do?

2   What is titanium: a metal, a star or a part of the human body?

3   What is three-tenths as a decimal?

4   Which P word is the machine made of ropes and wheels used to lift heavy loads?

5   What shape is the Moon a few days after a New Moon?

6   What does your body need about eight hours of every day?

7   What is helium?

8   What is charcoal?

9   What is the name for any flat shape with three or more straight sides?

10 Does hot air travel up or down?

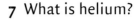

Question 6

★ BACKGROUND BONUS ★
The optic nerve carries signals to the brain from which part of the body?

42 Sporting Chance

1   How many kings are on a chessboard at the start of a game?

2   In baseball, what do the initials NL stand for?

3   What scores six points in a game of American Football?

4   In which sport might you perform a triple salchow?

5   Where would you find a hoop, a backboard and a three point line?

6   How many shots would a golfer have taken if scoring a birdie on a par 4 hole?

7   How many players are there in a basketball team?

8   In which sport do the New York Yankees attempt to win the World Series?

9   Which animal takes part in point-to-point races and steeplechases?

10 Which jockey achieved the Magnificent Seven at Ascot in September 1996?

Question 8

43 Written Word

1 In *The Jungle Book*, is Bagheera a black panther or a brown bear?

2 What gas is an anagram of the word none?

3 What word can precede print, bottle and bell?

4 Where did the Lost Boys live in *Peter Pan*?

5 What is the first animal mentioned in the nursery rhyme *Hey Diddle Diddle*?

6 What kind of creature is Jeremy Fisher in the Beatrix Potter tales?

7 What is the name of the train that takes Harry Potter to the wizard's school?

8 Which capital city is an anagram of the word more?

9 Which literary doctor created *The Cat in the Hat*?

10 What is the fifth *Harry Potter* book called?

Question 2

44 Lights, Camera, Action!

1 In which movie does a sheep dog called Fly become a foster parent to a pig?

2 What type of animal was voiced by Eddie Murphy in the movie *Shrek*?

3 Who stole Christmas in the 2000 movie?

4 Which character from *The Simpsons* has a teddy bear called Bobo?

5 Who plays Wanda in the movie "A Fish Called Wanda?

Question 4

6 What is Sid's dog in *Toy Story* called?

7 Which movie features a hen called Ginger and two farm owners called Mr. and Mrs. Tweedy?

8 In the movie *A Bug's Life*, Flik hires circus performers to defend his colony from what?

9 Manfred, Sid and Diego are all characters from which movie?

10 What is the name of the bear who befriends Mowgli in *The Jungle Book*?

45 Making History

1 Why did explorers often carry chickens and goats on board ship?

2 St. Francis of Assisi is the patron saint of what?

3 Was Amelia Earhart a famous flier, a lone sailor or a mountaineer?

4 What do Henry Irving, Laurence Olivier and John Gielgud have in common?

5 In the Bible, which unwilling prophet was swallowed by a whale?

6 Who was a famous English writer in the 1600s: John Milton, John Le Carré or John Keats?

7 Which continent did Columbus hope to find by sailing west?

8 Who wrote *The Faerie Queene* in the 1500s?

9 Nijinsky is famous for which performing art?

10 Who discovered the principle of how things float, in about 250BC?

Question 3

★ **BACKGROUND BONUS** ★
Buccaneers and corsairs were both types of what?

46 Scientifically Speaking

1 How many right angles does a right-angle triangle have?

2 Which machine is said to work like an electronic brain?

3 Which is the largest planet in our Solar System?

4 What is the smallest number divisible by both 3 and 4?

5 Which of your bones is shaped like a cage?

6 What silver metal is inside a thermometer?

7 Pb is the chemical symbol for which metal?

8 What material can you make from mixing newspaper, flour and water?

9 How many minutes long is the period of time starting at 6:15 and ending at 6:45?

10 What part of the Earth does a scuba diver explore?

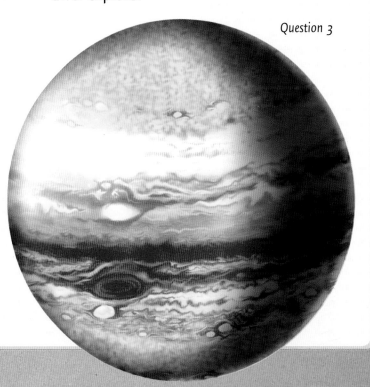

Question 3

47   Total Trivia

1   Who is the younger tennis player: Serena or Venus Williams?

2   In which country did kung fu originate?

3   What type of creature is the movie and TV character Flipper?

4   Which TV show stars Blossom, Buttercup and Bubbles?

5   In which sport do you get three strikes before you are out?

6   In which sport are there categories of bantamweight, flyweight and featherweight?

7   Which is the shortest month of the year?

8   What kind of bird is Hedwig in the *Harry Potter* books?

9   Which two U.S. states beginning with M are part of New England?

10 What mechanical animal is chased by greyhounds in a greyhound race?

Question 6

48   Global Matters

1   Which two continents are natural homes to the elephant?

2   Which U.S. state is known as The Grand Canyon State?

Question 6

3   How deep is the deepest part of the ocean: 1.6 km (1 mi), 4.8 km (3 mi) or 11.3 km (7 mi)?

4   If you ordered *tarte aux fraises* in a French restaurant, what would you get?

5   In which sea would you find the island country called Cyprus?

6   Which animal that builds a dam can be found in North America and Europe?

7   In which U.S. state would you be if you were staying in Orlando?

8   What type of natural feature is K2?

9   What is the capital of Thailand?

10 Which of these Caribbean Islands is the largest: Haiti, Cuba or Jamaica?

49 Natural Selection

1. Goose, albatross, cormorant: which can swim underwater?

2. Do poisonous frogs blend in well with their surroundings or stand out brightly?

3. Which insect product do humans often spread on bread?

4. Which animal is used to help herd sheep?

5. Are buttercups white or yellow?

6. Do fruit bats sleep in burrows or trees?

7. Is an armadillo a mammal or a reptile?

8. Do insects have two, three or four main body parts?

9. Do female rattlesnakes lay eggs or give birth to baby rattlers?

10. On which continent would you find llamas living in their natural habitat?

Question 7

50 Sporting Chance: Soccer

1. Which British soccer club did Dennis Wise captain to win the FA Cup?

2. What nationality is the soccer manager Alex Ferguson?

3. Which English soccer club is nicknamed "The Villains"?

4. How many minutes does each half last in a game of soccer?

5. What do the letters OG stand for in a soccer game?

6. Which Scottish soccer club has a five-letter name beginning with C, and is also a boy's first name?

7. Which is the only English Football League team beginning with the letter I?

8. For which country are Nicolas Anelka and Patrick Vieira team mates?

9. Which is the only English Football League team beginning with the letter Q?

10. In the soccer Premiership, how many points do teams receive for winning a game?

Question 2

★ BACKGROUND BONUS ★
What is the name for the peglike objects fixed to the sole of some sport footwear?

51 Written Word

1 Is the word fish a noun, a verb or both?

2 What is the silent letter in the word psychiatrist?

3 The cunning fox escaped from the hounds by hiding up a tree. Which word is the adjective?

4 How many vowels does the word vowels have?

5 What is the past tense of the word shoot?

6 Which three-letter word can precede ring, stone and hole?

7 Which Shakespeare play is commonly referred to as the Scottish play?

8 In the Roald Dahl story, which giant fruit did James sail in?

9 Which five-letter M word is given to the grinding teeth at the back of your mouth?

10 What term is used for setting fire to property on purpose?

Question 8

52 Natural Selection

1 Which has the keenest eyesight: eagle, duck or ostrich?

2 Which species of snake shares its name with a Cuban dance?

3 Does the sea anemone catch food with jaws or tentacles?

4 Is an albino animal white, black or brown?

5 Do vultures hover or soar in circles?

6 Which are taller: foxgloves or bluebells?

7 Leech, scorpion, chameleon: which is the reptile?

8 Which appeared first on Earth: spiders or dinosaurs?

9 Elephant, hippo, camel: which usually lives longest?

10 Are baby dolphins born on beaches or underwater?

Question 1

★ **BACKGROUND BONUS** ★
What birds are pink due to the shrimps and algae that they eat?

53   Scientifically Speaking

1   What kind of clock measures time by the Sun?

2   What is another name for perspiration?

3   What is the name for pieces of ice falling from clouds?

4   On a 24-hour digital clock, what numbers are displayed at 11:45 pm?

5   What is the name of our galaxy?

6   Which invention was first called a phonograph?

7   What part of your body works like a pump?

8   Which word describes how loud a sound is?

9   How many degrees is half a turn?

10 How many sides has an octagon?

Question 6

54   Total Trivia

1   *Vespa* is the Italian word for which insect?

2   What grew in length when the puppet boy Pinocchio told lies?

3   What is apiphobia a fear of?

4   What is the more common name for the capsicum?

5   Which shark is named after the shape of its head and is also the name of a tool?

6   What is the only dog breed to have a blue-black tongue?

7   Which is the lightest planet in our Solar System?

8   What is known as the Red Planet?

9   Who was the first woman mentioned in the Bible?

10 What kind of reptile is a basilisk?

Question 4

55   Lights, Camera, Action!

Question 6

1 In which bay is the Australian soap opera *Home and Away* set?

2 Which young wizard is played on screen by Daniel Radcliffe?

3 Which Disney movie features a *Brontosaurus* called Littlefoot?

4 Which actor appeared in *Seven*, *Snatch* and *Ocean's Eleven*?

5 Who is the cowboy character from *Toy Story*?

6 Which king of rock and roll starred in the movies *Jailhouse Rock* and *Blue Hawaii*?

7 What kind of animal is Kaa in the Disney movie *The Jungle Book*?

8 Who played one of Charlie's Angels and Mary in *There's Something About Mary*?

9 Name the actor who played the character of Neo in the movie *The Matrix*.

10 What is Batman's road vehicle called?

56   Scientifically Speaking

1 How many days are there in five weeks?

2 What is a monsoon?

3 Which kind of triangle has three equal sides?

4 You breathe air in through which two parts of your body?

5 What do you get if you mix red and blue?

6 What are constellations?

7 On a 24-hour digital clock, what numbers are displayed at 4 pm?

8 At what times of day can the sky become red?

9 What is the total of five 5s and ten 4s?

10 Which of the following will float in water: a cork, a nail, a coin?

Question 4

57 Total Trivia

1 Anaconda and cobra are species of what?

2 Which is the longest and narrowest country in the world?

Question 5

3 Who originally sang "Yellow Submarine"?

4 For how long does a human baby grow inside its mother?

5 Which of these is not a reptile: tortoise, alligator, octopus or snake?

6 What kind of insect is a scarab?

7 What kind of shape is an ellipse?

8 What is a space probe?

9 In *The Simpsons*, which musical instrument is played by Lisa Simpson?

10 What do 25, 16 and 9 have in common?

★ **BACKGROUND BONUS** ★
What type of bird would you find in a gaggle?

58 Sporting Chance

1 What is the ball hit with in a game of volleyball?

2 Which country hosts the Monte Carlo Grand Prix?

3 How many times has Michael Jordan been named Most Valuable Player?

4 In which sport is the ball slam-dunked through a raised hoop?

5 Which team won the NBA Championships 11 times in 13 seasons?

6 Which female WWE star is nicknamed "The Ninth Wonder of the World"?

7 What is worth 50 points on a dartboard?

8 In the game of golf, is an eagle or a birdie the better score?

9 In what word game is part of a gallows drawn for every wrong answer given?

10 Which player holds the all-time record for most points scored in the NBA?

Question 4

59 Natural Selection

1   Which is fastest: a swift or a sparrow?
2   Some butterflies migrate: true or false?
3   Is a boa a lizard or a snake?
4   Do llamas live in mountains or rainforests?
5   Which vegetable is made into a Halloween lantern?
6   Which bird of prey gathers in flocks to feed on dead animals?
7   Which has the most ribs: a snake or a crocodile?
8   Do stick insects rely on big jaws or camouflage to protect themselves from danger?
9   Which dogs pull sleds: labradors, huskies or corgis?
10 Male kangaroos have pouches and help raise their young: true or false?

Question 1

60 Total Trivia

1   Which flying machine has a propeller?
2   How can you tell if a shape is symmetrical?
3   Which is the odd one out: Asia, Australia, China, North America?
4   Which Australian marsupial looks like a bear?
5   What is the plural of knife?
6   Who killed Cock Robin?
7   What is a young deer called?
8   King William I was also known by what name?
9   In which country would you find the cities of Nice and Marseilles?
10 Which of these numbers are exactly divisible by 3: 6, 8, 12, 24?

Question 1

61 Scientifically Speaking

1. How many teeth in a full adult set?
2. Which planet is well known for its rings?
3. How many faces does a square-based pyramid have altogether?
4. When are baby animals usually born?
5. What part of your body has a hammer?
6. Which insect transmits malaria?
7. What is the distance between the middle and the edge of a circle called?
8. What is the name of a boat that carries cargo along a canal?
9. Does your heart beat faster or slower when you run?
10. What does vibrate mean?

Question 2

★ **BACKGROUND BONUS** ★
Where would you find solar flares and spots?

62 Making History

1. Why did early steamships have sails as well as engines?
2. What were the roofs of Bronze Age houses made of?
3. Which female leader rebelled against Roman rule in AD122?
4. In which century was the first all-iron bridge built at Coalbrookdale, England?
5. Who won the battle of Saratoga in 1777?
6. Who wrote the great Greek tragic play *Oedipus Rex*?
7. Who commanded HMS *Bounty* on a voyage to the Pacific in 1787?
8. Who composed *The Planets* suite between 1914 and 1917?
9. What are ancient Egyptian kings called?
10. What was the last planet in our Solar System to be discovered?

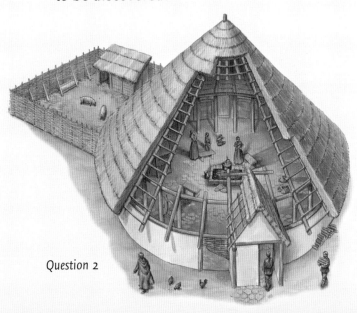

Question 2

63 Sporting Chance

1. The Arizona Diamondbacks beat which side to win the 2001 baseball World Series?

2. Which singer starred with Tom Hanks and Geena Davis in the baseball movie *A League of Their Own*?

3. Which team won the first Superbowl in 1967?

4. In the board game *Scrabble*, is the letter F worth three or four points?

5. Which five-letter P word is the name given to the prize money for a boxing bout?

6. In WWE, which wrestler is the brother of "The Undertaker"?

7. In which sport do competitors try to play below par?

8. Players in which sport throw projectiles from behind the oche?

9. Which WWE wrestler and commentator is nicknamed "The King"?

10. In which sport would the Detroit Tigers face the Chicago Cubs?

Question 7

64 Written Word

1. Which day of the week is also the name of Robinson Crusoe's manservant?

2. I visited the city of Paris yesterday. What is the proper noun in that sentence?

3. If a person is described as thrifty, are they generous or careful with money?

4. What word can precede pole, ship and stone?

5. What three-letter word can be a writing implement and an enclosure for animals?

6. How many books make up a trilogy?

7. The adjective equine refers to which animal?

8. In *The Lord of the Rings*, is Gandalf a witch, a wizard or a hobbit?

9. What is the name given to a young elephant, a young cow and a young whale?

10. What is the last vowel in the English alphabet?

Question 8

★ **BACKGROUND BONUS** ★
According to legend, where did King Arthur's sword, Excalibur, come from?

65   Total Trivia

Question 6

1. A river flows toward the sea: true or false?
2. How many grams are there in a kilogram?
3. What kind of fruit does a vine produce?
4. Which Disney movie features a monkey called Abu and a princess called Jasmine?
5. IA is the zip code for which U.S. state?
6. On a compass, which direction is 90° clockwise of west?
7. If a king or queen abdicates, what do they do?
8. Napoleon Bonaparte was a leader of which country?
9. Which sea lies between Africa and Europe?
10. What relation to you is your father's sister?

66   Natural Selection

1. The female hornbill bird is walled up in her nest until her eggs hatch: true or false?
2. What is the smallest breed of dog?
3. Which has more legs: a millipede or a centipede?
4. Do female whales lay eggs or give birth to babies?
5. Which E word describes trees that keep their leaves all year?
6. Would you find a crab spider hiding on a flower or in the sand on a beach?
7. Is the octopus related to the squid or the lobster?
8. What is a mammal called that has a pouch for its young: marsupial or placental?
9. Do winkles live on rocky shores or mudflats?
10. Is a Komodo dragon a lizard or a turtle?

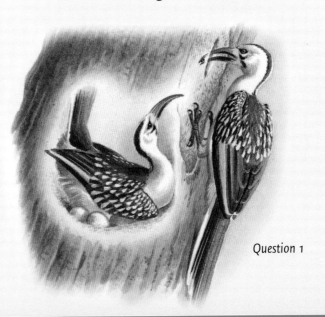

Question 1

67 Making History

1 Which mountain range did Hannibal cross with his army and their elephants?

2 Galleon, clipper and galley were all types of what?

3 Is the Humboldt current a part of a TV set or water in the ocean?

4 Who founded the U.S. state of Pennsylvania?

5 What was a "powder monkey" on a sailing warship?

6 About when did the first modern humans appear: 1,500,000BC, 150,000BC or 15,000BC?

7 What kind of farm machine did Cyrus McCormick invent?

8 Was the Egyptian pharaoh Tutankhamun buried in a pyramid or tomb?

9 In the book *Gulliver's Travels*, are the people from Lilliput large or small?

10 Who wore bellbottom trousers: sailors, soldiers or airmen?

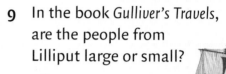

Question 2

> ★ BACKGROUND BONUS ★
> Which stone wall was built across Britain by a Roman emperor, to act as a frontier?

68 Scientifically Speaking

1 When animals and clothes blend in with their surroundings, what is it called?

2 What do you see in a planetarium?

3 Identical twins have the same fingerprints: true or false?

4 How many sides does a quadrilateral shape have?

5 Where would you find a pupil and an iris?

6 What do you get if you mix yellow and blue: dark red, green or orange?

7 If 2 February is Wednesday, what day will 6 February be?

8 What kind of work does a machine called an excavator do?

9 How many noughts are there in twenty thousand?

10 Natural history is the study of what?

Question 8

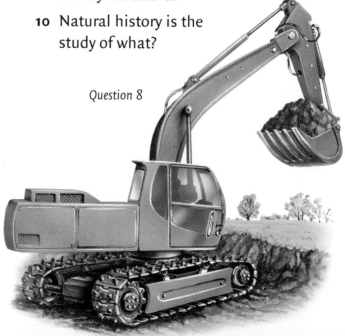

Written Word: The Bible

1 What did God create first, according to the words of Genesis, Chapter 1?

2 Who were Shem, Ham and Japheth?

3 What did Esau sell to his brother Jacob for a bowl of lentil stew?

4 What was Deborah's job?

5 Who lived to be 969 years old?

6 What is a parable?

7 On which road did the events described in the story of the Good Samaritan take place?

8 Which bird returned to Noah's ark with an olive twig in its beak?

9 What kind of tree did Zacchaeus climb so he could see Jesus?

10 How did Jesus die?

Question 8

 ## Natural Selection

1 Which black-and-white bird has a reputation as a thief?

2 Does the shingleback lizard have a tail shaped like its head or like a flower?

3 Do hummingbirds eat flowers or the nectar of flowers?

4 Which bird is associated with the United States?

5 What type of animal is an iguana?

6 Which are slower: hares or rabbits?

7 Are spiders related to ants or scorpions?

8 Which is smaller: a Shetland pony or a cart horse?

9 Are cornflakes made from wheat or maize?

10 Do sloths spend most of their time in trees or on the ground?

Question 2

71 Total Trivia

1 What H is another word for difficult?
2 Which forbidden fruit did Adam and Eve eat?
3 What is the plural of mother-in-law?
4 How many sides has an octagon?
5 Nancy Cartwright provides the voice of which member of the Simpson family?
6 Which star sign covers the first 21 days of December?
7 What is the world's biggest animal?
8 To a sailor, what is *mal de mer*?
9 What was the *Luftwaffe*?
10 What is the Great Barrier Reef made of?

Question 7

72 Making History

1 Which two countries began a "space race" in 1957?
2 Who laid down his cloak to keep Queen Elizabeth I's feet dry?
3 What is a blunderbuss?
4 Which Johnson was a famous aviator: Amy, Jack or Lyndon?
5 Who was the Norse god of thunder?
6 Robespierre was a leader of which revolution: the American, French or Russian?

7 Which great French scientist made the first vaccine against rabies?
8 Which Asian invaders were led by Attila the Hun in AD434?
9 During the Ice Age, sea levels dropped. How did this help the first people to reach America?
10 In which country is the kimono a form of national dress?

Question 10

73   Scientifically Speaking

1. What is one-quarter of 1,000?
2. Which is larger: 50% or 5/8?
3. How many degrees are there in a right-angle?
4. Which part of the body contains the cornea and the retina?
5. Which natural occurrence is caused by sunlight passing through falling raindrops?
6. If a number is multiplied, does it increase or decrease in size?
7. Frenchman André Ampère gave his name to a unit of what?
8. In total, how many sides would three rectangles and three triangles have?
9. In what part of a car might you find a cylinder, a piston and a spark plug?
10. Which gas do we need to breathe?

Question 5

74   Lights, Camera, Action!

1. In which country is the Disney movie *Mulan* set?
2. What kind of creepy crawlies featured in the movie *Arachnophobia*?
3. What kind of dinosaur is the movie monster Godzilla?
4. Robbie Williams sang "We Are The Champions" for which movie?
5. How many of the Seven Dwarfs have a name beginning with S?
6. In the 2002 animated movie, what is the name of the stallion of the Cimarron?

Question 3

7. What is the name of the bird that Stuart Little rescues from the clutches of a falcon?
8. Which 1997 animated movie features the characters of Pain and Pegasus?
9. In their second movie, the Spy Kids venture to which islands?
10. Who is Fred Flintstone's best friend?

★ BACKGROUND BONUS ★
The name of which 2001 movie translates into English as "red windmill"?

75 Making History

1 What people invented the magnetic compass?

2 Which holy book was first written down by the Prophet Muhammad?

3 Which country attacked Pearl Harbor in 1941?

4 Which explorer, who discovered America, sailed in the *Santa Maria*?

5 What language did the Romans speak?

6 What fell on Newton's head, according to one story?

7 In which war were V-1 flying bombs used?

8 Which river flowed through ancient Egypt?

9 What device helped the Greeks to capture the city of Troy?

10 In which century did the Industrial Revolution begin?

Question 6

76 Sporting Chance: Soccer

1 Which member of England's 2002 World Cup squad has the first name of Solberg?

2 For which British soccer club did Alan Shearer score his 200th Premiership goal in 2002?

3 Who won the 2002 soccer World Cup?

4 Who were the beaten finalists in the 2002 soccer World Cup?

5 What nationality is the soccer player Thierry Henry?

6 Before 2002, when was the last soccer World Cup held?

7 Which member of England's 2002 World Cup squad has sons called Brooklyn and Romeo?

8 Mick McCarthy managed which international soccer side in 2002?

9 Are the home shirts of Italy's national soccer team red, blue or yellow?

10 Bayern Munich FC is based in which country?

Question 3

77   Global Matters

1   Is Philadelphia northeast or southwest of New York?

2   Stockholm is the capital of which country?

3   Danish people are citizens of which country?

4   On which continent does Luxembourg lie?

5   What is the world-famous bridge in San Francisco called?

6   Which D word is the name given to the language spoken by people from Holland?

7   What is the longest river in Asia?

8   Is California on the west or east coast of the United States?

9   The design of Blackpool Tower in England is based on which French landmark?

10 Of which country is Budapest the capital city?

Question 5

★ BACKGROUND BONUS ★
In its local language, this city is called
Firenze. What is its English name?

78   Natural Selection

1   What is the second largest living fish: the basking shark or the thresher shark?

2   Did the dinosaur *Tyrannosaurus rex* live in water or on land?

3   What raids beehives for honey: hawkmoths, hornets or dragonflies?

4   Do hippos avoid sunburn by sheltering under trees or staying in the water?

5   What type of animal is a gecko?

6   For what do whales use baleen?

7   Which eats the most each year: a large snake or a small rat?

8   Do some ants live alone?

9   Giraffes have horn-like growths on their heads: true or false?

10 Do crabs release their eggs on land or in the sea?

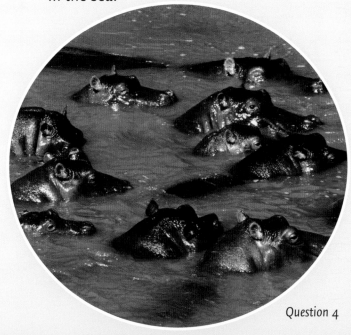

Question 4

79 Sporting Chance

1 Which country does Jennifer Capriati represent at tennis?

2 Which team won Superbowls XVI, XIX, XXIII, XXIV and XXIX?

3 In which British race do competitors negotiate fences called The Chair and Becher's Brook?

4 How many wheels does a unicycle have?

5 Tim Montgomery broke the world record for the 100 m in 2002 when he ran what time: 8.72, 9.78 or 10.02 seconds?

6 What is the ice hockey equivalent of a ball?

7 Would you see Evander Holyfield skiing down a hill, scoring a touchdown or throwing a punch?

8 In gymnastics, what piece of apparatus is 5 m (16 ft) long?

9 What name is given to the starting area in a Formula One Grand Prix race?

10 What is the second fastest swimming stroke?

Question 1

★ BACKGROUND BONUS ★
Which breed of dog is used for racing?

80 Total Trivia

1 What name is given to a young beaver?

2 What are back, breast and crawl?

3 What were zeppelins?

4 What is behind your ribs?

5 Where are the British Crown Jewels kept?

6 Which country is famous for canals and windmills?

7 How many sides does a cube have?

8 How many people play or sing in a quartet?

9 What sank the SS *Titanic*?

10 Which animal never forgets?

Question 5

81   Natural Selection

1 How many chicks do penguins have at one time: one, four or seven?

2 Eel, sea horse, sea snake: which is the odd one out?

3 Which bird is the fastest flier: the peregrine falcon or the bald eagle?

4 What sort of animal was Black Beauty?

5 Which live longer: reptiles or insects?

6 Are lobsters hunters or scavengers?

7 Is coffee made from leaves or beans?

8 What is a young kangaroo called?

9 Does a kangaroo fight with its feet or its teeth?

10 Equids include which striped animal?

Question 10

82   Lights, Camera, Action!

1 Are ET's eyes green, brown or blue?

2 What is the name of the knights that appear in the *Star Wars* movies?

3 In the movie *Home Alone*, what is the first name of the boy that is left home alone?

Question 4

4 What kind of animal is Rocky in *The Adventures of Rocky and Bullwinkle*?

5 Which movie features the characters of Fred, Velma, Daphne, Shaggy and a talking dog?

6 What is the name of the piggy bank in the movie *Toy Story*?

7 Which 2000 animated movie sees Emperor Kuzco transformed into a llama?

8 In the movie *Dinosaur*, what is the name of the leader of the dinosaurs?

9 What is the name of the white family cat in the movie *Stuart Little*?

10 In which movie is Bugs Bunny assisted by basketball superstar Michael Jordan?

83 Natural Selection

1   Which birds have strong talons and hook-shaped beaks: waders or birds of prey?

2   Which lays its eggs in water: the newt or the lizard?

3   What is a scorpion: an insect or arachnid?

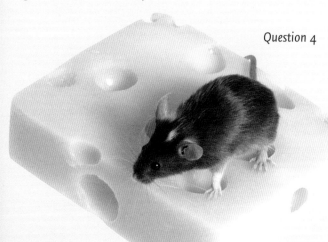

Question 4

4   Which small rodent famously has a weakness for cheese?

5   Is ebony wood very light or very heavy?

6   What sort of yellow bird is the cartoon character Tweetie Pie?

7   Did plant-eating dinosaurs walk mainly on two or four legs?

8   Which are larger: stag beetles or rhinoceros beetles?

9   Do clams live in sandy seabeds or attached to seaweed?

10 Does the marine otter live on land or at sea?

> ★ **BACKGROUND BONUS** ★
> Which plant is thought to bring good luck
> if you find one with four leaves?

84 Total Trivia

1   Which island is at the southern tip of Italy?

2   Who are the infantry?

3   The Chinese were making ice cream some 5,000 years ago: true or false?

4   What people wrote in hieroglyphics?

5   Which creature did St. George slay?

6   What is the capital of Germany?

7   What is another word for unite?

8   In *The Simpsons*, what is the name of Mr. Burns' aide?

9   What shape is a cylinder?

10 What is marine algae?

Question 5

Eye Spy

85

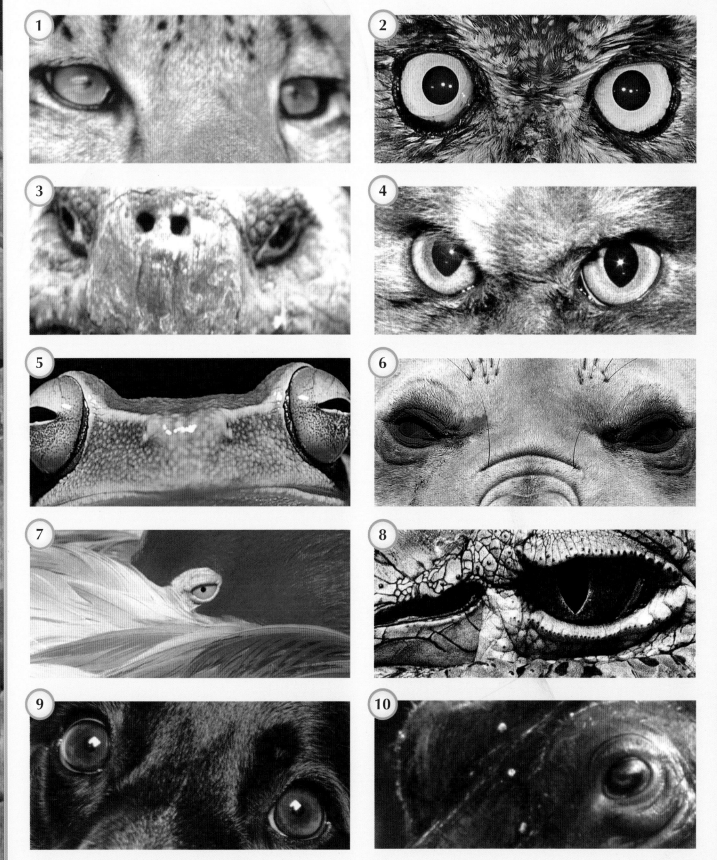

1
2
3
4
5
6
7
8
9
10

Can you identify these animals?

86   Total Trivia

1. Which game is played in a four-walled court with a small rubber ball?
2. In what country was tea first grown?
3. Which plant is used to make pasta?
4. What boy's name is also the name for a rabbit's home?
5. What is the shape of one side of a cube?
6. What is the coldest continent?
7. Which country was first ruled by shoguns?
8. What is another word for suspend?
9. Which animal is said to have nine lives?
10. What is the name for the imaginary line around the middle of the Earth?

Question 9

★ BACKGROUND BONUS ★
What is the name of the traditional hip-swaying dance from Hawaii?

87   Natural Selection

1. Which very tall and long-legged wading bird is usually pink?
2. What kind of bird is a scarlet macaw?
3. What does a butterfly use its proboscis for: to fight rivals or drink nectar?
4. Some snakes hibernate: true or false?
5. What do frogs eat: insects or plants?
6. What sort of dog was the movie star Lassie: a labrador, a collie, a St. Bernard, an Alsatian?
7. Which flower has the same name as part of your eye?
8. Does the octopus give birth to babies or lay eggs?
9. Do willow trees like damp or dry conditions?
10. Eurasian, American, honey and Palawan stink are all varieties of which carnivorous animal?

Question 6

88 Making History

1 Who wrote *Kidnapped*?

2 Was Dr. Crippen a famous murderer or the inventor of *Snakes and Ladders*?

3 Who was nicknamed the "Lady of the Lamp" during the Crimean War?

4 How many of Magellan's ships sailed home after circling the world in 1522?

5 What was the first mass-produced car in 1908?

6 What invention changed the way books were made in the 1400s?

7 How many children has the British Queen Elizabeth II?

8 Who had ships known as longships?

9 Which Russian composer wrote the *1812 Overture*?

10 To which country did Marco Polo journey?

Question 5

89 Music Mania

1 "No crib for a bed" is the second line in which Christmas carol?

2 Which Californian "surfing" group was founded by the Wilson brothers?

3 Which rock group had a transatlantic hit in 1994 with "Please Come Home For Christmas"?

4 Which hit song contains the line: "No hell below us, above us only sky"?

5 Which U.S. female singer had a hit with "Beautiful" in 2003?

6 The name of which British pop group is also the name for a fertile spot in a desert?

7 Which actress sang "What If" and which 2001 animated movie did it feature in?

8 The song "Take My Breath Away" featured in which 1986 movie starring Tom Cruise?

9 Who wrote the song "White Christmas"?

10 Which singer sang the words "I'm not that kind of girl" in 2001?

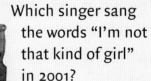

Question 1

90   Written Word

1 What group of animals does the word brood describe?

2 Which book about four sisters was written by Louisa May Alcott?

3 What word describes a person turning pink with embarrassment?

4 Who wrote the book *Frankenstein*?

5 Which famous poet was the author of *Frankenstein* married to?

6 Which great detective's last case was described in the book *Curtains*?

Question 1

7 Which famous writer had her book *Pride and Prejudice* rejected by a number of publishers?

8 Which T word describes a group of dancers?

9 What book about a young lord was written by Frances Hodgson Burnett?

10 Which female author wrote *Malory Towers*, *The Secret Island* and the *St Clare's Naughtiest Girl* series?

> ★ BACKGROUND BONUS ★
> Name Keats' poem with the first line:
> "Season of mists and mellow fruitfulness..."

91   Making History

1 Did the first bicycles have pedals?

2 In which country were Europe's first banks?

3 What was the system called under which serfs worked for the lord?

4 Was a trireme a Roman warship, a Greek council of war or a Saxon drink?

5 In which year was the Magna Carta signed: 1180, 1215 or 1300?

6 Who invented the lightning rod?

7 Which English county is named after the East Saxons?

8 What were Greek hoplites?

9 Which island in the South Pacific features 600 mysterious stone head statues?

10 Was Leonardo da Vinci born near Florence, Italy or in Vienna, Austria?

Question 8

92 Music Mania

1. Who, with Midge Ure, wrote the song "Do They Know It's Christmas"?

2. Which female singer's hugely successful album is called *Come Away With Me*?

3. In what type of tree was the partridge found in the song "The Twelve Days of Christmas"?

4. Which 1996 movie starring Keanu Reeves was also the title of a 1986 hit song for Diana Ross?

5. What are crotchets, semibreves and quavers?

6. Which U.S. female singer had a solo hit with "Heaven Is A Place On Earth"?

7. Whose album includes the songs "Superman" and "Sing for the Moment"?

8. Which famous German composer wrote nine symphonies?

9. Which song was a hit for Harry Belafonte and Boney M?

10. What is the title of the album released by Michael Jackson in 2001?

Question 4

93 Total Trivia

1. How long does it take for the Earth to revolve around the Sun?

2. Olivetti, Benetton and Fiat are all companies from which country?

3. Was Alfred Nobel, the inventor of dynamite, Swedish, English or German?

4. Traditionally, what measurement is used for the height of horses?

5. Which two U.S. states begin with the letter K?

6. Which animal from Scandinavia is closely linked with Father Christmas?

7. In which Asian country is Mount Fuji?

8. Which Egyptian statue of a lion with a king's face is found near Cairo?

9. In which continent would the Rhine River be found?

10. On which continent would you find the fewest people?

Question 8

94 Total Trivia

1 Which flower commemorates the war dead?

2 What is another word for begin?

3 How many bones are in the human body: 58, 206 or 520?

4 Which country's rugby team is called the All-Blacks?

5 What would you call a group of birds?

6 What are Scottish lakes called?

7 What is irrigation?

8 Who wrote *Twelfth Night* and *Macbeth*?

9 Which book told the adventures of Toad of Toad Hall?

10 Where is the Amazon rainforest?

Question 1

95 Scientifically Speaking

1 Iron, steel and copper are examples of what?

2 What are Sirius, Betelgeuse and Polaris examples of?

3 How many hours are there in a day?

4 What is the name for three babies born at the same time?

5 What happens to water at 0°C (32°F)?

6 What is the name for the strip where an aircraft lands?

7 Which times table are these numbers part of: 14, 28, 49, 56?

8 What happens to paper and wood when they become very hot?

9 In total, how many legs do six spiders have?

10 What travels faster: light or sound?

Question 9

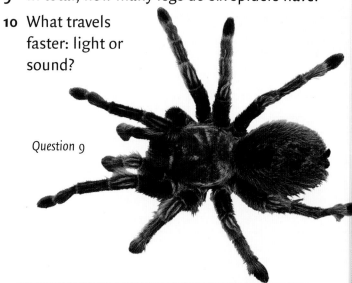

★ BACKGROUND BONUS ★
Which thin, glass object is used in chemical tests and experiments?

96 Lights, Camera, Action!

1 In which 1999 movie did Brendan Fraser play the all-action hero Rick O'Connell?

2 Who played the title role in the 2001 movie *Miss Congeniality*?

3 What is the title of Steven Spielberg's 1991 adaptation of the story of Peter Pan?

4 Which 2002 movie starring Tom Cruise is set in the year 2054?

5 In which movie do a gang of children search for the treasure of One-Eyed Willy?

6 Jafar is the name of the villain in which 1992 Disney movie?

7 What is the three-letter name of the little girl in the movie *Monsters, Inc.*?

8 In 2002, the first Oscar for Best Animation was awarded to which movie?

9 In which city is the movie *Wall Street* set?

10 Who provided Mickey Mouse's voice in the cartoon character's debut appearance?

Question 1

97 Sporting Chance

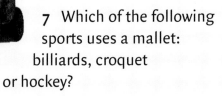

1 On what type of surface does the game of curling take place?

2 Rocky Marciano was World Champion of which sport?

3 Where do you find a golf link course?

4 In which sport has Greg Rusedski represented Britain?

5 What is the area surrounding the golf hole called where a putter is used?

6 What game is played using the fruit of the horse chestnut tree?

7 Which of the following sports uses a mallet: billiards, croquet or hockey?

8 In tennis, which V word means hitting the ball before it bounces?

9 Which side won the Stanley Cup five times in the 1950s and 1960s and six times in the 1970s?

10 What three-letter word is given to the forward sail on a yacht: jig, jag or jib?

Question 7

98 Scientifically Speaking

1 What is the total of four 2s and two 4s?

2 What part of your body has a drum?

3 What is the name of a little boat that tows a big ship?

4 What sort of vehicle did Sir Christopher Cockerell invent?

5 What would you find at the core of the Earth?

6 What is the largest kind of ship?

7 What fills with air when you breathe in?

8 What is the middle of an atom called?

9 What is the next number in this sequence: 30, 27, 24, 21?

10 Is cotton a natural or manufactured material?

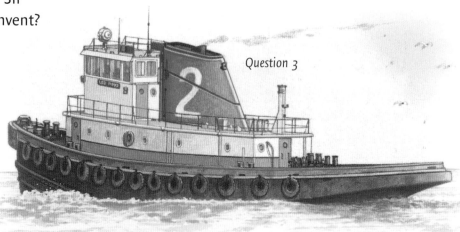

Question 3

99 Total Trivia

1 What is a noun?

2 Which brass instrument has a sliding section?

3 What is the capital of Northern Ireland?

4 What is created when a meteorite hits a planet?

5 What do we do when we have a nap?

6 What did David use to kill Goliath?

7 Why do you sneeze?

8 Which was the biggest dinosaur?

9 Which bird has big, round eyes at the front of its head?

10 What is a cat-o'-nine-tails?

Question 9

100 Written Word

1 What kind of creature was Bilbo Baggins?
2 Which fictional detective had an enemy called Moriarty?
3 Which detective's first appearance was in the book *The Mysterious Affair at Styles*?
4 Which Charles wrote *Great Expectations*?
5 Who wrote tales about Brer Rabbit?
6 How many actors speak in a monologue?
7 Who is the boy who never grew up?
8 In which story would you find Smaug the dragon?
9 Who wrote the book *The Iron Man*?
10 In which horror story does Jonathan Harker hunt down a vampire?

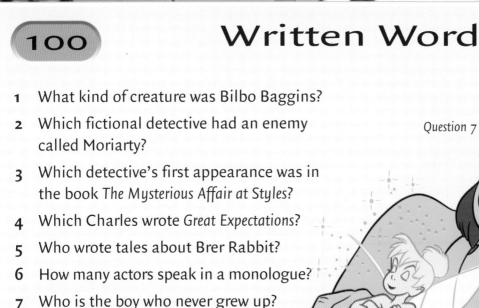

Question 7

101 Lights, Camera, Action!

1 In Disney's *Bambi*, what animal was Flower?
2 In which city is the 1972 musical *Cabaret* set?
3 What kind of animal is Pummba in the movie *The Lion King*?
4 Which award-winning movie tells the story of a flower girl called Eliza Doolittle?
5 Which star of TV's *X Files* had a lead role in the comedy sci-fi movie *Evolution*?
6 In which 2001 movie did Ewan McGregor play Christian?
7 Which movie featured a feline called Mr. Tinkles and a puppy named Lou?
8 What animal is Colonel Hathi in *The Jungle Book*?
9 In which movie did Jonathan Pryce play Madonna's husband?
10 Which 1979 movie was set at the New York School of Performing Arts?

Question 9

★ BACKGROUND BONUS ★
What kind of music-making facility is in Abbey Road in London?

102   Natural Selection

1   Which has the beautiful tail: the female peahen or the male peacock?

2   In which country would you find a wallaby in the wild?

3   What type of animal is a Great Dane?

4   Are any bats vegetarian?

5   Which grows taller: a pine tree or an apple tree?

6   Which has the longer beak: the heron or the swan?

7   Which bird of prey shares its name with a flying toy?

8   Is sleeping sickness spread by a spider, a fly or a beetle?

9   Which member of the horse family has stripes?

10   Does clover grow in open meadows or thick woods?

Question 1

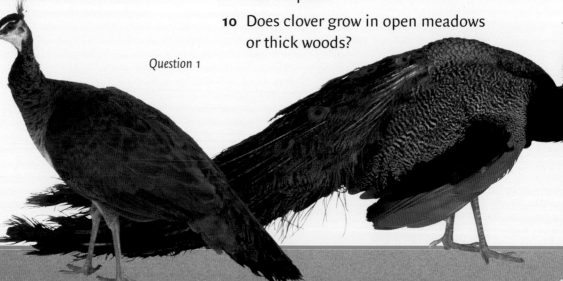

103   Making History

1   In which decade did World War II begin?

2   Which was the first nation to give women the vote: the United States, Australia or New Zealand?

3   Which came first: the Stone Age or Bronze Age?

4   How many British kings have been called George?

5   What were the followers of Oliver Cromwell called?

6   Which mountain did Edward Wymper climb in 1869?

7   "Watson come here, I want you" were the first-ever words spoken on the what?

8   Which U.S. president was assassinated in November 1963?

9   In ancient Egyptian times, what was the name given to the people who could write?

10   Which British queen died in 1901?

Question 7

★ BACKGROUND BONUS ★
Which temple was built as a dedication to the Greek goddess, Athena?

104   Sporting Chance

1 What is the American Football equivalent of a try in rugby?

2 How many serves is a tennis player allowed on each point?

3 What are rugby players doing if they are selling dummies?

4 At which Japanese sport do wrestlers attempt to push each other out of a ring?

5 Which of the following sports do horses not take part in: polo, dressage, hurling?

6 If the Astros play the Cardinals, which two U.S. cities are in opposition?

7 What name is given to the small peg from which a golf ball is driven?

8 What is the official national sport of the United States?

9 At which sport do competitors perform a Fosbury Flop?

10 In which sport do participants say *touché* if a hit has been scored?

Question 9

105   Global Matters

1 Which city in Scotland has the highest population?

2 In which country might you eat paella, drink sangria and hear flamenco music?

3 The largest gorge in the world is in the United States. What is its name?

4 Which London building boasts a dome that stands 111.56 m (366 ft) above the ground?

5 Melbourne is the capital of which Australian state?

6 Which Italian city is famous for its Grand Canal?

7 Which is the farthest south: South Africa, South America or the South Pole?

8 On a map of Europe, which country is shaped like a boot?

9 Which currency was adopted by 12 EU countries on 1 January 2002?

10 Which is the largest country in South America?

Question 4

106   Total Trivia

1. Who are the Harlem Globe Trotters?
2. What is 15 divided by 2.5?
3. How many minutes are there between 10:15 and 11:05?
4. What is the singular of dice?
5. What title is given to the eldest son of an English sovereign?
6. Does a west wind blow from the west or to the west?
7. Who was the Roman god of the sea?
8. Which of these words is a noun: hopped, laughing, road, because?
9. What creature can unhinge its jaws?
10. How many legs has a quadruped?

Question 7

107   Making History

1. With which European nation did the United States conclude the Louisiana Purchase by buying nearly 600 million acres of land?
2. What was the name of the ship in which the Pilgrim Fathers sailed from Devon, England, in 1620?
3. Which British Votes for Women organization was founded by Emmeline Pankhurst in 1903?
4. In 1959, what became the 50th U.S. state?
5. Anne Boleyn was the mother of which queen of England?

6. In what century did the astrologer Nostradamus live?
7. Who was the first U.S. president to resign from office?
8. Which Italian artist painted a mural of *The Last Supper* around 1495?
9. How many Scottish kings have been called Kenneth: one, two or three?
10. In the 1850s, which American woman invented a new kind of practical clothing for women?

Question 3

108 Sporting Chance

1 Which sport featured in the movie *Cool Runnings*, starring John Candy?

2 What is the only object that is thrown in the women's heptathlon?

3 In 1997, which 21-year-old became the youngest winner of golf's U.S. Masters?

4 Magic Johnson was named Most Valuable Player three times while playing for who?

5 What did Eddie Charlton carry in 1956 and Muhammed Ali in 1996?

6 Which ice hockey team had Stanley Cup victories in 1997 and 1998?

7 How many players are in a netball team?

8 What side lost in four consecutive Superbowls in the early 1990s?

9 What is the national sport of Ireland?

10 What is not an event in the decathlon: 1,500 m, pole vault or triple jump?

Question 1

★ BACKGROUND BONUS ★
What sport is played by the Cleveland Browns?

109 Music Mania

1 "Never Ever" was a hit for which girl band?

2 Who couldn't get you out of her head in 2001?

3 Irish musician James Galway is particularly associated with what instrument?

4 Which opera house was opened in 1973 and looks like yachts in full sail?

5 At what time of the day is a serenade traditionally sung?

6 Who had a hit with "It's Raining Men" in 2001 and entertained British troops in Oman?

7 In 1993, which chart topper sang "I'd Do Anything For Love, But I Won't Do That"?

8 Courtesy of the 1990 World Cup finals, who enjoyed a hit single with "Nessun Dorma"?

9 Which musical percussion instrument is named after its geometrical shape?

10 Gordon Sumner and Stuart Copeland were members of which 80s band?

Question 4

110 Scientifically Speaking

1 Which six-sided object does a group of snow crystals form?

2 How does a gyroscope move?

3 What are Orion, Cassiopeia and Virgo?

4 How long does it take for a meal to go through your digestive system: four hours, three days or one week?

5 The invention of what machine brought about the Industrial Revolution of the 1700s and 1800s?

6 What is a trawler?

7 How many equal sides has an isosceles triangle?

8 What metal is a mixture of copper and tin?

9 What would you measure with a hygrometer?

10 What gas do you breathe out: oxygen or carbon dioxide?

Question 2

★ BACKGROUND BONUS ★
Forked, streak and ribbon are forms of which natural occurrence?

111 Total Trivia

1 Who are the Wallabies?

2 What country is the world's largest consumer of tea?

3 For what does G.M.T. stand?

4 How many noughts has a million?

5 In the Lewis Carroll story, which animal faded away leaving only its grin?

6 What might you find in an oyster?

7 In which sport do you do butterfly or crawl?

8 Who was William Gladstone?

9 What is a Camberwell beauty?

10 Which U.S. civil rights leader was assassinated in 1968?

Question 9

Famous Faces

112

Can you identify these famous people?

113 Global Matters

1. On which thoroughfare in London does the Cenotaph War Memorial stand?

2. What is the name of the New York avenue associated with the advertising industry?

3. Which capital city provided the title of a 1981 hit record for Ultravox?

4. Which is the only U.S. state that begins with the letter P?

5. What is the national flower of Scotland?

6. On what river does the city of New Orleans stand?

7. Which Scottish city gave its name to a type of cake?

8. In France, what kind of vehicle is the T.G.V.?

9. Which Mediterranean island's flag includes an image of the George Cross?

10. On which Caribbean island is the resort of Montego Bay?

Question 5

★ **BACKGROUND BONUS** ★
Simpson, Atacama and Kalahari are examples of what?

114 Total Trivia

1. What does the spine protect?

2. Which navigational instrument is named for its shape?

3. How many seconds in ten minutes?

4. What type of energy is made up of electrons?

5. Is kinetic energy movement or heat energy?

6. In a manual car, what pedal do you press to change gear?

7. What protects the Earth from the heat of the Sun?

8. Is an alloy a pure metal or a mixture of metals?

9. Do you grow more when you are awake or asleep?

10. What kind of vehicle was a Lanchester?

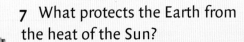

Question 2

115   Lights, Camera, Action!

1 In which 2000 movie did Richard Harris play Emperor Marcus Aurelius?

2 Who played an oil driller called Harry Stamper in the movie *Armageddon*?

3 To which decade did Marty McFly travel back in the 1985 movie *Back to the Future*?

4 The 2001 movie, *Planet of the Apes*, is a remake of a 1968 movie starring which Hollywood star?

5 What is the title of the 1997 movie that features a talking pug dog called Frank?

6 Trinity, Tank and Mouse are all characters in which 1999 movie?

7 What was the world's top box office movie of the 1970s?

8 In which 1993 movie is Dr. Richard Kimble wrongly accused of murdering his wife?

9 *Thelma and Louise* starred which two famous actresses?

10 Which 1991 movie sequel is subtitled *Judgment Day*?

Question 1

116   Sporting Chance

1 What nationality is motor racing star Jacques Villeneuve?

2 Which Korean city hosted the 1988 Summer Olympics?

3 With what sport would you associate the promoter Don King?

Question 2

4 Who was the first athlete to jump in excess of 18 m in the triple jump?

5 What was won four times by Brazil in the 20th century, in 1958, 1962, 1970 and 1994?

6 In what century were the Wimbledon Tennis Championships first contested?

7 Which Derby-winning horse was kidnapped in 1983?

8 What sport is played by the San Antonio Spurs?

9 What sport uses balls with a blue dot, a white dot, a red dot and a yellow dot?

10 What is the maximum number of clubs a golfer is allowed to take onto the course?

117 Making History

1 In which country were rockets probably invented over 700 years ago?

2 Who was the first woman to swim the English Channel?

3 What country was reformed by Kemal Atatürk during the 1920s?

4 What short cut did Magellan take from the Atlantic to the Pacific?

5 In what way was the longbow a better weapon than the crossbow?

6 Of which country did Fidel Castro become leader in 1959?

7 What was the job of a knight's squire?

8 Who was the youngest ever president of the United States?

9 Who is the patron saint of Scotland?

10 What pushed steamships along before the invention of the screw propeller?

Question 10

★ BACKGROUND BONUS ★
Isla de Pascua is the Spanish name for what island in the eastern Pacific?

118 Total Trivia

1 What are a clove hitch and a reef?

2 The world's fourth largest island lies off the east coast of Africa. What is it called?

3 What made the craters on the Moon?

4 What vegetable is sauerkraut made from?

5 Which boy didn't want to grow up?

6 Who were the Boers?

7 Why does water flow downhill?

8 What country was led by General de Gaulle?

9 Name the four citrus fruits.

10 What is a male chicken called?

Question 10

119   Lights, Camera, Action!

1 What town do the Flintstones come from?

2 Who, early in his career, appeared in the Australian soap opera, *Neighbours*, before finding screen fame playing a gladiator?

3 Who plays Dana Scully in *The X Files*?

4 Which *Friends* character is played by actor David Schwimmer?

5 Which TV show features a radio psychologist who lives with his father and his father's dog?

6 Burgess Meredith and Danny DeVito have both played which archenemy of Batman?

7 In which city is the TV show ER set?

8 Which female singer starred in the movie *The Bodyguard*?

9 Who won an Oscar for his role in the movie *Philadelphia*?

10 What is the name of the cartoon character known as the friendly ghost?

Question 7

120   Sporting Chance

1 What type of ball has three holes and weighs 7.25 kg (16 lb)?

2 The Anaheim Angels beat what side to win their first World Series in 2002?

3 What athlete broke Bob Beamon's 23-year-old long jump world record in 1991?

4 Larry Bird is a NBA legend for what side?

5 What game developed from wooden balls being hit through hoops of willow?

6 Who was No. 1 seed in the men's singles at the 2002 Wimbledon Tennis Championships?

7 What golfer won the U.S. Open in 2002?

8 In table tennis, after how many points do the players change serve?

9 In which game do you use a tolley?

10 What is longer: a baseball bat or a tennis racket?

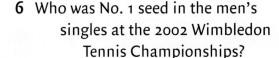

Question 9

121 Sporting Chance: Soccer

1 Who was the first French soccer player to be voted PFA Player of the Year?

2 In September 2001, who scored a hat-trick for England against Germany?

3 Which soccer club finished second in the 2002 Premier League in England?

4 Aged 42, which Cameroon striker was the oldest player to score a goal in the World Cup finals?

5 For which English soccer club was Kevin Phillips the leading scorer in the Premiership in the 1999/2000 season?

6 What nation was beaten in the 1994 soccer World Cup final on a penalty shoot-out?

7 Who did Celtic beat in the final when they became the first British soccer club to win the European Cup?

8 Who won 108 caps for England from 1962 to 1973?

9 In which country was the 1990 soccer World Cup held: Italy, Spain or France?

10 What is the only country to have played in every World Cup finals from 1930 to 2002?

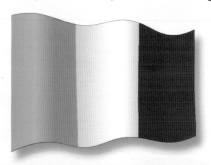

Question 9

122 Lights, Camera, Action!

1 The 1999 teen movie, 10 Things I Hate About You, was based on which Shakespeare play?

2 Which 1996 movie is based on the life of pianist David Helfgott?

3 What movies featured terrifying creatures called raptors?

4 Which movie, starring Jane Fonda, was based on a comic strip by Jean Claude Forest?

5 What actress played the leading lady alongside Bob Hope and Bing Crosby in the Road To... movies?

6 Who played the clumsy inspector in the 1968 movie, Inspector Clouseau?

7 The 1970 movie, The Music Lovers, was based on the life of which classical composer?

8 What was the title of the first sound movie that featured Mickey Mouse?

9 Which 1953 movie starring Richard Burton was the first ever to be filmed in cinemascope?

10 In which 1995 movie did Sophie Marceau play Princess Isabelle?

Question 10

123   Natural Selection

1 Which bird, native to the island of Mauritius, became extinct in 1681?

2 A painted lady and monarch are both species of what?

3 From what animal is the meat venison obtained?

4 Which B word is the name given to whale fat?

5 How many stomachs does a cow have?

6 What is the world's tallest bird?

7 What is stored in a camel's hump?

8 What shape are honeycomb cells in a beehive?

9 What kind of leaves provide the silkworm's staple diet?

10 A male pig and a male bear share the same name. What is it?

Question 10

★ **BACKGROUND BONUS** ★
Which is the fastest land mammal?

124   Making History

1 In what year was the silicon chip invented: 1925, 1955 or 1975?

2 Which U.S. president was forced to resign in 1974?

3 What was the nickname of pirate Edward Teach?

4 Which Brontë sister wrote the novel *Jane Eyre*?

5 What kind of engine was Thomas Newcomen famous for inventing?

6 Which Wonder of the World was built on the orders of the Egyptian king, Cheops?

7 How many sets of wings had a triplane?

8 What country was historically known as New France?

9 Who was emperor of China when Marco Polo arrived in 1275?

10 Which Communist leader ruled China from 1949?

Question 8

125 Scientifically Speaking

1 What instrument would a scientist use to see a micro-organism?

2 Which of these foods is not protein: meat, eggs, cabbage, cheese?

3 When it is summer in Europe, what season is it in Australia?

4 Do the north poles on two magnets pull together or push apart?

5 Does an astrologer or an astronomer study the effect of the stars on human lives?

6 What are the factors of 22?

7 Do things look larger or smaller through a convex lens?

8 What does a food chain always begin with: green plants, insects or animals?

9 What is the name of an angle between 90° and 180°?

10 What numbers show on a 24-hour digital clock at a quarter to nine in the evening?

Question 1

126 Natural Selection

1 What animal is a cross between a mare and an ass?

2 Is the saki a type of rat, fish or monkey?

3 What is a stinkhorn?

4 What name is given to a male horse or pony that is less than four years old?

5 What part of a flower produces pollen?

6 What is the alternative name for a cranefly?

7 Is a young seal called a kitten, a pup or a cub?

8 What is the only bird that has nostrils?

9 What is a Manx cat missing?

10 From what flowers do we obtain opium?

Question 5

127 Total Trivia

1 Dates, coconuts and raffia all come from what?

2 Who wrote the operas *Don Giovanni* and *The Magic Flute*?

3 Where is the volcano Mount Etna?

4 What game has knights, castles and bishops?

5 Which two sea creatures squirt out inky fluid to escape from an enemy?

6 What have taken the place of glass valves in radios?

7 Which large sea mammal has two long tusks?

8 What cereal grain is grown in paddies?

9 How often in 24 hours does the tide rise and fall?

10 In what year did World War I begin?

Question 4

128 Sporting Chance

1 What sport begins with a storke-off?

2 Cobi, the official mascot of the 1992 Olympics, was what type of animal?

3 On what shape of pitch is Australian Rules Football played?

4 What did Thomas Burgess become the second man to do in September 1911?

5 What was first achieved by Edmund Hillary and Tenzing Norgay in May 1953?

6 In tennis, what is the score in a set when the tie-break comes into play?

7 On what side of a yacht is the starboard side?

8 In which equestrian event did Bonfire win gold at the 2000 Olympics?

9 In which sport can competitors use the Western Roll?

10 What nationality was the long distance runner Ingrid Kristiansen?

Question 5

★ BACKGROUND BONUS ★
In which sport would players deliver a combination of jabs, hooks and uppercuts?

129 Total Trivia

1 Woodwind, percussion and brass are three sections of an orchestra. What is the fourth?

2 What do we call a tropical fruit with yellow skin, yellow flesh and spiky leaves?

3 If you go aft in a boat, where do you go?

4 Which jazz singer was known as "Lady Day"?

5 Which garment, worn mainly by Hindu women, is made by wrapping cloth around the body?

Question 2

6 What part of the body is affected by conjunctivitis?

7 If you were in Cuzco visiting the sites of the Incas, In which country would you be?

8 What sport is Le Mans famous for?

9 Which king of England was called The Lionheart?

10 What is the name of Moscow's chief square?

130 Natural Selection

1 What is the world's largest amphibian?

2 Do frogs have dry scales or a thin, damp skin?

3 Do butterflies eat small insects, plant nectar or green leaves?

4 Is a haddock a type of octopus, oyster or fish?

5 Do all zebras have exactly the same stripe pattern or are they all different?

6 Do burrowing owls nest in pine trees, abandoned prairie dog burrows or hollow logs?

7 Does a newt egg hatch into a little newt or a tadpole?

8 Which animal from the American plains was almost hunted to extinction in the 19th century?

9 Is vanilla a member of the orchid, rose or lily family?

10 Which part of a radish do we eat: the leaf, the flower or the root?

Question 9

131 Written Word

1. Is the spear side the male or female side of the family?

2. According to the proverb, what sort of men tell no tales?

3. According to the proverb, what makes the heart grow fonder?

4. What do the initials VHF stand for?

5. Which C word is the name given to an official in charge of a museum?

6. On a ship, which instrument, used for showing direction, is housed in a binnacle?

7. Which H word is the name given to the small stroke separating two words, as in re-enter?

8. The Penny Black was the first what in the world?

9. In Roman numerals, what is D: 50, 500 or 5,000?

10. What is the shared name for a natural container for peas and a group of dolphins?

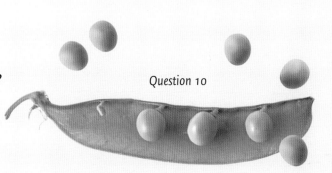

Question 10

132 Lights, Camera, Action!

1. Name the knighted actor who died in August 2000 and who, on screen, played a Jedi knight.

2. Which child actress starred in *National Velvet*?

3. In 1928, who made his movie debut in *Plane Crazy*?

4. In which city is *A Room with a View* set?

5. Which member of the Addams Family did Christina Ricci play?

6. On TV, which monastic sleuth has been portrayed by Sir Derek Jacobi?

7. In Disney's adaptation of *The Jungle Book*, what kind of animal is Shere Khan?

8. Which movie star first shot to fame playing a disco dancer in *Saturday Night Fever*?

9. In which movie did Tommy Lee Jones and Will Smith play agents J and K?

10. Who plays the title role in the TV show *Ally McBeal*?

Question 7

★ **BACKGROUND BONUS** ★
Which successful British romantic comedy starred Hugh Grant and Andie MacDowell?

133 Making History

1 What kind of weapon was a ballista?
2 Who invented the phonograph, an early kind of record player?
3 Which planet in our Solar System was discovered in 1930?
4 What are teachers called in the Jewish religion?
5 Which famous structure was built by an Indian emperor as a tomb for his wife?
6 Which World War II fighter pilot had false legs?
7 Which U.S. state was founded by William Penn?
8 According to William Shakespeare who said, "Cry havoc and let slip the dogs of war"?
9 What do architects use a buttress for?
10 When did plastic surgery begin: 2,000 years ago, 100 years ago or 10 years ago?

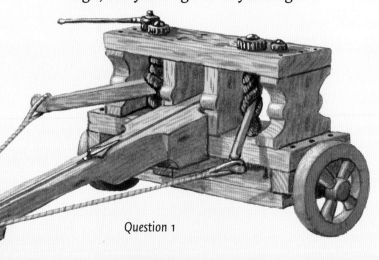

Question 1

134 Global Matters

1 The timber wolf comes from what continent?
2 Which country produces more diamonds than all the world's nations put together?
3 If you were a Bruxellian, In which city would you live?
4 Captain James Cook was the first European to discover which U.S. islands?
5 Arthur's Seat and The Royal Mile are found in which British city?
6 Did the Renaissance start in Poland, France or Italy?
7 What currency is used in Canada?
8 The U.S. city of St. Louis is famous for which monument?
9 Porto is a city in which European country?
10 In which two countries would you come across the region known as Patagonia?

Question 8

Music Mania

135

1   Which member of the boy band Five is known by a single letter of the alphabet?

2   In 2001, which pop superstar released the album *Invincible*?

3   Whose music provided the score for the movie *The Sting*?

4   What is the alternative name for an English horn?

Question 7

5   Which duo released the EP *Abba-esque* in 1992?

6   Which musical TV show featured Miss Sherwood, Leroy, Coco and Bruno?

7   What is the name of Kid Creole's backing singers?

8   Which boy band were the first Irish group to have five No. 1 hits in the U.K.?

9   A choir generally consists of four voice parts: soprano, alto, tenor and what?

10 Which British group produced a successful album in 1994 called *Parklife*?

★ BACKGROUND BONUS ★
Which musical instrument was invented in 1700 by German, Johann Christoph Denner?

Total Trivia

136

Question 1

1   Which English king reigned from 1660 to 1685?

2   Which dwarf could spin straw into gold?

3   What is one third of 51?

4   What is a Jewish place of worship called?

5   Which crop does corn come from?

6   Who saw Cock Robin die?

7   Are cornflowers blue, white or yellow?

8   What is the climate like in a tropical forest: hot and dry or hot and wet?

9   Did the Crusades take place in the Middle Ages or the Dark Ages?

10 What fish makes spectacular leaps to return to its birthplace?

137 Lights, Camera, Action!

1 Which actor battled with aliens in *Independence Day* and with dinosaurs in *Jurassic Park*?

2 Which singer won an Oscar for her role in the movie *Moonstruck*?

3 The James Bond movie, *A View to a Kill*, involves a scene set on which bridge ?

4 Which movie tells the story of Jim Garrison's investigation into a 1963 assassination?

5 What was Marilyn Monroe's first name in *Some Like it Hot*?

6 What is the third movie to feature the character of Indiana Jones?

7 Which actor was born Archibald Leach?

8 Which Hollywood legend was the subject of the 1983 movie *Mommie Dearest*?

9 What is the title of the 1991 movie in which Billy Crystal embarks upon a cattle-driving vacation?

10 In which 1976 movie did Jodie Foster play a gangster's moll?

Question 6

138 Great and Famous

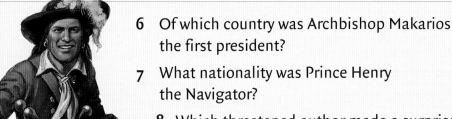

1 Was Frank Sinatra once married to Mia Farrow, Lulu or Cher?

2 Who was the inventor of the *Peanuts* cartoon strip?

3 Which international statesman received the Nobel Peace Prize in 1990?

4 What did Mary Read do for a living?

5 What was George Bernard Shaw's profession?

6 Of which country was Archbishop Makarios the first president?

7 What nationality was Prince Henry the Navigator?

8 Which threatened author made a surprise appearance at a 1993 U2 concert?

9 What weapon was Sir Barnes Wallis famous for building?

10 In what year did Prince Charles and Diana marry?

Question 4

★ BACKGROUND BONUS ★
Which inhospitable terrain was explorer Roald Amundsen the first to cross in 1911?

139   Natural Selection

1 How did the cuckoo get its name?

2 Do lizards store fat in their legs, tails or heads?

3 Do caterpillars eat mainly leaves or fruit?

4 Which has tufted ears: the red squirrel or the grey squirrel?

5 Are the seeds of holly spread by wind or by birds?

6 What does a bird have that no other animal has?

7 Snakes have voices: true or false?

8 What do mosquitoes, vampire bats and leeches have in common?

9 In summer, do caribou graze in the Arctic tundra or on southern prairies?

10 Do turtles have teeth or beaks?

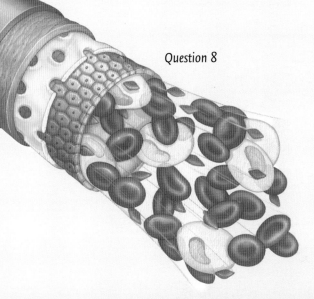

Question 8

140   Making History

1 Who exhibited his painting *Impression: Sunrise* in 1874?

2 Which Scotsman made the first steam engine to use cranks and pistons in 1769?

3 Which Soviet leader called himself "Man of Steel"?

4 Who designed a helicopter and a parachute over 500 years ago?

5 Which Australian folk hero was hanged in Melbourne in 1880?

6 Which war was ended by the Treaty of Appomattox?

7 What birds live at the Tower of London?

8 Who became British prime minister in 1940?

9 Who was Queen Elizabeth I's mother?

10 Which South Seas volcano blew up in 1883?

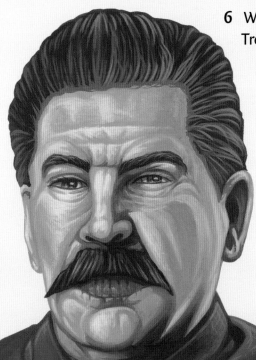

Question 3

141 Making History

1 What nationality was Charlie Chaplin?

2 What name was given to the poisonous juice that Jean Nicot extracted from tobacco in 1562?

3 What was a castle's portcullis?

4 Was the 19th-century English novelist George Eliot a man or a woman?

5 What kind of weapon is a bayonet?

6 When did sailors first use the magnetic compass: 1000BC, AD1000 or AD1500?

7 How many British kings have been called Charles?

8 What new kind of aircraft engine was developed by Frank Whittle in the 1930s?

9 Who wrote the novel *Far From the Madding Crowd*?

10 Who tried to invade Russia in 1812?

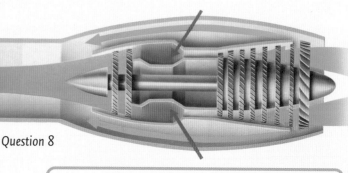

Question 8

> ★ BACKGROUND BONUS ★
> In which cathedral is Peter the Great buried?

142 Lights, Camera, Action!

1 Who provided Mikey's voice in the movie *Look Who's Talking*?

2 Which actress played the role of Honey Rider in *Dr. No*?

3 The movie *Gone With the Wind* was set against which war?

4 In which Oscar-winning movie epic did Oliver Reed make his screen farewell?

5 What is the title of the 2002 psychological thriller starring Al Pacino and Robin Williams?

6 In which movie did Graham Chapman play King Arthur?

7 What is the title of the movie sequel to *Bill and Ted's Excellent Adventure*?

8 Alphabetically, who is the last Marx Brother?

9 In which 2000 movie comedy does Jim Carrey play a state trooper with a split personality?

10 Which infamous brothers were played by Gary and Martin Kemp in the 1990 movie?

Question 10

Great and Famous

 143

1 Who wrote the novel *The Great Gatsby*?

2 Who was the first person to meet Christ after the crucifixion?

3 Which pianist and composer wrote *Maple Leaf Rag* and other ragtime songs?

4 Whose famous art studio in the 1960s was called The Factory?

5 Which cartoonist's first job was drawing pictures for a barber, receiving 25 U.S. cents or a free haircut per picture?

6 Which Peter's biography, full of stories of his acting and writing days, was called *Just Me*?

7 Dashiell Hammett created which tough, fictional detective?

8 Which French painter, together with Pablo Picasso, created the style known as Cubism?

9 The novel *Brighton Rock* was written by which English author?

10 Which U.S. male tennis player was known as "Superbrat" and "Motormouth"?

Question 10

Total Trivia

144

1 Who led the Israelites out of captivity in Egypt?

2 What is the correct term for ancient Egyptian picture writing?

3 Which process for preserving food was named after Louis Pasteur?

4 Which fungus is used to make bread, beer and wine?

5 How many people are there in a quintet?

6 Which Indian and African doglike animal makes an uncanny laughing noise?

7 What empire did Genghis Khan found?

8 Which animals shed their antlers and grow new ones every year?

9 What proportion of the air is oxygen: one fifth, one eighth or one tenth?

10 What is 20 percent of 100?

Question 8

145 Total Trivia

1 Where might you find the Abominable Snowman?

2 What bear is called the Lord of the Arctic?

3 What mountains divide Spain from France?

4 Howard Carter discovered which Egyptian pharaoh's tomb in 1922?

5 How many players are there in an ice hockey team?

6 What is the name for a French castle or a large mansion?

7 What is a bream?

8 What instrument did Chopin play?

9 "Elementary, my dear Watson." Who said this?

10 Which speckled freshwater fish belongs to the salmon family?

Question 4

146 Sporting Chance

1 Roger Craig, Joe Perry and Ricky Watters all played for which NFL team?

2 What team holds the record for the least points scored in a Superbowl?

3 What did the basketball legend Lew Alcindor change his name to?

4 Which sport, popular in Ireland, is played using a ball called a sliothar?

5 Who was the No. 1 seed in the women's singles at the 2002 Wimbledon Championships?

Question 8

6 Along with the Buffalo Bills, which two other sides have lost in four Superbowls?

7 Which piece of sporting equipment has a maximum length of 96.5 cm (38 in) and a maximum width of 10.8 cm (4.25 in)?

8 What country was the host of the Olympic Games when Judo made its debut?

9 What nationality is skier Jean-Claude Killy?

10 How many hurdles does each runner negotiate in a 110 m hurdle race?

147   Scientifically Speaking

1 Do your back or front teeth grind up your food?

2 What is 2.3 + 0.7?

3 What is a vacuum?

4 What is the name for the study of points, lines and flat, solid shapes?

5 How many faces does an octahedron have?

6 What invention by Joseph Lister allowed him to reduce the number of deaths from surgery?

7 In what industry was William Caxton a pioneer?

8 On a cold day, from which part of your body does most heat escape?

9 Where in the body is the smallest muscle, the stapedius?

10 What does a geologist study?

Question 7

> ★ **BACKGROUND BONUS** ★
> Which C word describes the board on which electronic data is handled and arranged?

148   Making History

1 Who made the first successful wireless, in 1895?

2 What kind of instrument is a clavicord?

3 Who brought the first horses to North America?

4 Why were canaries once taken down coal mines?

5 What kind of plane was a Stuka?

6 Which pack animal was known as "the ship of the desert"?

7 What is the companion story to Lewis Carroll's *Alice in Wonderland*?

8 The island of Réunion became a colony of what country in 1764?

9 James Cook's first ship was a collier. What kind of ship was this?

10 In 1769, a French priest designed a waistcoat filled with cork. What was it?

Question 1

149 Scientifically Speaking

1 How many hours are there in a week?

2 What do builders use a spirit level for?

3 What kind of boat has wings called foils?

4 Which husband and wife team discovered radium?

5 How many degrees colder is −5°C than 1°C?

6 What do seismic waves travel through?

7 What shape is a volcano?

8 What kind of operation is used to give someone a new heart?

9 What does an angle of 180° look like?

10 Did *Thrust 2* break the land, water or air speed record?

Question 10

150 Written Word

1 Semaphore is a system using arm signals and what else?

2 What do the initials CB in CB radio stand for?

3 Is an epilogue at the beginning or at the end of a book?

4 Choreography is the art of arranging what?

5 What do the initials I.C.U. stand for in a hospital?

6 Which four-letter word can come before ache, light and phone?

7 According to the grammatical rule, which letter comes before E except after C?

8 Which A word is the name given to a drug that counteracts a poison?

9 Is hypothermia when your body gets very hot or very cold?

10 What does the letter P stand for in POW?

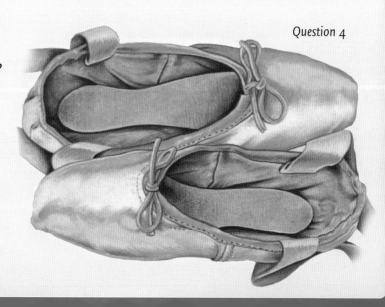

Question 4

151　Lights, Camera, Action!

1　Which *Friends* star appeared in the movie *Lost in Space*?

2　In which 2000 children's comedy movie did Jonathan Lipnicki play a young bloodsucker?

3　Which of the Seven Dwarfs wears glasses?

4　Indiana Jones is terrified of what creatures?

5　What kind of animals are Scar and Simba?

Question 7

6　Which Disney movie features Thomas O'Malley and Duchess?

7　In which movie do two dogs and a cat called Chance, Shadow and Sassy attempt to find their way home?

8　*The Adventure Home* and *The Rescue* are both sequels to what movie about a killer whale?

9　The song "Walking In The Air" is heard in which seasonal animated movie?

10　What city did Batman try to protect?

> ★ BACKGROUND BONUS ★
> In which 1998 animated movie does Woody Allen provide the voice for Z?

152　Total Trivia

Question 6

1　Which ancient people invented paper?

2　What is the mongoose famed for killing?

3　What do three dots represent in the Morse Code?

4　What two countries make up the Iberian Peninsula?

5　Tibet is ruled by what country?

6　Which tropical bird has bright plumage and an enormous beak?

7　What is the capital of Turkey?

8　Where is urine made in your body?

9　What ocean lies between Africa, Asia, Australia and Antarctica?

10　What is the name for a male goose?

153 Total Trivia

1 In which city is the Louvre?

2 What rodent spread the Plague?

3 Alligators, crocodiles and snakes are all what?

4 Which rock is formed from grains of sand?

5 What is the most common animal in Australia?

6 What does supersonic mean?

7 What are your biceps?

8 What are you doing if you are performing the quickstep?

9 How many sides has a cube?

10 Which of the Seven Wonders of the World still stands?

Question 4

154 Lights, Camera, Action!

1 What is the name of the black-and-red-faced villain in *Star Wars: The Phantom Menace*?

2 What kind of plant is Count Dracula repelled by?

3 In which Christmas movie does Dudley Moore play an elf?

4 What movies are based on the best-selling novels by J.K. Rowling?

5 According to the fairy tale, who falls in love with Prince Charming?

6 Who played Ethan Hunt in *Mission Impossible*?

7 Which rap artist played the Fresh Prince of Bel Air on TV?

8 Which actor links the roles of Han Solo and Dr. Kimble?

9 Who played the title role in the movie *Bean*?

10 What is Jim Carrey's occupation in the movie *Liar, Liar*?

Question 4

155 Natural Selection

1 What flying insect is known for spreading malaria?

2 Do scorpions produce live young or lay eggs?

3 Which B word is the name given to the study of plants?

4 What is the more common name for a eucalyptus tree?

5 What name is given to a female foal?

6 A Wessex Saddleback is a breed of which farm animal?

7 What kind of creature is a natterjack?

8 Which species of snake has varieties called green tree, reticulated, Indian and Burmese?

9 What breed of dog connects Beethoven, Schnorbits and the patron saint of mountaineers?

10 A rookery is the name given to a collection of which fast-swimming birds?

Question 9

★ BACKGROUND BONUS ★
African tiger, blue coral and Cuban wood are all types of what creature?

156 Scientifically Speaking

1 What is the more common name for sodium chloride?

2 Which material is made from oil: plastic, glass or rubber?

3 What is a negative number?

4 What is the name of the machine that weaves thread into cloth?

5 What is ornithology: the study of bones, birds or precious metals?

6 What happens to a boy's voice when it breaks?

7 What is another word for data?

8 Where on your body is your skin the thinnest?

9 Which of these shapes is not a polygon: triangle, decagon, tetrahedron, octagon?

10 What did Edmond Halley have named after him?

Question 4

157 Lights, Camera, Action!

1   What is the name of the emperor who is Buzz Lightyear's archenemy?

2   Which U.S. rock group recorded the song "I Don't Want To Miss A Thing" for the movie *Armageddon*?

3   Which Christmas novel was written by Charles Dickens?

4   Which star of the sitcom *Friends* appears in the movies *Dr. Doolittle II* and *Analyze This*?

5   Who plays the title role in the 2002 movie *Pluto Nash*?

6   In Disney's *Aladdin*, Robin Williams provides the voice for which character?

7   Which of Batman's foes was played by Jack Nicholson?

8   In which series of sci-fi thrillers does Sigourney Weaver play Ellen Ripley?

9   Which U.S. pop sensation made her big screen debut in the movie *Crossroads*?

10   What is the name of the Hobbit played by Elijah Wood in the *Lord of the Rings* trilogy?

Question 3

158 Global Matters

1   In which country would you find the cities of Kyoto and Osaka?

2   What is the current population of Easter Island: 200, 2,000, 20,000 or 200,000?

3   Would you find Hilo Bay in the English Channel, Hawaii or the Canary Islands?

4   The Olympic flame is found at Mount Olympus in which country?

5   If you were sitting in Wenceslaus Square, would you be in Warsaw, Prague or Budapest?

6   Is the Rila Monastry found in Bulgaria, Hungary or France?

7   Is a small, rounded hill called a knoll, a coll or a poll?

8   Was Montezuma a famous Aztec, Inca or Mongol leader?

9   The Sahara Desert is home to which nomadic tribe?

10   In which South American country would you find the Nazca Plains?

Question 9

159 Scientifically Speaking

1 What was the name of the first artificial satellite?

2 What did Charles Macintosh invent in 1823?

3 In your body, where would you find marrow?

4 In your home, which device breaks an electric circuit?

5 Do things look larger or smaller through a concave lens?

6 In which flying machine does the pilot hang below the wings?

7 How many right-angles are there in a rectangle?

8 Does it take more muscles to smile or to frown?

9 What foods give you vitamin C?

10 What does REM stand for?

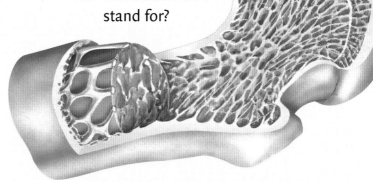

Question 3

> ★ **BACKGROUND BONUS** ★
> Which gas of the chemical symbol, Ne, was named after the Greek word for new?

160 Sporting Chance: Soccer

1 Which 1966 World Cup winner went on to manage the Republic of Ireland in the World Cup finals?

2 In which country did Gary Lineker play for Grampus 8?

3 At the 1998 World Cup, which nation was known as "The Reggae Boys"?

4 Which Italian Chelsea star scored the quickest ever goal in the 1997 FA Cup final?

5 Which was the first British club that Eric Cantona played for?

6 Who was England's manager in the 1990 World Cup?

7 In the 1920s, which legendary Everton striker scored 60 goals in a single season?

8 Who were England's first opponents in the 2002 World Cup finals?

9 Who was the first soccer player to score 100 goals in England's Premiership?

10 Which soccer club was Brian Clough managing when he announced his retirement from the game?

Question 3

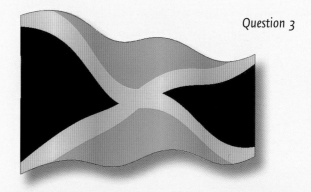

161 Global Matters

1 What was the island of Sri Lanka known as before 1948?

2 What design is on the flag of Canada?

3 Where did Quasimodo ring the bells?

4 What is the capital of Thailand?

5 In which European capital city could you visit the Tivoli Gardens?

6 The island of Zanzibar lies off the east coast of which continent?

7 What is the name of the straits that separate Anglesey from mainland Wales?

8 Which Israeli port gave its name to a variety of orange?

9 Palm trees are native to what kind of natural habitat?

10 What is the national bird of India?

Question 9

★ **BACKGROUND BONUS** ★
In what industry would you use a subsoiler, windrower and baler?

162 Total Trivia

1 What is a census?

2 What is special about a catamaran?

3 Which edible blue-black shellfish is found in clusters on coastal rocks?

4 What is the capital of Israel?

5 Which animal is yellow with black spots and is called a panther in India?

6 What is the name of the technique used to send people into a trance-like sleep?

7 What star sign follows Taurus?

8 In which ocean do the Falkland Islands lie?

9 What landmark is the French city of Chartres famous for?

10 Stockholm is the capital of what country?

Question 5

163 Sporting Chance

1   Johnny Weissmuller went on to play Tarzan after winning five Olympic golds In which sport?

2   Wilt Chamberlain holds the NBA record for most points in a baseball game. How many points?

3   In 1986, who became World Heavyweight Boxing champion after defeating Trevor Berbick?

Question 8

4   In which city did Australian Rules Football originate?

5   In gymnastics, what is a backward handspring known as?

6   What sport is played by the Doncaster Belles?

7   Is the Happy Valley racecourse in New York, Paris or Hong Kong?

8   What piece of sporting equipment shares its name with a character from Shakespeare's *A Midsummer Night's Dream*?

9   In what type of car did Paddy Hopkirk and Henry Widden win the 1964 Monte Carlo Rally?

10 In polo, with what do you hit the ball?

164 Natural Selection

1   Where does the harvest mouse live: above ground in tall grass or in woodland leaf litter?

2   When do rattlesnakes rattle: to threaten enemies or when they are ready to breed?

3   Which South American rodent is the size of a pig and has webbed feet: the capybara or the coypu?

4   Which prickly American desert plant sometimes swells up when it rains: the cactus or the yucca?

5   Which wild, red-furred European member of the dog family lives in cities?

6   Which yellow, sausage-shaped fruit is grown throughout the Caribbean Islands?

7   Do turtles lay their eggs in underwater nests or on land?

8   Which seabird did sailors consider it bad luck to kill: the gannet, the tern or the albatross?

9   What proportion of all living species are made up by insects: one-tenth, one-quarter or over half?

10 Which creatures create the dawn chorus: mice, birds or insects?

Question 5

165 Great and Famous

1 In the Bible, what were the names of Adam's two sons?

2 Was Sir Christopher Wren an architect, a British prime minister or a naval captain?

3 What nationality was the sculpter Alberto Giacometti?

4 Is Henry Moore known as a sculptor, a poet, a playwright or a painter?

5 Which U.S. president was known as "Honest Abe"?

6 Who did Melinda, a product manager at Microsoft, marry in 1994?

7 U.S. naval officer, Robert Peary, was the first to reach which part of the world?

8 In which country did Eva Perón live?

9 Who sentenced Jesus to death?

10 How was writer Herbert George Wells better known?

Question 8

166 Total Trivia

1 What does the word "medieval" mean?

2 Which element in the air was discovered by Lavoisier in the 1780s?

3 Which Russian composer caused a riot with his ultra-modern *The Rite of Spring* in 1913?

Question 5

4 What was a lord's "demesne" in the Middle Ages?

5 What country was crossed for the first time by Burke and Wills?

6 What is the largest public square in the world?

7 What vegetable was struck by disease, causing Ireland's "Great Hunger" after 1845?

8 What was the first full-length movie picture with sound, made in 1927?

9 Which famous iron construction was designed in 1889 for an exhibition?

10 Who is the Buddhist leader of the Tibetan people?

167 Natural Selection

1 Where do flying swans land: in riverside trees, on the water or in flat meadows?

2 What are pattern, withers, muzzle and hock?

3 Which gas, essential to animal life, is produced by green plants: hydrogen, oxygen or carbon dioxide?

4 Do geckoes hunt mainly in the day or at night?

5 Is a whelk a kind of lobster, an eel or a shellfish?

6 Do salmon leap waterfalls going upstream or downstream?

7 When turning into frogs, do tadpoles grow their front or back legs first?

8 Where do spider monkeys spend most of their time?

9 Crabs, lobsters and shrimps all have the same number of legs. How many?

10 What sort of bird is Wol in the *Winnie the Pooh* stories?

Question 10

168 Scientifically Speaking

1 What is a microchip made of?

2 What do long-sighted people see more clearly: things that are near or farther away?

3 Which German physicist worked out the theory of relativity?

4 What is three-quarters as a decimal fraction?

5 Does drag slow things down or speed them up?

6 Which solid shape has a circular base and a curved surface rising to a point?

7 Does incoming air pass through your lungs or your windpipe first?

8 Where would you find black smokers: in a city, on the ocean floor or in a factory?

9 What force is produced when two surfaces rub together?

10 The patella is another name for which bone found in the leg?

Question 3

★ BACKGROUND BONUS ★
Amateur British weather scientist, Luke Howard, identified ten types of what?

169   Lights, Camera, Action!

1 In which Disney movie does a spaniel fall in love with a mongrel?

2 In which movie did Demi Moore shave off her hair to join the U.S. Navy Seals?

3 In the *Harry Potter* movies, what is Hagrid's three-headed dog called?

4 In Disney's *The Aristocats*, what kind of waddling creatures are Abigail and Amelia?

5 In which 1990 movie did Johnny Depp possess metal hands?

6 Who played the bride in the 1997 romantic comedy *My Best Friend's Wedding*?

7 In which movie did an alien phone home with the help of Elliott?

8 In what decade was Robin Williams born?

9 Which U.S. wrestler appeared in the movies *Rocky III* and *Muppets From Space*?

10 Which 1995 animated movie told the story of Captain John Smith, who fell in love with an American-Indian princess?

Question 10

170   Global Matters

1 In which city was Terry Waite taken hostage in 1987?

2 The French town of Dijon is famed for the manufacture of which condiment?

3 The River Taff flows through which British capital city?

4 What is the nickname for the state of Kansas?

5 In which European city are the headquarters of the Red Cross?

6 What is the former name of China's capital?

7 In what century did the British rule of India end?

8 Which building in the seaside resort of Brighton, England, was built for King George IV?

9 Which U.S. state is the nearest to Russia?

10 Which famous statue in the United States was built on Bedloe's Island?

Question 10

171   Scientifically Speaking

1 What liquid is made when your mouth waters?

2 In Roman numerals, what is 1,000?

3 What is the process called when water disappears into the air?

4 What was Yuri Gagarin's historic achievement?

5 What kind of vehicle has a conning tower?

6 What is the word for the Earth's path around the Sun?

7 Where are the smallest bones in the body?

8 What part of a light bulb glows?

9 What part of the body has buds?

10 How many seconds in three and a half minutes?

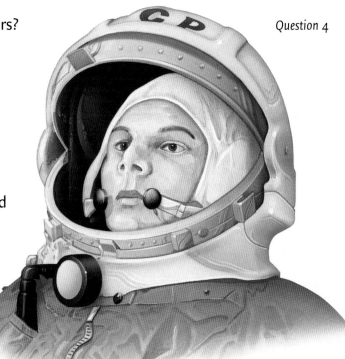

Question 4

172   Natural Selection

1 What does the flamingo use its beak for: to filter food from water and mud or to catch small fish?

2 Which animal often works in the flooded rice fields of Asia: the camel or the water buffalo?

3 What is a female horse aged five or more known as?

4 How far can a gliding frog glide: 7 m (23 ft) or 70 m (230 ft)?

5 Which is the odd one out: mint, sage, thyme or tomato?

Question 7

6 Is the woodlouse related to spiders, shrimps or cockroaches?

7 What is the tallest, thickest kind of grass and also provides food for the giant panda?

8 Do dates grow on pine trees, palm trees or vines?

9 Is the rhinoceros an omnivore, a carnivore or a herbivore?

10 Would you look for limpets on a sandy beach, a shingle beach or a rocky beach?

★ BACKGROUND BONUS ★
Which Asian mammal has an extra "thumb" which it uses to grasp food?

173   Total Trivia

1 Which musical instrument consists of a long pipe and is played by Aborigines?

2 What do you dry to get a prune?

3 Who were the greatest road builders of the ancient world?

4 What substance makes fireworks explode?

5 Which black-and-white seabird has a red, blue and yellow bill?

6 What are the four cavities in the bones of your skull called?

7 What is the name for a high female singing voice?

8 What does it mean to nip something in the bud?

9 What religion did the Romans adopt in the AD300s?

10 What is an egress?

Question 5

174   Lights, Camera, Action!

1 What is the name of the tomb raider played on screen by Angelina Jolie?

2 Which *Friends* actress married movie star David Arquette in 1999?

3 Which man of steel is weakened when exposed to kryptonite?

4 In the movie *Grease*, does Danny fall in love with Sindy, Sandy or Mandy?

5 Which sport features in the movie *The Bad News Bears*?

6 What kind of toy bird is Wheezy in *Toy Story II*?

7 What is the name of Popeye's girlfriend?

8 Which movie opens with the words: "A long time ago, in a galaxy far, far away..."?

9 In which country was Arnold Schwarzenegger born?

10 In which 1998 movie did Lindsay Lohan play twin sisters?

Question 6

175 Making History

1 In the Middle Ages, what job did a spinster do?

2 What planet did William Herschel discover in 1781?

3 What nationality is Pope John Paul II?

4 Who wrote *The Invisible Man* in 1897?

5 Which common tool is associated with the Swiss army?

6 Which Himalayan peak is named after the man who mapped the area?

7 Who were the Fauves: a group of artists, poets or jazz musicians?

8 In what year was the CD invented: 1959, 1979 or 1999?

9 Which Italian city minted its own gold coins called "florins"?

10 What was the name of the ruling council in ancient Rome?

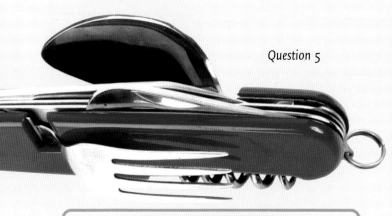

Question 5

★ **BACKGROUND BONUS** ★
Is a fresco a Renaissance wallpainting or an Impressionist outdoor painting technique?

176 Scientifically Speaking

1 The bark of the willow tree was originally used to make what kind of painkiller?

2 How do you write one thousandth as a decimal fraction?

3 What happens to light when it shines through a prism?

4 What is the name of the natural fountains found on top of old volcanoes?

5 Who uses a barometer, a thermometer and an anemometer?

6 What are you doing when you inhale?

7 What is the Beaufort Scale used to measure?

8 Where can the strongest muscles in your body be found?

9 What is the name of the robot spacecraft sent into space to take close-up pictures and measurements?

10 What is the name for numbers that can only be divided by themselves and 1?

Question 3

177 Total Trivia

Question 3

1 Where is the ski resort of St. Moritz?

2 Who ate Turkey Lurkey?

3 What food is eaten by most of the world's people?

4 Pneumonia affects which part of the body?

5 Where would you find your adenoids?

6 What is 0.2 x 10?

7 Which melon has pink flesh and lots of large, black seeds?

8 The Secretary General is the head of what organization?

9 Which German city was divided by a wall?

10 Who went to sea in "a beautiful pea-green boat"?

178 Sporting Chance

1 Which new American Football team fought the 2000 Superbowl against the Rams?

2 In which country did speedskating originate?

3 Which player holds the major league baseball record for most home runs?

4 Which British athlete broke the world record for the javelin in 1990?

5 Which sporting body has the initials WBO?

6 Bernard Hinault is a national hero in France for which sport?

7 Which player holds the major league baseball record for most strikeouts?

8 In which sport might you achieve a strike or a spare?

9 Who became Formula One World Champion after winning the Japanese Grand Prix in October 1996?

10 British Ice Dance champions Torvill and Dean are associated most with which piece of music?

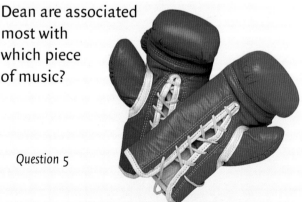

Question 5

★ BACKGROUND BONUS ★
In which sport was Marcus Grönholm the 2002 World Champion ?

179 Global Matters

1 Is Chomu Lonzo a mountain in Nepal, China or India?

2 Does the area of Brazil represent less or more than half of South America's total land?

3 How many horses can be found in the United States: 60,000, 600,000, or 6 million?

4 The mistral is a strong, dry, cool type of what?

5 Kuala Lumpur is the capital city of what country?

6 Seat cars are made In which country?

7 What country does singer Björk come from?

8 How long is a baby kangaroo at birth: 2.5 cm (1 in), 10 cm (4 in) or 25 cm (10 in)?

9 In which country is the River Ebro?

10 If you are giggling at the Melbourne Comedy Festival, what country are you in?

Question 5

180 Making History

1 Which two bodies of water were linked by the Suez Canal in 1869?

2 Which president of the United States, from 1913 to 1921, was awarded the 1920 Nobel Peace Prize?

3 Which Chicago gangster was nicknamed "Scarface"?

4 What people were scattered throughout the world in the diaspora?

5 Which kind of rocket launched the U.S. Moon expedition in 1969?

Question 9

6 What is the name for the wooden sailing ships that have been used in the Far East for thousand of years?

7 What king began the Anglo-Saxon Chronicles in AD891?

8 Why was the Pacific Ocean so-called by early European sailors?

9 Which silent movie actor was known as the "Great Lover"?

10 Where was the capital of the ancient Hebrew kingdom?

181 Sporting Chance

1 In which sport would you see a baranie, a seat drop or Randolph?

2 What is the name of the machine that picks up the pins in tenpin bowling?

3 How many golf shots would you have taken if you had an eagle on a par 5 hole?

4 In the United States, in which sport is the Royal Rumble contested?

5 In which sport is a series of bouts called a barrage?

6 Who inflicted a defeat on Mike Tyson in November 1996?

7 Three cushions is a form of which game?

8 What is the age limit for racehorses in nursery stakes?

9 Where did the 2002 Winter Olympics take place?

10 Which monocle-wearing boxer made his ring entrances to Tina Turner's hit "Simply The Best"?

Question 4

182 Lights, Camera, Action!

1 What kind of dinosaurs chased two children around the kitchen in the movie *Jurassic Park*?

2 Which Disney movie featured a wicked witch called Maleficent?

3 What kind of insect attempts to be the conscience of Pinocchio?

4 Which 2001 animated movie tells the story of a white blood cell cop called Ozzy?

5 In which movie do two dogs share a plate of spaghetti outside an Italian restaurant?

6 Which 2002 animated movie features a character called Chihiro whose parents are turned into pigs?

7 Which Disney movie, set in the jungle, is based on a novel by Edgar Rice Burroughs?

8 *Honey I Blew up the Kids* is the sequel to which movie?

9 In which country are the Bollywood movies made?

10 Which of the Muppets played Benjamina Gunn in *The Muppets' Treasure Island*?

Question 3

★ **BACKGROUND BONUS** ★
Which Hollywood actress started her career in movies such as *Lassie Come Home*?

183   Making History

1 What country was led by the Ayatollah Khomeini?

2 What was the magical land created by C.S. Lewis in a series of books?

3 What nationality was the poet Horace?

4 Who was the first European to cross the Indian Ocean?

5 Who was emperor of Japan during World War II?

6 The Battle of Lexington sparked off which major American war?

7 Which Roman emperor founded the city of Constantinople?

8 Which jazz composer and bandleader was known as "Duke"?

9 Which country did Britain and its allies fight against in the Crimean War?

10 What natural disaster destroyed the Italian town of Pompeii in AD79?

Question 10

184   Natural Selection

1 What flatfish has a whiplike tail often equipped with a sting: the halibut, the ray or the plaice?

2 Which of these countries has no snakes: France, New Zealand or Japan?

3 Which flower-like sea creature fastens itself to rocks and catches prey with stinging tentacles?

4 What is the ferret-like mammal renowned for killing snakes: the mink or the mongoose?

5 What insects guard the nest and workers as large-jawed soldiers?

6 Were prehistoric woolly mammoths similar to rhinos, elephants or sheep?

7 Is the gharial a type of bird, snake or crocodile?

8 Is the hobby a fish or bird of prey?

9 Cactus plants never bear flowers: true or false?

10 Is salmon flesh white, brown or pink?

Question 6

185 Lights, Camera, Action!

1 The character of Milo Thatch appears in which Disney movie about a lost empire?

2 What type of vehicle did Elliott use to escape from government officials?

3 What letter of the alphabet is the code name for James Bond's boss?

4 In which movie did King Louie sing "I Wanna Be Like You"?

5 What kind of animals are Skip, Benji and Rin Tin Tin?

6 In the 1991 sequel to *An American Tail*, in which direction does Fievel travel?

7 What is the name of the wood where Winnie the Pooh lives?

8 Who starred alongside Renée Zellweger as Velma in the 2002 movie *Chicago*?

9 Which 1999 teen comedy is also the title of a 2000 hit for Madonna?

10 During which war is the movie *Pearl Harbor* set?

Question 9

186 Total Trivia

1 What country is known for its mountains, watches and chocolate?

2 Which of these is not an African country: Gambia, Ghana, Guyana, Congo?

3 Which metal costs three times as much as gold?

4 How does the possum try to avoid capture?

5 What is the highest numbered segment on a dart board?

6 What is the only bird that can fly backward and hover?

7 In which country is the Algarve?

8 What is gnocchi?

9 How many years are there between 15BC and AD15?

10 Julius Caesar sailed from Gaul to England. What is Gaul now called?

Question 6

187 Natural Selection

1. What is a young owl called?
2. Which weasel-like animal catches fish and is more at home in water than on dry land?
3. Do ants communicate with one another by sound, sight or with their antennae?
4. Which of these cats has the longest hair: Siamese, Persian or Manx?
5. What is used to make porridge: barley, wheat or oats?
6. What bird uses its long, sharp beak to drill a nest hole and to dig out insects from bark?
7. Which has waterproof skin: the frog, the newt or the snake?
8. Most apes are too heavy to climb trees: true or false?
9. Mustard belongs to what vegetable family?
10. Which slow land creature carries its home?

Question 4

188 Music Mania

1. Which top-selling girl group of the 1980s had a U.S. hit with "Venus"?
2. The Beatles are the only group to have had more U.K. top 10 hits than this British group. Can you name the group?
3. Rapper star Dr. Dre had a U.S. No.1 and U.K. Top 10 hit with which track?
4. What was George Michael's first solo chart-topping hit?
5. As well as reaching No. 1, what did Sandie Shaw's "Puppet on a String" achieve?
6. Whose first hit was the 1978 "Hit Me With Your Rhythm Stick"?
7. Which hugely successful rap single of 1997 was a tribute to Notorious B.I.G.?
8. What band recorded "Help" and "A Hard Day's Night"?
9. What is Fleetwood Mac's only U.K. No. 1 single, from 1968?
10. What was Madonna's first U.S. No. 1 single?

Question 9

★ **BACKGROUND BONUS** ★
With which U.S. band would you associate the tracks "Give it Away" and "Don't Stop"?

189   Total Trivia

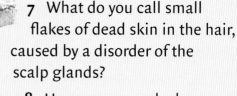
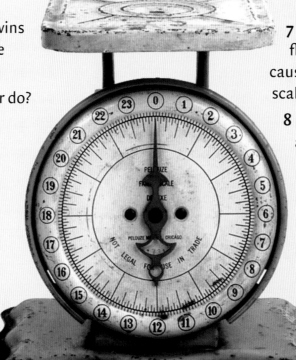

1   What is the name for twins joined together at some part of their bodies?

2   What does your bladder do?

3   What is a group of bees called?

4   What country does the island of Corsica belong to?

5   What kind of animal is a narwhal?

6   What are rings, parallel bars and the pommel horse?

7   What do you call small flakes of dead skin in the hair, caused by a disorder of the scalp glands?

8   How many people dance a *pas de deux*?

9   What symbol is associated with the star sign, Libra?

10   Which country was at war with Iran for eight years from 1980?

Question 9

190   Scientifically Speaking

1   How many hundreds are there in two thousand five hundred?

2   Does a light bulb give out heat as well as light?

3   The temperature is −4°C. How many degrees must it rise to reach 6°C?

4   Why is stainless steel good for making cutlery and cooking equipment?

5   Is your stomach positioned above or below your intestines?

6   What instrument is used to measure angles?

7   What, in terms of computers, is the monitor?

8   What is longer: your small or large intestine?

9   How long does it take for the Earth to spin around once?

10   What is the mechanism that drives a ship through the water?

Question 10

★ BACKGROUND BONUS ★
What is formed in space from a cloud of dust and gas called a nebula?

World Wonders

191

Can you identify these famous buildings and landmarks?

192   Sporting Chance

1   Which sport takes place in a velodrome?

2   At which sport was Kate Howey of Great Britain a world champion in 1998?

3   Who did Mary Decker collide with in the 1984 Olympic 3,000 m final?

4   Which ice hockey legend scored a total of 2,857 points in a career starting with the Edmonton Oilers?

5   Which team did the Dallas Cowboys beat to win their fifth Superbowl in 1996?

6   Who connects the New York Yankees and Marilyn Monroe?

7   What is a table tennis ball made of?

8   At which sport did Suzanne Dando represent Great Britain?

9   What is the minimum depth of the pool in water polo?

10 What boxing weight category comes between bantamweight and lightweight?

Question 1

193   Lights, Camera, Action!

1   What is the second *Harry Potter* novel to be adapted into a movie?

2   In *One Hundred and Two Dalmatians*, what is the name of the 102nd dalmatian?

3   In *The Lion King*, Shenzi and Banzai are what kind of animal?

4   Which 2000 movie features the characters of Misty and Ash?

5   How many thieves accompany Ali?

6   Which movie, with a large feline cast, features a sinister butler called Edgar?

7   In which movie do we meet a sea witch called Ursula?

8   Which movie character has a pet elephant who thinks he is a dog?

9   In the movie *The Borrowers*, what drink does Pea Green dislike?

10 Who wrote the plays on which the movies *Hamlet* and *Henry V* are based?

Question 3

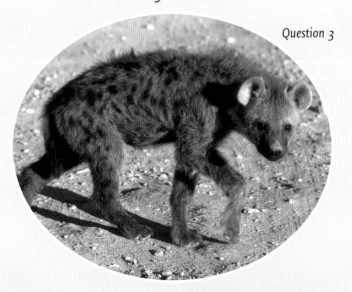

194   Music Mania

Name each band from its band members:

1 Kurt Cobain, Krist Novoselic, Dave Grohl.

2 Beyoncé Knowles, LeToya Luckett, LaTavia Roberson, Kelly Rowland.

3 Roger Daltrey, Pete Townshend, John Entwhistle, Keith Moon.

4 Bill Berry, Peter Buck, Mike Mills, Michael Stipe.

5 Mick Jagger, Keith Richards, Brian Jones, Bill Wyman, Charlie Watts.

6 Gwen Stefani, Tom Dumont, Tony Kanal, Adrian Young.

7 Kevin Richardson, Nick Carter, Brian Littrell, A.J. McLean, Howard Dorough.

8 Chris Martin, Guy Berryman, Jonny Buckland, Will Champion.

9 Francis Rossi, Rick Parfitt, Alan Lancaster, John Coghlan.

10 Marc Bolan, Steve Peregrine Took.

Question 10

195   Written Word

1 Who wrote *The Secret Garden*?

2 Who writes fantasy novels about Discworld?

3 Who wrote *The Origin of Species*?

4 What is the opposite of encourage?

5 When you add -ly to an adjective, what type of word do you normally create?

6 In Greek mythology, which character's weak point was his heel?

7 Who is author of the hugely successful series called *Horrible Histories*?

8 What is the meaning of the word turmoil?

9 Which member of the Royal Family wrote *The Old Man of Lochnagar* in 1980?

10 Which Shakespearean character was known as the Prince of Denmark: Othello, Hamlet or King Lear?

Question 9

★ BACKGROUND BONUS ★
Which popular food is an Italian term for the word "dough"?

196 Scientifically Speaking

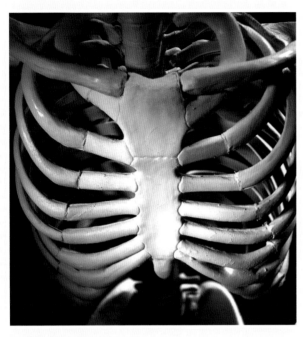

Question 8

1 What did alchemists try to turn ordinary metals into?

2 What is one-quarter of 28?

3 If something contracts, does it get bigger or smaller?

4 Which household machine has a rotating drum, a motor and a water outlet?

5 What is 9.35 + 1.45?

6 How many seconds in a quarter of a minute?

7 What kind of vehicle is used for the radar warning system AWACS?

8 Which bones protect your lungs?

9 What kind of energy is solar energy?

10 What pollution falls from the clouds?

197 Total Trivia

1 What sort of animal is a pug?

2 Who were the first people to grow potatoes, maize, tomatoes and tobacco?

3 In which ocean is the island of Fiji?

4 In which country is New Mexico?

5 Who wrote *Pride and Prejudice*?

6 If someone's bank account is in the red, what does it mean?

7 What is the name for a baby hippo?

8 In French it is *jeudi*, in German it is *Donnerstag*. What day of the week is it?

9 How long has a couple been married if they celebrating their diamond wedding?

10 Which cereal crop grows underwater?

Question 10

198 Great and Famous

1 Which religious leader's real name is Karol Jozef Wojtyla?

2 Which movie, with the lead played by John Hurt, was about the real life of John Merrick?

3 Which U.S. president gave his name to the teddy?

4 Who was the first woman to fly solo from England to Australia?

5 What did John Paul Getty III lose when kidnapped in 1974?

6 Who directed the movies *The Color Purple*, *E.T.* and *Jaws*?

7 Which Belgian-born actress has won a record four Oscars in major roles?

8 Which English king was known as "The Unready"?

9 What country did the writer Leo Tolstoy come from?

10 Who founded the Boy Scouts?

Question 1

★ **BACKGROUND BONUS** ★
Siddhartha Gautama is also known as who?

199 Sporting Chance

1 What type of wood are hurling sticks made from: willow, ash or yew?

2 Which Olympic gold medal-winner of 1968 went on to become World Heavyweight Boxing champion?

3 Who worked as a sports commentator before becoming a U.S. president?

4 What sport is played by the New Jersey Devils?

5 Which Italian boxer holds the record for being the heaviest ever World Heavyweight champion?

Question 4

6 Which track star beat a racehorse over a sprint course in 1936?

7 Hakeem Olajuwon was named Most Valuable Player in 1994 and 1995 for which basketball side?

8 Who was first to fly solo around the world in a hot air balloon?

9 Which ice hockey side was coached to Stanley Cup victory four times by Al Arbour?

10 Which was the first motorcycle manufacturer to register 400 Grand Prix wins?

200 Global Matters

1 In which ocean does Sri Lanka lie?

2 Suriname can be found in which continent?

3 Do stalactites or stalagmites hang down from the roofs of caves?

4 If your airline baggage was tagged MMA, would you be going to Malmo, Manchester or Milwaukee?

5 What term describes a volcano that has not been active for a time?

6 What is the Matterhorn: a church, a lake, a mountain or a massive cave?

7 What country makes up the world's largest island chain?

8 The highest navigable lake in the world is found in which continent?

9 What is the main meat eaten in Asia?

10 What continent is home to Lake Superior, the world's largest freshwater lake?

Question 10

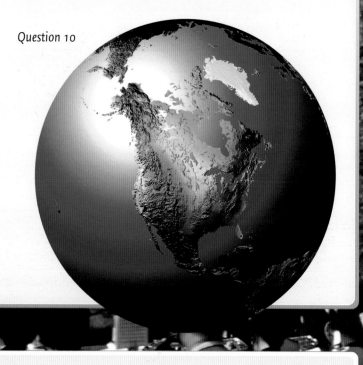

201 Total Trivia

1 Which group of sea mammals has flippers for swimming, lives in herds and barks?

2 Who was Moses' brother?

3 Which Scottish doctor explored Africa in the 19th century?

4 Which tall plant has huge, yellow flowers and has seeds that are rich in oil?

5 The human brain is getting bigger over time: true or false?

6 What country produces the most coffee?

7 The beam, the arch and the suspension are three kinds of what?

8 What river do the Great Lakes flow into?

9 What type of insect is an Apollo?

10 Where is Jesus said to have been born?

Question 1

202   Making History

1. How many Crusades were there?
2. In which English town was William Shakespeare born?
3. Which great African river was explored by H.M. Stanley in 1889?
4. Which steamship of 1843 was the first to cross the Atlantic using a screw propeller?
5. After 1935, Persia became known by what new name?
6. Who was the last tsar of Russia?
7. What is Constantinople now known as?
8. Which revolutionary type of firearm was invented by Richard Gatling in 1862?
9. Which Russian revolutionary leader changed his name to "Man of Iron"?
10. Which of the Seven Wonders of the World was in Babylon?

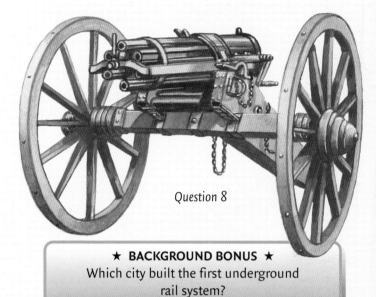

Question 8

★ **BACKGROUND BONUS** ★
Which city built the first underground rail system?

203   Natural Selection

1. What kind of animal is a shark?
2. Which are longer: a frog's front legs or its back legs?
3. What is the name of the tree on which the cocoa seed grows?
4. Is a shellfish with a hinged double shell called a univalve or a bivalve?
5. Which European weed causes a stinging rash called urticaria if it touches bare skin?
6. What do some birds swallow to help grind up tough seeds?
7. Which is the heaviest of the sea reptiles: the sea snake, the marine turtle or the marine iguana?
8. Is the sandhopper, which is usually found under rotting seaweed, related to mice or crabs?
9. Which of these has webbed feet: the fish eagle, the penguin or the kingfisher?
10. Which mammal never has fleas: the lion, the wolf or the zebra?

Question 7

204   Written Word: The Bible

1   Did the three Wise Men travel to see the baby Jesus from the north, south, east or west?

2   What creature represented the devil in the Garden of Eden?

3   Which festival is also known as The Purification of The Virgin Mary?

4   Where in the Bible does it say "You shall not kill"?

5   In the Bible, Jesus was placed in a manger. What is a manger?

6   How many books are there in the Old Testament: 29 or 39?

7   What does the word advent actually mean?

8   In which city can you find the Wailing Wall?

9   What was the name of King Herod's wife?

10 Who did David kill with a stone from his catapult?

Question 10

205   Lights, Camera, Action!

1   Who played Mel Gibson's leading lady in the comedy thriller, *Bird on a Wire*?

2   Which character has been played on TV by Phil Silvers and on film by Steve Martin?

3   Which country and western singer rode alongside John Wayne in the movie *True Grit*?

4   The 1976 movie, *All the President's Men*, chronicled the Watergate scandal. Which newspaper was central to the plot?

5   Which 1998 movie starred Catherine Zeta Jones and Antonio Banderas?

6   Which famous vet has been played on film by Simon Ward and John Alderton?

7   *Il Buono, il Brutto, il Cattivo* is the Italian title of which spaghetti western?

8   Who provided the voice of Mrs. Potts in the Disney adaptation of *Beauty and the Beast*?

9   When Michael Caine played Scrooge in the 1992 movie, who played Bob Cratchit?

10 Who played the title role in the 1996 movie, *Michael Collins*?

Question 9

206 Sporting Chance

1 In which sport has Victor Barna won world titles?

2 In 1875, Aristides became the first winner of which race?

3 Which British rower won his fifth successive Olympic gold medal at the Sydney Olympic Games?

4 What is the nationality of tennis star Lleyton Hewitt?

5 What skater won an Olympic gold for Britain in 1976?

6 Which swimming stroke made its Olympic debut in 1956?

7 Which tennis star, nicknamed "Little Mo", was the first woman to win the Grand Slam?

8 What is the most popular indoor sport in the United States?

9 Which member of The Monkees pop group was a former apprentice jockey?

10 From which country does the mother of Tiger Woods hail?

Question 10

207 Making History

1 What does Genghis Khan's name mean?

2 Who was the first European to cross the Australian outback?

3 In which two countries did the ancient Maya culture exist?

4 In which circular building in London were most of Shakespeare's plays first performed?

5 Of which country was Cleopatra the queen?

6 Which royal house did both Edward I and Richard II belong to?

7 Which European country did Garibaldi fight to unite in 1860?

8 In what century did Marco Polo visit China?

9 Where did Columbus actually land after crossing the Atlantic in 1492?

10 Which dynasty, famous for its vases, ruled China between 1368 and 1644?

Question 5

★ **BACKGROUND BONUS** ★
In 1987, which Van Gogh painting was auctioned for a record $39,921,750?

208 Total Trivia

1 Which missionary organization is structured like an army with ranks and uniforms?

2 Which small fish hangs upright in the water, holding on to seaweed stems with its tail?

3 What plant is the emblem of Ireland?

4 What is the official language of Brazil?

5 In which continent is the Zambezi River?

6 Which is the largest of the apes?

7 What animal represents the star sign, Taurus?

8 In which building in central Rome did the Romans hold contests between gladiators?

9 What is the capital of Canada?

10 What word describes a book written by a person about their own life?

Question 6

209 Global Matters

1 What are gauchos?

2 Which name, beginning with G, is given to the boats that carry visitors around Venice?

3 If you were in the Northern Hemisphere in October, what season would it be?

4 What would you find at Tulum in Mexico: Maya ruins, rare flowers or rock formations?

5 Valetta is the capital of which Mediterranean island?

6 The Rhine, Rhone and Danube all have their sources in which range of mountains?

7 Are California and Florida famous for growing oranges, corn or wheat?

8 Where would you find the Ural Mountains?

9 In which U.S. state is Key West?

10 Meteorology is the study of what Earth feature?

Question 1

210   Natural Selection

1. Does the skunk beetle get its name because it has black-and-white stripes or a smelly spray?

2. How does the frilled lizard scare its enemies?

3. Where does the queen honey bee lay her eggs?

4. Which North American mammal has a pouch for its young?

5. A kangaroo sometimes drowns enemies by holding them underwater: true or false?

6. Which European freshwater fish sometimes catches and eats ducks: the eel, the pike or the carp?

7. Where does the bracket fungus flourish: on dung heaps or attached to tree trunks?

8. Are birds warm-blooded or cold-blooded?

9. Are catkins fruits or pollen-bearing flowers?

10. Did plants first appear on Earth in the sea or on land?

Question 2

★ **BACKGROUND BONUS** ★
What is the name of the mass of flowers that bloom on some trees during spring?

211   Sporting Chance: Soccer

1. In which tournament did Paul Gascoigne become famous for crying?

2. Robbie Fowler was a Liverpool supporter as a boy: true or false?

3. With which French club did Thierry Henry and Emmaunuel Petit begin their careers?

4. What nationality is Nwankwo Kanu?

5. Who scored the winner for Arsenal in the 1994 European Cup-Winners' Cup final?

6. With which British club did John Barnes begin his career?

7. Who was manager of Leeds when they won the League title in 1992?

8. What team lost both the 1993 League Cup and FA Cup finals to Arsenal?

9. What club did Eric Cantona play for before he joined Manchester United?

10. Which U.K. Division One side achieved a record number of points in the 1998 to 1999 season?

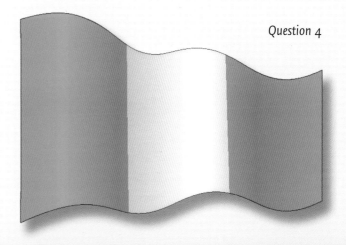

Question 4

212 Natural Selection

1. What kind of animal is a tuatara?
2. Does the Australian thorny devil lizard get its water from rain, rivers or dew?
3. Eel, mussel, oyster, clam: which is the odd one out?
4. Which tail-less, furry and popular European pet is eaten by some people in South America?
5. Which nut, often ground into a sandwich spread, grows underground?
6. What is the smallest mammal baby?
7. Why is the mistle thrush also called the stormcock?
8. Which poisonous spider relative pulls its prey apart with its massive claws?
9. How does the golden wheel spider escape attack?
10. How many types of oak tree are there: 10, 150 or more than 400?

Question 8

213 Total Trivia

1. What rodent is covered with long, sharp, black-and-white spikes called quills?
2. What name is given to the text of an opera?
3. What is another name for ping-pong?
4. What is the device for showing the movement of stars and planets on a curved ceiling?
5. According to the Christmas carol, when did King Wenceslas last look out?
6. Who invented radio?
7. What queen was called Bloody Mary?
8. What strait connects the Mediterranean Sea to the Atlantic Ocean?
9. Which prehistoric reptiles died out 65 million years ago?
10. Which is the highest mountain in Europe?

Question 9

214　Scientifically Speaking

1　In which bodily substance is plasma found?

2　What part of the body is affected by conjunctivitis?

3　What paper is used to measure acids and alkalis?

4　How many decades are there in a millennium?

5　Which type of body tissue expands and relaxes in order to let you move?

6　What is produced by a solar cell?

7　What are the names of the three segments of an insect?

8　What are the three states of matter?

9　What term describes half of the diameter of a circle?

10　What word describes a region's average weather over a long period of time?

Question 3

215　Music Mania

1　Which enduring U.K. pop artist had a Christmas hit with "Saviour's Day"?

2　Which U.S. musician is a direct descendant of Herman Melville, the author of *Moby Dick*?

3　Which country music goddess starred in the 1989 movie *Steel Magnolias*?

4　According to the song, what did Molly Malone sell in the streets of Dublin?

5　"Somethin' Stupid" was a U.K. hit in 2001 for Robbie Williams and Nicole Kidman. Who sang it originally?

6　Which Cuban singer enjoyed a 1992 festive hit with "Christmas Through Your Eyes"?

7　What kind of Christmas did Elvis Presley have in the 1964 charts?

8　What group did Paul McCartney form after the break up of The Beatles?

Question 8

9　Which Bond theme did Sheena Easton perform?

10　What is the last name of the punk princess Toyah?

★ BACKGROUND BONUS ★
Tico Torres is best-known for what?

216 Making History

1 Michael Collins was a famous revolutionary In which country?

2 What is the large medieval catapult that was used to attack castles called?

3 Which Roman god was ruler of the Underworld?

4 In which country did samurai warriors live?

5 Which 1947 invention made pocket-sized radios possible?

6 Who ruled the Soviet Union from 1924 to 1953?

7 In ancient Egypt, what was a nilometer used for?

8 What year was the first digital computer made?

9 Which oath, taken by modern doctors, is named after a Greek physician?

10 How many kings of England have been called Henry?

Question 2

217 Natural Selection

1 What came first: dinosaurs or crocodiles?

2 What spider has a hinged, flaplike entrance to its nest?

3 Which American mammal once roamed the prairies in enormous herds?

4 What ape is most closely related to humans?

5 Which is the largest member of the ray family?

6 What creatures live in groups called shoals?

7 How does the marine toad deter its enemies: by growling, squirting venom or biting?

8 Which is the largest land predator in Africa?

9 Where does the wombat live?

10 What is a skink?

Question 5

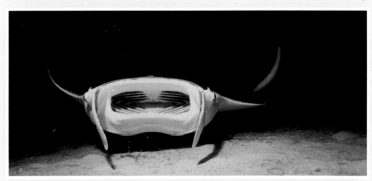

★ BACKGROUND BONUS ★
What spider makes a wheel-shaped web?

218 Lights, Camera, Action!

1 What lighter-than-air substance was invented by the Absent Minded Professor?

2 What actor connects the movies *Jurassic Park*, *The Omen*, and *The Final Conflict*?

3 In which 1989 movie did Daniel Day Lewis play the writer Christie Brown?

4 The 1993 movie *Backbeat* told the story of the early days of which superstar pop group?

5 What outlaw was played by Paul Newman in the movie *The Left Handed Gun*?

6 On which Greek island is *Zorba the Greek* set?

7 Which movie star played the title role in the 1998 historical drama, *Elizabeth*?

8 Which *Oliver* star also played a Sherwood Forest outlaw in *Robin Hood, Prince of Thieves*?

9 What is the only musical movie to win ten Oscars?

10 Which Disney character fell in love with a prince called Eric?

Question 5

219 Scientifically Speaking

1 What is the name of the molten rock that is thrown up from a volcano?

2 The disease Rubella is also known by what other name?

3 How many weeks are there in five years?

4 What does a dermatologist study?

5 What fraction of a circle is a section measuring 270°?

6 What part of your body has vertebrae?

7 What comes in varieties called bar, horseshoe and electro?

8 At room temperature, is helium a gas, a liquid or a solid?

9 What is the name of the light-sensitive lining behind the eye?

10 Glass is mainly composed of what?

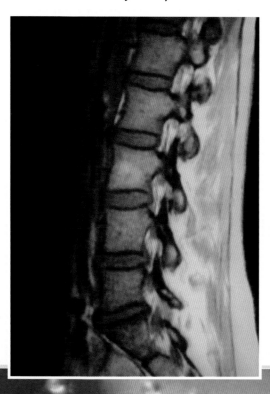

Question 6

220   Total Trivia

1. In which country was the environmental organization, Greenpeace, founded?
2. How long is a leap year?
3. What is the capital of Albania?
4. Which parts of a tree trap sunlight and make food for the tree?
5. What is pyrophobia a fear of?
6. What is the word fax short for?
7. What is India's main religion?
8. In which American state is Amarillo?
9. Which girl's first name is the Italian name for woman?
10. What does "long in the tooth" mean?

Question 10

221   Making History

1. What nationality was the scientist Niels Bohr?
2. Where was the great gold rush of 1849?
3. What crop did Jimmy Carter grow before he became U.S. president?
4. Which two important metals were mined in England during Roman times?
5. Which science-fiction story caused a panic in the United States in 1938?
6. In which Asian country was the Khmer empire founded in about AD900?
7. Which British prime minister had the forenames Margaret Hilda?
8. Was the first globe of the Earth made in 1350, 1492 or 1796?
9. What land did Cartier claim for France in 1534?
10. What is the name of the pyramid-like platforms built in ancient Mesopotamia?

Question 5

222   Music Mania

1 What opera is subtitled *The Lass That Loved a Sailor*?

2 In which city was the singer Gloria Estefan born?

3 Who performed the title song for the Bond movie *Never Say Never Again*?

4 Who wrote the Tina Turner hit "Private Dancer"?

5 Which best-selling song of the 20th century was written by Bernie Taupin?

6 Who replaced Keith Moon in The Who?

7 How old was Buddy Holly when he died?

8 On whose novel is the musical *Les Misérables* based?

9 On what island was Nana Mouskouri born?

10 With which musical instrument is Sonny Rollins associated?

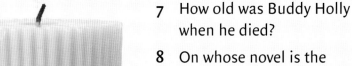

Question 5

223   Lights, Camera, Action!

1 When were the Oscars first awarded?

2 In which country was the 1984 movie *The Killing Fields* set?

3 What is the first name of Baron Frankenstein?

4 What connects the movies *Raising Cain*, *Dead Ringers* and *The Man in the Iron Mask*?

5 In which 1985 movie comedy did Richard Pryor inherit millions of dollars?

6 In which movie, starring Nicholas Cage and John Travolta, did Archer "borrow" Troy's face?

7 What movie saw David Tomlinson "bobbing along on the bottom of the beautiful briny sea"?

8 Which of the Marx Brothers was born with the first name of Leonard?

9 In which 1995 movie did Michelle Pfeiffer play an ex-marine who becomes a schoolteacher at a tough inner city school?

10 The 1993 movie *Dragon* is a biopic of which martial arts hero?

Question 5

★ **BACKGROUND BONUS** ★
In *The Adventures of Rocky and Bullwinkle*,
what kind of animal is Bullwinkle?

224 Total Trivia

1 Which kind of pedigree domestic cat has cream fur and blue eyes?

2 What is the capital of Egypt?

3 What country's name is Spanish for "rich coast"?

4 Who wrote *David Copperfield*?

5 Which precious stone is purple?

6 Who is Mickey Mouse's girlfriend?

7 What river flows through Paris?

8 Who led Britain for much of World War I?

9 *Papillon* is the French word for what?

10 What do you call a toy with mirrors that creates random regular patterns?

Question 4

225 Scientifically Speaking

1 What is the body's largest joint?

2 How much water is there in urine: 10 percent, 60 percent or 95 percent?

3 Where would you find your femur bone?

4 Acoustics is the study of what?

5 Which vitamin, found in liver and green vegetables, helps with clotting blood?

6 What planet is known as the red planet?

7 Ancient scientists believed that there were only four elements: earth, fire, air and what else?

8 What is petrology the study of?

9 What is nausea?

10 What does a nutritionist specialize in?

Question 10

> ★ BACKGROUND BONUS ★
> In a laboratory, what is the name of the dish on which bacteria are grown?

226 Sporting Chance

1 Who won Olympic gold medals for the long jump in 1984, 1988 and 1992?

2 In which country was the tennis star Monica Seles born?

3 Who moved to the New York Yankees from the Boston Red Sox in 1921 for a fee of $125,000?

4 Who was World Professional Billiards champion from 1968 to 1980?

5 In which city did Allan Wells win an Olympic gold medal?

6 Who was ranked as Britain's No. 1 male tennis player in 2001?

7 From which wood were longbows traditionally made?

8 Which B word is the name of a form of hockey played on ice with a ball?

9 Who was the first South African golfer to win the U.S. Open?

10 What is swimmer Ian Thorpe's nickname?

Question 2

227 Music Mania

1 Which group was Lionel Richie the lead singer of?

2 In which horror movie were extracts from Mike Oldfield's *Tubular Bells* used?

3 Falco had a hit with "Rock Me Amadeus" from the movie *Amadeus*. Where is Falco from?

4 "Stuck in the Middle with You" is in which Quentin Tarantino movie?

5 Underworld's "Born Slippy" shot to No. 2 in the U.K. after featuring In which movie?

6 Which solo artist recorded the album *Listen Without Prejudice*?

7 Who recorded the theme to the 1973 Bond movie *Live and Let Die*?

8 What movie helped Huey Lewis up the charts with "The Power of Love"?

9 Whose career was documented in *The Great Rock'n'Roll Swindle*?

10 *Desperately Seeking Susan* starred which female singer?

Question 3

228 Total Trivia

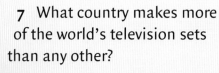

1 What is another name for the sea creature called an orca?

2 Managua is the capital of what country?

3 Where can the Metropolitan Museum of Art be found?

4 Which president of the Soviet Union introduced Perestroika in the 1980s?

5 Which is the fastest-moving snake in the world?

6 Who composed "Air on a G String"?

7 What country makes more of the world's television sets than any other?

8 In which country is the Brenner Pass?

9 Khartoum is the capital of what country?

10 In what year was John Lennon shot?

Question 4

229 Natural Selection

1 Where would you be most likely to find a hornets' nest?

2 What kind of fish is the halibut?

3 Which of the following has a hinged shell: winkle, mussel or barnacle?

4 In what hemisphere are penguins found?

5 Frogs and toads make up almost nine-tenths of amphibians: true or false?

6 What is a kumquat?

7 Apart from some lizards, what other kinds of reptile can leap from trees and glide?

8 Which exotic spice is obtained from the stigmas of the crocus flower?

9 What do we call a group of chimpanzees?

10 Which nut tree did the Romans introduce to Britain: the hazel, the walnut or the sweet chestnut?

Question 7

★ BACKGROUND BONUS ★
What is special about the whistling swan?

230   Scientifically Speaking

1. What is the only mammal that can fly?

2. What job does bile perform in the body?

3. Which type of insect makes huge mounds more than 2 m (6 ft) tall in Australia?

4. Which is the brightest planet, as seen from Earth?

5. How many sides has a parallelogram?

6. Barbary apes live in only one small part of Europe. Where is it?

7. Where in the human body is the trapezium?

8. What is the square root of 64?

9. If a doctor recommends taking insulin regularly, from what disorder is the patient suffering?

10. About 95 percent of the body's calcium is found In which two areas?

Question 3

231   Lights, Camera, Action!

1. Who connects the movie epics *Lawrence of Arabia*, *Zorba the Greek* and *Barabbas*?

2. What character has been played on film by Bo Derek, Dorothy Dunbar and Maureen O'Sullivan?

3. Who played the president of the United States in the movie *Primary Colors*?

4. How are Curly, Larry and Mo collectively known on film?

5. Who played Oscar Madison in the movie *The Odd Couple*?

6. What board game is played by Steve McQueen and Faye Dunaway in *The Thomas Crown Affair*?

7. Who was the first British movie star to win a Best Actress Oscar?

8. What actor played Mel Gibson's partner in the *Lethal Weapon* movies?

9. What writer did Virginia McKenna portray in the movie *Born Free*?

10. In the movie *Peter's Friends*, which British comedy star played Peter?

Question 8

232 Total Trivia

1. Which Spanish percussion instrument is made of two wooden shells?
2. How many holes are there on a golf course?
3. Currants and raisins are dried what?
4. Which German brothers wrote a famous collection of fairy tales?
5. What is the capital of Denmark?
6. A lawyer by the name of Billy Flynn is a character in which musical?
7. What is a private eye?
8. What is a newborn horse called?
9. What does a shark's skeleton comprise of?
10. If someone has a nest egg, what do they have?

Question 3

233 Sporting Chance

1. In Judo, what is an *ippon*?
2. In golf, what is a mulligan?
3. What sport featured in the book *Death in the Afternoon*?
4. Who defeated Lennox Lewis in April 2001?
5. What is the first throwing event in the decathlon?
6. On what would you find a boom yang?
7. Which racket sport made its Olympic debut in 1992?
8. In which sport is a female contestant known as a wahine?
9. What sporting body has the initials ISU?
10. In horse racing, what is a scurry?

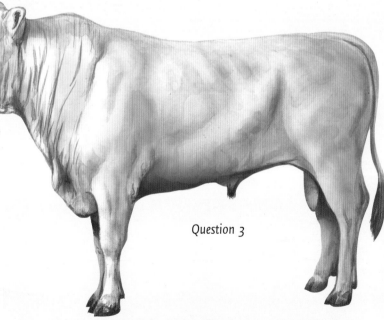

Question 3

★ BACKGROUND BONUS ★
In what event did the United States beat Australia 76–54 at the 2000 Olympics?

234 Natural Selection

1 What is a thrush's anvil?

2 What does the Malaysian horned toad disguise itself as?

3 What happens to a honey bee after it uses its sting?

4 Which African mammal uses its head and very long neck as a club when fighting?

5 Why does the woodpecker have a liquid cushion inside its skull?

6 Which umbrella-like tree has no branches?

7 What does the antlion dig to catch its prey?

8 What is a caecilian?

9 Which rainforest mammal spends most of its life hanging upside down?

10 Where do tigers originate?

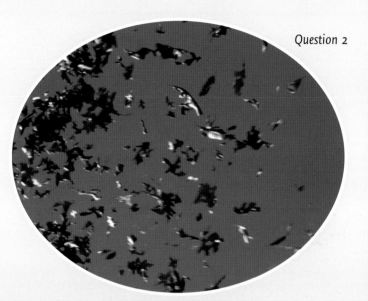

Question 2

235 Written Word: The Bible

1 Who was the first person to see Jesus after his resurrection?

2 Who was created from Adam's rib?

3 An angel appeared to Joseph telling him to take Mary and Jesus to what country?

4 What is the Seventh Commandment?

5 What was the name of Herod's stepdaughter?

6 How many books are there in the New Testament?

7 Who visited Mary to inform her that she was pregnant with the Son of God?

8 Which gospel writer was known as The Beloved Physician?

9 The Three Wise Men are believed to be buried in which German cathedral?

10 Who is the patron saint of tax collectors?

Question 3

236   Making History

1 In what year did India become independent of Britain?

2 What was built across the United States in 1869?

3 Which German composer, born in 1685, wrote *The Messiah* and the *Water Music*?

4 How many thousands of years ago did the first modern humans appear?

5 Which English poet wrote *Kublai Khan*?

6 Who won the battle of Austerlitz in 1805?

7 Who became president of the United States in 1929, the year of the Wall Street Crash?

8 Across what mountains did Lewis and Clarke lead an expedition?

9 Who were Ginger Rogers and Fred Astaire?

10 After which Greek god was the American manned Moon-landing spacecraft named?

Question 2

237   Total Trivia

1 Where is singer Jim Morrison buried?

2 John, Ringo and George were three of the Beatles. Who was the fourth?

3 What kind of plant is marjoram?

4 What shape is *farfalla* pasta?

5 In which sea is the island of Crete?

6 Who wrote *Robinson Crusoe*?

7 Of which city were the Crusaders fighting for control?

8 What is the name for a small explosive charge that sets off a bomb?

9 Who was the only ruler of Britain who ruled instead of a king or a queen?

10 Which is the world's largest country?

Question 9

238   Natural Selection

1   What goose migrates from Greenland to Mexico: the barnacle, Canada or snow goose?

2   How fast can tortoises move: 1 km/h (0.6 mph), 2 km/h (1.2 mph) or over 3 km/h (1.8 mph)?

3   The 37 species of toucan all live on what continent?

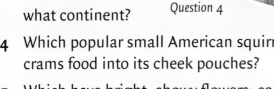

Question 4

4   Which popular small American squirrel crams food into its cheek pouches?

5   Which have bright, showy flowers: cone-bearing trees or broad-leaved trees?

6   Why do vultures have naked heads and necks?

7   Why do some South African geckoes have webbed feet?

8   What kind of animal is the sea mouse?

9   What is the odd one out: tuna, dolphin, dugong, sea otter?

10   Do the cones of the Australian bunya pine weigh: 1 kg (2.2 lb), 3 kg (6.6 lb) or 5 kg (11 lb) each?

239   Global Matters

1   In which country was the world's first public television service?

2   What country's flag features a blue globe in a yellow diamond on a green background?

3   Larnaka airport serves what island in the Mediterranean?

4   What is the name given to the outer surface of the Earth?

5   In which country are the ruins of the ancient city of Troy?

6   Which two nations have dominated pop music from its start in the 1950s?

7   What tree appears on the national flag of Lebanon?

8   Which city in British Columbia sits opposite an island of the same name?

9   Caracas is the capital of what country?

10   Frankfurt is the major financial hub of what country?

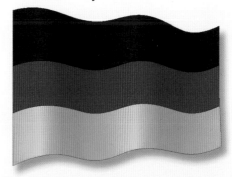

Question 10

★ BACKGROUND BONUS ★
What did the Western Wall in Jerusalem used to be known as?

240 Scientifically Speaking

1 What type of instrument uses two or more lenses to make small objects appear much larger?

2 What in the body are the *rectus abdominus* and *deltoid* examples of?

3 What type of medical professional performs root canal treatments?

4 What name is given to the graphic recording of the electrical changes in the heart?

5 What metal does the chemical symbol Zn represent?

6 What is the closest natural satellite to Earth?

7 What did Ladislao Biro invent in 1933?

8 Which black-and-white mammal is of the genus *Equus*?

9 If an insect flaps its wings 30 times a second, how many times will it flap them in two minutes?

10 Pneumonia affects what part of the body?

Question 3

> ★ BACKGROUND BONUS ★
> What flower takes its name from the Turkish word for "turban"?

241 Sporting Chance

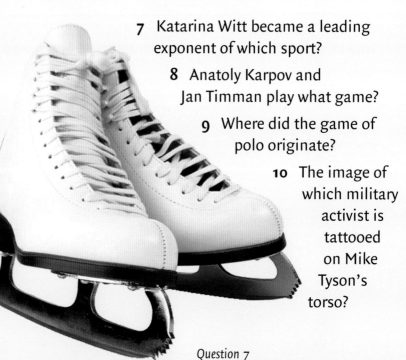

1 In which city did Lennox Lewis beat Mike Tyson in June 2002?

2 How many laps is the Indianapolis 500?

3 Which three-letter word is the name given to a replayed point in tennis?

4 In which sport did Dawn Fraser compete in three consecutive Olympics?

5 In which weight category did the Irish boxer Barry McGuigan become world champion?

6 How many players play at any one time in a water polo team?

7 Katarina Witt became a leading exponent of which sport?

8 Anatoly Karpov and Jan Timman play what game?

9 Where did the game of polo originate?

10 The image of which military activist is tattooed on Mike Tyson's torso?

Question 7

242 Written Word

1 Which Shakespeare play is set during the Trojan War?

2 The address 2 Devonshire Place, London, was used as a surgery or study by what author?

3 What novel was narrated by Nick Carraway?

4 In *The Lord of the Rings*, who is the maker of the ring?

5 Who wrote *National Velvet*?

6 What poet lived in a house called *Alloway*?

7 What is the surname of Anne of Green Gables?

8 Delores Haze is a central character of which controversial novel?

9 What do the initials H.E. stand for in the name of the author H.E. Bates?

10 What is the name of the fictional village where Dr. Doolittle lives?

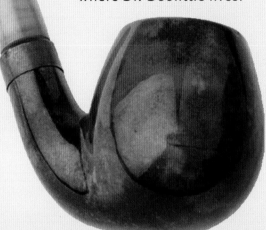

Question 2

243 Making History

1 Which U.S. army unit did Custer lead at the Battle of Little Big Horn?

2 Which real-life Tudor inspired a play and a movie called *A Man For All Seasons*?

3 Which river in Africa did 19th-century explorers strive to find the source of?

4 Which bridge in London, completed in 1894, can open and close?

5 In 1971, East Pakistan became an independent country. What was it called?

6 What kind of prehistoric works of art were found in caves at Lascaux, France?

7 Balboa was the first European to see what, in 1513?

8 Was the *Turtle* of 1778 an early submarine, a tank or a rocket?

9 What country was the first to introduce the metric system of weights and measures, in 1795?

10 What islands was the Portuguese sea captain, Magellan, visiting when he was killed in a fight between rival tribes?

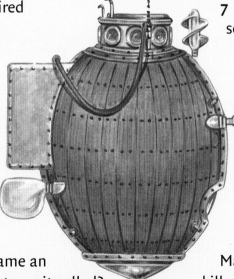

Question 8

244 Lights, Camera, Action!

1 Who did Kenneth Williams play in the movie *Carry On Cleo*?

2 In the *Addams Family*, what is the name of the uncle?

3 On TV, what is the name of Roseanne's sister in *Roseanne*?

4 Name the actor who played Chief Engineer Scott in *Star Trek*.

5 Who played the villain Harvey Two Face, in the 1995 movie *Batman Forever*?

6 Which Belgian actor played a law enforcer in the movie *Timecop*?

7 What vehicle was Jock Ewing in when he was killed in the TV soap, *Dallas*?

8 Which female criminal was the subject of the movie *Dance With a Stranger*?

9 What author wrote the dramas *Pennies From Heaven* and *The Singing Detective*?

10 Which *Friends* star married Brad Pitt?

Question 1

245 Natural Selection

1 Does the American bullfrog lay up to 500, 5,000 or 25,000 eggs?

2 The world's smallest frog, at less than 12 mm (0.4 in) long, lives on which Caribbean island?

3 Why is the banded shrimp known as a "fish doctor"?

4 Which North American mammal weighs up to half a ton and can run at 50 km/h (30 mph)?

5 Why does seaweed not grow in the darkest depths of the ocean?

6 Which member of the heron family removes parasites from rhinos?

7 Where does Darwin's frog guard its tadpoles: on its back, in its throat or on its feet?

8 Which ten-limbed seabed-dweller can have a leg span of over 3 m (10 ft)?

9 What member of the camel family was tamed 4,000 years ago in the Andes?

10 What bird of prey has New World and Old World varieties?

Question 9

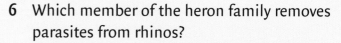

> ★ **BACKGROUND BONUS** ★
> Which kind of camel has one hump?

246　Sporting Chance

1　What city hosted the first World Athletics Championship?

2　In which U.S. city is the Pimlico horse racing track?

3　What sport employs the Stableford scoring system?

4　In which city is the Flinders Park tennis stadium?

5　Who was the first female tennis player to achieve the Grand Slam?

6　In which U.S. city can the Kronk boxing stadium be found?

7　In the 1970s, what team won the World Series in three consecutive years?

8　Where is the world's highest golf course?

9　At what event was Al Oerter crowned Olympic champion in four successive games?

10　For which car company did Enzo Ferrari drive racing cars

Question 10

247　Scientifically Speaking

1　Which is larger: Mars or Saturn?

2　In 1782, which French brothers made a flight in a hot air balloon?

3　Combustion is the scientific term for what process?

4　In what disease do some of the body's cells go out of control and multiply?

5　Iron will only rust if exposed to air and what other substance?

6　What line of tropic runs through South America, Africa, and Australia?

7　If an engineer is measuring a moving object's RPMs, what is being checked?

8　Which two muscles are used to lift the forearm?

9　Which small weapon did Samuel Colt invent in 1835?

10　A block and tackle is a group of what?

Question 5

248   Total Trivia

1 What have larger ears: African or Indian elephants?

2 Could you jump higher on the Moon or on Earth?

3 Why do spiders build webs?

4 What countries make up Scandinavia?

5 What happens when an eclipse of the Sun occurs?

6 What does "to throw in the towel" mean?

7 Who wrote *The Twits*?

8 In which sport can you make a hole-in-one?

9 What was the code name for the day the Allied forces landed in Normandy during World War II?

10 What is the collective name for knives, forks and spoons?

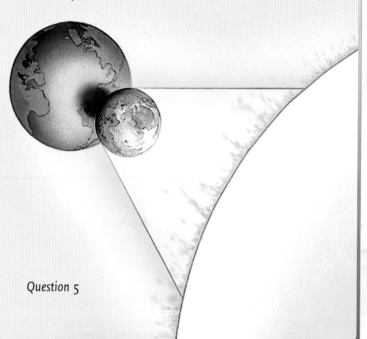

Question 5

249   Making History

1 What ruler was known as "The Little Corporal"?

2 What queen became empress of India in 1876?

3 What was the city of New York originally called by Dutch settlers?

4 Which islands off Ecuador inspired Charles Darwin's theory of evolution?

5 Which Greek thinker was condemned to die by drinking poison?

6 On what planet did the space probe *Venera 7* land in 1970?

7 What is the setting for Verdi's opera *Aida*?

8 What did Jesus's 12 disciples become known as after his death?

9 Who was the longest-serving Australian prime minister?

10 What is the only part left standing of the ancient Temple of Jerusalem?

Question 7

250 Written Word

1. Who is the world's most successful horror writer, with books including *Misery*, *Rose Madder* and *The Shining*?

2. What was the name of Winnie the Pooh's small friend?

3. What word can mean to hobble and is also used to describe something that is floppy?

4. If canine equals dog what does vulpine equal?

5. Is a rotunda a round, domed building, a round, musical instrument or a round brooch?

Question 4

6. Which English word derives from the Italian meaning "little ball": balloon, ballot or ballet?

7. Who wrote *Sons and Lovers*?

8. Is a coracle: a prophet, a council meeting place, or a boat?

9. How does *Anno Domini* translate into English?

10. Dendrophobia is the morbid fear of what?

★ **BACKGROUND BONUS** ★
Which play by Alfred Uhry was made into an Oscar-winning movie?

251 Sporting Chance: Soccer

1. In the 1940s, why was Maine Road host to Manchester United's home games?

2. Despite qualifying for the 1950 World Cup, why was India banned from competing?

3. Who was sacked as manager of Leeds United FC in June 2002?

4. Which paint company sponsored Liverpool when they won the double in 1986?

5. Which former Italian international soccer player was sacked as manager of Watford FC in 2002?

6. In 1931, what was the first London club to win the League title?

7. Who scored the winner when West Germany won the 1974 World Cup?

8. What team plays at the Nou Camp?

9. What nationality is former Arsenal player Christopher Wreh?

10. Which World Cup winner was sacked as manager of Portsmouth in 1999?

Question 9

252 Global Matters

1 What was the name of Austria's currency before the euro?

2 Valparaiso is a city in which South American country?

3 What is the capital of Australia's Northern Territory?

4 The Tagus and Douro Rivers are found in which European country?

5 Which Asian country builds one in six of the world's ships: Japan, South Korea or Taiwan?

6 What nationality was the writer Mark Twain?

7 An artificial lake used to store water for drinking or to make electricity is known as what?

8 In which country would you find the city of Shanghai?

9 The Great Mosque at Djenne is in which African country?

10 If you were watching cricket at Galle or Kandy, what country would you be visiting?

Question 2

253 Lights, Camera, Action!

1 Which 2003 movie sees Nick Nolte playing the father of Dr. Bruce Banner?

2 What actor was America's most decorated soldier of World War II?

3 Who played the writer Joan Wilder in both *Romancing the Stone* and *Jewel of the Nile*?

4 In which movie did Jennifer Grey play the character of Baby Houseman?

5 Elliot Carver is the name of the villain in which Bond movie?

6 Which 1990 movie features Leonardo, Donatello, Michelangelo and Raphael?

7 In which 1982 movie did Dustin Hoffman play the characters of Michael and Dorothy?

8 What was Cary Grant's real name?

9 In which movie did Elton John sing "Pinball Wizard"?

10 Who plays the role of Leo Getz in the *Lethal Weapon* movies?

Question 6

★ **BACKGROUND BONUS** ★
Which Sinbad movie features a feline in its title?

Music Marvels

254

Can you identify these singers and musicians?

255　Making History

1　Which Native American people defeated Custer at the Battle of Little Big Horn?

2　Who was the leader of the team that reached the South Pole in second place?

3　What was the last battle fought by Horatio Nelson?

4　Who did Britain fight in the 1839 Opium War?

5　What emperor announced in 1946 that he was no longer a god?

6　Who wrote *The Lord of the Flies*?

7　At what siege did Davy Crockett die in 1836?

8　Which drink was invented by Dom Perignon?

9　Which waterfall in Africa was named after a British queen?

10　What pair of aviators first flew the Atlantic in 1919?

Question 1

256　Total Trivia

1　Which novel opens with the line: "The great fish moved silently through the water"?

2　What is the name of the main river running through Hamburg?

3　Which movie actress is the mother of the actress Kate Hudson?

4　What is the name for a tube that carries blood to the heart?

5　The Christian Mission was the original name for what army?

6　What type of berries are used in the alcoholic spirit, gin?

7　Which Japanese delicacy is considered to be the world's most dangerous food?

8　What is a quetzal?

9　In which country will you find the Mato Grosso plateau?

10　Who wrote *Waiting for Godot*?

Question 1

257 Sporting Chance

1 How many players comprise a Canadian football team?

2 What do the initials WTA stand for in the world of sport?

3 Which British tennis star wrote an autobiography entitled *Courting Triumph*?

4 In which sport do competitors race head to head in an event called the parallel giant slalom?

5 At what sport have Michael and John Whittaker represented Great Britain?

6 Which U.S. football team won the most Super Bowls in the 1980s?

7 What form of bowling is played on a green with a raised middle area?

8 Former Olympian Geoff Capes is a leading breeder of which popular pets?

9 Which popular children's game was called nuts in ancient Rome?

10 Which Formula One racing team have an emblem in the form of a prancing horse?

Question 4

★ **BACKGROUND BONUS** ★
Yogi Berra, Johnny Bench and Gary Carter all played in which position in baseball?

258 Written Word

1 Which book about a horse did Anna Sewell write?

2 Who wrote *My Family and Other Animals*?

3 Which Shakespeare play features the characters Viola, Malvolio and Sir Toby Belch?

4 What is the literal English translation of the Italian word *veto*?

5 In the novel *1984*, what language do the authorities try to introduce?

6 Which S word is the name given to the highest order of angels in the celestial hierarchy?

7 *Captain Corelli's Mandolin* is set on which Greek island?

8 Bathsheba Everdene is the heroine of which novel by Thomas Hardy?

9 What is unusual about the word "facetious"?

10 What is a *croque monsieur*?

Question 10

259 Written Word

1 What part of the body is affected by glossitis?

2 What name is shared by a heavily spiked club and the spice made from nutmeg?

3 Which A word describes a circular coral reef growing on top of a submerged mountain?

4 Which F word is the name given to the metal ribs on the fingerboard of a guitar?

5 What is the name of the sequel to *Bridget Jones's Diary*?

6 What king was portrayed by Shakespeare as a murderous hunchback?

7 Eugenics is the study of what?

8 If a meeting is held *sub rosa* what does this mean?

9 Which Italian poet wrote the *Divina Commedia*?

10 In which city is Shakespeare's *Romeo and Juliet* set?

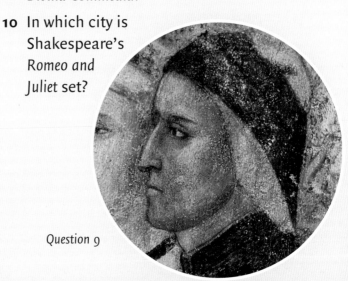

Question 9

260 Total Trivia

1 What is the main ingredient in mayonnaise?

2 What is the second heaviest land mammal?

3 How many seconds are there in an hour?

4 What is an accurate seagoing clock called?

5 In which country are the cities of Arequipa and Nazca?

6 Which great Austrian composer wrote over 600 pieces of music, including many famous operas?

7 What is the capital of Hungary?

8 Who is the Roman god of love?

9 What is a dhow?

10 Which four-sided shape has equal sides and equal angles?

Question 1

261 Natural Selection

1 Which cartoon character was always trying to make a meal out of Road Runner?

2 What leaves provide the staple diet of koalas?

3 A male donkey is called a Jack. Which girl's name provides the name of a female donkey?

4 Which stinging creature represents one of the signs of the Zodiac?

5 What could a dodo not do?

6 What species of monkey gave its name to a protein found in blood?

7 Is a boomslang a frog, a snake or a bird of prey?

8 Brock is another name for which carnivorous mammal?

9 What animal's name means "little thief" in Latin?

10 How many arms does a starfish have?

Question 9

★ BACKGROUND BONUS ★
What familiar yellow flower blooms
early in spring?

262 Scientifically Speaking

1 What do you call an open sore on the lining of the intestine?

2 How many degrees has a quadrant?

3 What is sorghum?

4 What does the prefix "iso" mean in the words isosceles and isobar?

5 British scientist William Fox Talbot was a pioneer in what field?

6 Where will you find your occipital lobe?

7 What cords vibrate when we talk?

8 Fe is the chemical symbol for what metal?

9 What is mitosis?

10 What kind of electricity does a Van de Graaff generator create?

Question 5

263 Total Trivia

1 What country has borders with France, Germany and Holland?

2 Which sea creature has species called European, Norway, spiny and American?

3 In which ocean is the island of Mauritius?

4 In which city are the main administrative offices of the European Union?

5 What type of animal is a grebe?

6 What country invaded Kuwait in 1990?

7 Which dish from New Orleans consists of rice, seafood, green peppers and spices?

8 What is an anemometer?

9 What is the capital of Mexico?

10 What do you call the coat of a sheep?

Question 9

264 Making History

1 In 63BC, who became the first Roman emperor?

2 What animals did armies in India and Cambodia use like tanks?

3 In what century was Michelangelo born?

4 The artist Canaletto painted many views of which Italian city?

5 In what year did the first Gulf War start?

6 What connects the monarchs Richard II, Edward II and Edward VIII?

7 What did Queen Elizabeth II and President Mitterand officially open in May 1994?

8 Did Vikings first invade Britain in the 7th, 8th or 9th century?

9 In which country was the medical treatment called acupuncture developed?

10 What does the B stand for in the name of former U.S. president, Lyndon B. Johnson?

Question 1

265 Scientifically Speaking

1   What is amnesia?

2   What planets, apart from Saturn, have rings?

3   What proportion of the air is oxygen: one-fifth, one-eighth or one-tenth?

4   Where would you find a stamen and an anther?

5   In computing, what do the initials ROM stand for?

6   What kind of test would an audiologist give?

7   What part of the body does arthritis affect?

8   What is the boiling point of water in the Celsius scale?

9   Inches, pounds and miles are all measurements in what system?

10   What organ in the body does a dialysis machine replace?

Question 4

★ **BACKGROUND BONUS** ★
Which U.S. spacecraft lands back on Earth like a plane?

266 Lights, Camera, Action!

1   If Pokémon means pocket monsters, what does Digimon mean?

2   What actress connects the movies *The Accused*, *Bugsy Malone* and *Taxi Driver*?

3   Name the actor who plays Hagrid in *Harry Potter and the Philosopher's Stone*.

4   In which 1993 movie blockbuster did Sam Neil play Dr. Alan Grant?

5   Who played boat owner Charlie Allnut in the movie *The African Queen*?

6   In which country was *Dr. Zhivago* set?

7   In which country was Omar Sharif born?

8   In which 1987 movie did Michael Douglas play stockbroker Gordon Gecko?

9   Who provided the voice of Z-4195 in the 1998 movie *Antz*?

10   What bird inspired Walter Lantz to create his famous cartoon character, Woody?

Question 4

267 Lights, Camera, Action!

1 Which famous composer was played by Tom Hulce in a 1984 Oscar-winning movie?

2 The movie *The Killing Fields* was set in what country?

3 Is Grandpa Simpson called Isaac, Abraham or Jacob?

4 What is the name of Bruce Wayne's butler in *Batman*?

5 What was the last movie that James Dean starred in?

6 In the movie *Romancing the Stone*, what kind of animal did the writer Joan Wilder own?

7 What is the title of the 1997 movie in which John Travolta plays an angel?

8 Which Hollywood actor, star of the movie *Some Like it Hot*, died in 2001 aged 76?

9 Who plays the character of Molly Brown in the 1997 movie *Titanic*?

10 What instrument plays the theme music to the movie *O Brother, Where Art Thou?*

Question 8

268 Global Matters

1 Which European capital city has an old quarter called the Plaka?

2 What is the state capital of Texas?

3 What country is nearest to the Greek island of Rhodes?

4 What is the national flower of India?

5 Which African country gained independence from Britain in 1962?

6 In which U.S. state is the city of Tucson?

7 Khartoum is the capital of which African country?

8 What is the name of Japan's largest island?

9 Which European capital city lies mainly on the island of Zealand?

10 Which English city did the Romans call *Aquae Sulis*?

Question 4

★ BACKGROUND BONUS ★
In the Islamic religion, what is the name given to a place of worship?

269   Making History

1. In which country did the poets Keats and Shelley die?

2. Who reached the Bahamas and thought he had reached India?

3. How long did an early musket take to reload: ten seconds, one minute or two minutes?

4. Which native peoples call Creation "The Dream Time"?

5. Which famous American playwright married Marilyn Monroe?

6. How did France's Queen Antoinette die?

7. Who wrote the first draft of the U.S. Constitution: Jefferson, Lincoln or Grant?

8. Of what country was Augusto Pinochet once dictator?

9. In which English cathedral was Archbishop Thomas á Becket murdered in 1170?

10. Where is China's Forbidden City?

Question 4

270   Natural Selection

1. What is the world's smallest owl?

2. What is the loofah the skeleton of?

3. Which eight-armed distant relative of the snail moves both by crawling and jet propulsion?

4. What carnivore follows polar bears to scavenge their kills?

5. Which is the fastest bird in level flight?

6. How are parrot toes arranged?

7. What type of animal lives in a sett?

8. Is the nautilus a close cousin of the crab or octopus?

9. Which rabbit relative stores plant material for winter: the hare, the pika or the jackrabbit?

10. Is the world's tallest tree, the Australian mountain ash 80 m (262 ft), 100 m (328 ft) or 150 m (492 ft) tall?

Question 4

271   Total Trivia

1   What is the hottest planet in our Solar System?

2   Where would you find a ligament?

3   Which western European nation has the largest population?

4   What river flows through Vienna?

5   Which emperor died in St. Helena?

6   One-third is approximately what as a decimal fraction?

7   What insect has larvae called daphnia?

8   Which African country takes its name from the Spanish for lion mountains?

9   What do the lachrymal glands produce?

10 What is the Irish name for Ireland?

Question 9

272   Global Matters

1   Colombo is the capital of what country?

2   In which South American country is the highest capital city situated?

3   In what country would you find the Wollomombi waterfalls?

4   What is the world's biggest industry?

5   Is the Alcazar in Toledo, Spain, a fortress, a hill range or a set of caves?

6   In what country is the Yucatán Peninsula?

7   What is "Old Faithful"?

8   What is the name of Haiti's capital: Princessville, Port au Prince or Princetown?

9   The river Lo flows through which Scandinavian capital?

10 What is the odd one out: Cologne, Bonn, Berlin or Prague?

Question 7

273 Music Mania

1 Father Abraham was the guiding light for which tiny hit-making figures?

2 Who wrote the U.S. single "We Are The World"?

3 Who wrote the Madonna hit song "Justify My Love"?

4 Who legally adopted a symbol to replace his name in 1993?

5 Who recorded "We All Stand Together" with The Frog Chorus?

6 "When I Need You" was a U.K. hit for what singer?

7 *The Rise and Fall* and *Keep Moving* were 1980s albums for which U.K. band?

8 Who joined Eurythmics on "Sisters Are Doin' It For Themselves"?

9 What rapper performed at Bill Clinton's inauguration?

10 "Hangin' Tough" was a No.1 hit for which U.S. boy band?

Question 6

★ BACKGROUND BONUS ★
In the 1500s, the Italian town of Cremona was famous for producing what instrument?

274 Sporting Chance

1 Petra Felke was the first woman to throw what over 80 m (260 ft)?

2 Which animal gives its name to an ice-skating move?

3 What type of sporting hall has a name that literally means naked exercise?

4 In chess, what piece moves with a rook in a move known as castling?

5 What is the highest grade awarded in judo?

6 Which former Wimbledon champion was knocked out of the 2002 tournament by an unseeded Swiss?

7 In tennis, what makes the ball travel faster: a grass court or a clay court?

8 What sport is sometimes described as "bowls on ice"?

9 How many attempts is a pole-vaulter allowed at each height?

10 In 1980, what became the first communist country to win the Davis Cup in tennis?

Question 8

275 Sporting Chance

1. In what decade were women's track and field events introduced to the Olympics?

2. In what sport would you find a telltale, a service box and a tin?

3. Which F word is the name given to a pigeon breeder or racer?

4. In a triathlon event, is swimming, running or cycling the last discipline?

5. What city is to host the 2006 Winter Olympics?   *Question 2*

6. Which Olympic gold medal-winner of the 1996 games went on to become a star in the World Wrestling Federation?

7. In what sport was the Walker Cup named after George Herbert Walker?

8. Who was the first boxer to beat Lennox Lewis in a professional fight?

9. What athlete did Ian Charleston play in the movie *Chariots of Fire*?

10. Who was the only U.S.-born winner of the ladies singles at Wimbledon in the 1990s?

276 Lights, Camera, Action!

1. In what country was *The Lord of the Rings* trilogy filmed?

2. Which star of the sitcom *Cheers* featured in the movie *Three Men and a Baby*?

3. Which famous model played the leading lady in *The Boy Friend*?

4. What is the name of the acting brother of Jeff Bridges?   *Question 8*

5. Who links the movies *Seven*, *Along Came a Spider* and *The Shawshank Redemption*?

6. Which superstar singer played Breathless Mahoney in *Dick Tracy*?

7. What food do the Teenage Mutant Ninja Turtles particularly like?

8. Which James Bond comedy co-starred David Niven, Peter Sellers and Woody Allen?

9. Which pretty woman married Danny Moder in July 2002?

10. Who played the role of Gertie in *ET*?

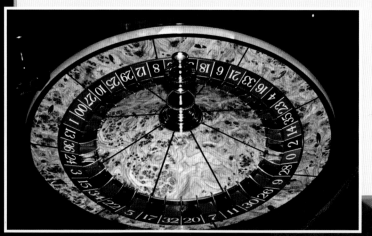

> ★ BACKGROUND BONUS ★
> What actress starred in the 1935 movie *Anna Karenina*?

277 Making History

1 What was Dutchman Hans Lippershey the first to look through in about 1600?

2 Of which ancient country was Akhenaten a ruler?

3 Which conflict was called "the war to end all wars"?

4 Who was the Amazon River named after?

5 Of which country was Antonio Salazar once dictator?

6 What name was given to the first Spanish invaders of Central and South America?

7 Which world statesman was once imprisoned on Robben Island off the African coast?

8 From what country did the United States buy Alaska in 1867?

9 Which U.S. president was a famous general during World War II?

10 What nationality was the composer Sibelius: Danish, Finnish or Romanian?

Question 3

278 Scientifically Speaking

1 What important gas did Joseph Priestley discover in 1774?

2 What item of clothing shares its name with the process of starting up a computer?

3 On what planet did the *Pathfinder* mission land, in 1966?

4 What part of a fan pushes the air?

5 Which three letters would a ship's radio operator send out as an emergency call?

6 How many sides has a pentagon?

7 How many days are there in seven weeks?

8 What type of biologist studies the plants and animals of the oceans?

9 What is one-third squared?

10 Eating too much of a fat called cholesterol can lead to what type of disease?

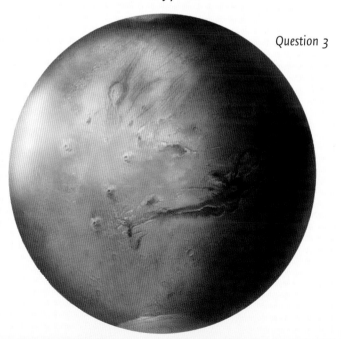

Question 3

279 Scientifically Speaking

1. Which famous table did the Russian, Dmitri Mendelev, produce?

2. What number did an Indian by the name of Vyas invent in the 7th century AD?

3. What computer device was invented by Douglas Englebart?

4. What blood vessels take blood from the heart to the different parts of the body?

5. Vitamin D keeps which two parts of the body strong and healthy?

6. What did Alessandro Volta invent in 1800?

7. What planet takes 247.7 years to orbit the Sun?

8. Which geological era does the Jurassic period belong to: Palaeozoic, Mesozoic or Cenozoic?

9. Taste bud cells distinguish four basic flavours: sweet, sour, bitter and what?

10. How many stars are estimated to be in the Milky Way: 200 million, 20 billion or 200 billion?

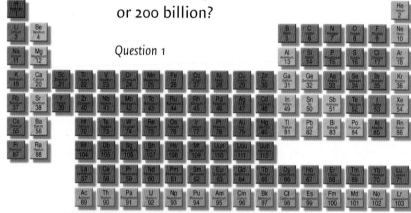

Question 1

280 Written Word

1. What is the collective name for a group of angels?

2. What book featured Meg, Jo, Beth and Amy March?

3. What special feature do words or phrases that are palindromes have?

4. Which American writer wrote *The Grapes of Wrath*?

5. Which famous diarist finished each entry with the words "and so to bed"?

6. Beginning with K, what is the name of the Indian drama consisting of dance and music?

7. What is the plural of roof?

8. What do you call a word having the same sound or spelling as another?

9. Does the word "festinate" mean tasty or hasty?

10. Who wrote the poem *Paradise Lost*?

Question 6

★ BACKGROUND BONUS ★
In his poem *Daffodils*, Wordsworth wandered lonely as a what?

281 Global Matters

1 Rudolph Hess was the last prisoner to be held in what building in England's capital?

2 In what country is the most westerly point of South America?

3 What type of plant features on Mexico's flag?

4 In what ocean are the Maldives?

5 In which Italian city was Christopher Columbus born?

6 What country would you be visiting if you spent a dirham in the capital city of Rabat?

7 Hammerfest, Europe's most northerly town, lies in what country?

8 In which European country are the headquarters of the Heineken Brewing Company?

9 Where is the source of the river Rhine?

10 What is the largest province in Canada?

Question 3

282 Total Trivia

1 Which European country is also known as the Hellenic Republic?

2 His thoughts were published in a little red book. Who was he?

3 There are two kinds of electric current. One is direct current or DC, what is the other?

4 How old is the Earth: 3 billion, 3.5 billion, 4 billion or 4.5 billion years?

5 Reykjavik is the capital of what country?

6 Which famous statue stands high above Rio de Janeiro?

7 What was the name of Nelson's flagship at the Battle of Trafalgar?

8 How many eyes did the Cyclops have?

9 Which Greek mythological hero killed the gorgon Medusa?

10 From which language do the words "tafetta", "bazaar" and "caravan" originate?

Question 6

283   Music Mania

1. Who had a posthumous U.K. No. 1 in 1993 with the song "Living on My Own"?

2. A sackbut was the old name for which musical instrument?

3. In what year was Britney Spears born?

4. Which song, written by Neil Diamond, was a hit for UB40 in 1983?

5. In October 2001, which Rolling Stone qualified for his old age pension?

Question 4

6. Who composed the song "Land of Hope and Glory"?

7. In which country was Cliff Richard born?

8. In *The Muppet Show*, what instrument is played by Zoot?

9. The song "Lady Marmalade" featured in which 2001 movie starring Nicole Kidman?

10. Christine McVie was once a member of which group?

284   Total Trivia

1. What do you call people who have no permanent home and move about in search of pasture?

2. What country is made up of two main islands: North Island and South Island?

3. What is an air-breathing gastropod mollusc with a spiral shell better known as?

4. Which teeth are your canine teeth?

5. In what city will you find the ancient cathedral of Hagia Sophia?

6. Which P word are chickens, ducks, geese, partridges and pheasants?

7. Which word, beginning with P, means to put off until another time?

8. Heat travels by conduction, convection and which other way?

9. Of which country is Colonel Qaddafi the head?

10. In the 15th century, what was the name of the dispute between the English noble families of York and Lancaster?

Question 10

285 Making History

1 Who was called the "Liberator" of South America?

2 By what title was bandleader William Basie known?

3 In which year did Julius Caesar first land in Britain: 550BC, 55BC or AD55?

4 Which human body part was the first to be successfully transplanted in 1954?

5 In what country is the ancient Walloon language spoken?

6 Which Apache chief died in 1909?

7 Who was defeated at Orleans in 1429 by an English army?

8 How many countries joined the European Community when it was started in 1957?

9 Who would wear chaps?

10 What do the initials RAF stand for?

Question 9

★ **BACKGROUND BONUS** ★
Which famous bell first tolled in 1859?

286 Sporting Chance

1 Who is the only heavyweight boxer to have won all of his professional fights?

2 To make a perfect score of 300 in tenpin bowling, how many successive strikes must be registered?

3 What nationality is the tennis star Marcelo Rios?

4 To a golfer, what is a nervous disability affecting the putting?

5 On a chessboard, what are the files?

6 On what flag are the words *Citius, Altius, Fortius* written?

7 What do the initials ICC stand for in the world of sport?

8 In 2000, Jackie Joyner Kersee set a new world record in what event?

9 What sport took its name from the Tibetan word for ball?

10 Who partnered Martina Navratilova to consecutive Wimbledon doubles titles from 1981 to 1984?

Question 3

287 Natural Selection

1 What is a male badger called: a bull, a dog or a boar?

2 Britain's largest is the Death Head, the world's largest is called the Hercules: what are they?

3 What material forms a shark's skeleton?

4 What animals have the largest teeth?

5 Which seabird shares its name with a greedy person?

6 What is a young otter called?

7 What animal has the largest brain?

8 What swims faster: the great white shark or the marlin?

9 Of all the rivers in the world, which one contains the greatest amount of water?

10 To which fish family do goldfish belong?

Question 7

★ BACKGROUND BONUS ★
In Chinese culture, what flower was known as the "plant of king's fragrance"?

288 Making History

1 What is the old name for Ethiopia?

2 Which part of China passed from British rule in 1997?

3 Which expanse of water did the steamship *Savannah* cross in 1819?

4 Which Sioux leader appeared in Buffalo Bill's Wild West Show?

5 Who is the patron saint of sailors?

6 In what country is the Islamic holy city of Mecca?

7 What kind of weapon was a Lee Enfield?

8 Who wrote the play *The Importance of Being Earnest*?

9 Which two countries fought out the Hundred Years War?

10 What important body in Iceland is called the Althing?

Question 8

289   Total Trivia

1   What were the pyramids in ancient Egypt used for?

2   To what group of animals do rats belong?

3   What is a part of the circumference of a circle called?

4   What was J.M.W. Turner famous for?

5   Passover is a festival celebrated in which religion?

6   St. Petersburg was renamed Leningrad. What is it called now?

7   What is the official language of Macao, Mozambique and Angola?

8   From what plant is linen made?

Question 4

9   What does the abbreviation PTO mean?

10 Who were Virgil and Ovid?

290   Lights, Camera, Action!

1   What is the name of the doctor who is the archenemy of Austin Powers?

2   What singer did Val Kilmer play in the 1991 movie *The Doors*?

3   Which movie starring Whoopi Goldberg is also the title of a Rolling Stones hit record?

4   Who did Rosie O'Donnell play in the 1994 movie *The Flintstones*?

5   In which 1997 movie did Mel Gibson play a paranoid character called Jerry Fletcher?

6   Which 1950 musical told the story of the Wild West heroine Annie Oakley?

7   *Jason Takes Manhattan* is the subtitle of the eighth movie in what series of horror flicks?

8   In which 1993 movie does Kevin Kline impersonate the president of the United States?

9   In what movie does a weatherman have to live the same day over and over again?

10 Which 1998 movie saw Wesley Snipes vanquishing vampires?

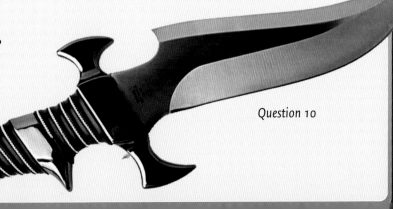
Question 10

291 Sporting Chance

1 Who was Wimbledon men's singles champion in 1976?

2 In which U.S. state was the first Ryder Cup contested?

3 Which U.S. golfer died in a plane crash in 1999?

4 What has a racehorse done if it has spread a plate?

5 What is the middle division on a backgammon board called?

6 What do the initials TP signify to an archer?

7 In what country is the world's oldest golf course?

8 What do the initials SSS signify in golf?

9 In which Texan city can the Astrodome Stadium be found?

10 What pastime is enjoyed by a piscatologist?

Question 10

★ **BACKGROUND BONUS** ★
Allen Johnson and Colin Jackson are famous for competing in what event?

292 Natural Selection

1 Which mammal lives in Egyptian pyramids?

2 What is the world's tallest ruminant?

3 Which Indian Ocean island is home to all 30 or so species of the hedgehog-like tenrec?

4 What timid burrowing animal has a name meaning earth pig?

5 What types of animals are the eland and impala?

6 What crime would you associate with the collective name for a group of crows?

7 Moray, black ribbon and leopard are all species of which sea creature?

8 What comical looking birds were named after the Spanish word for clown?

9 Black Norfolk and Beltsville are both breeds of which large bird?

10 If an animal is described as vermivorous, does it feed on rodents, insects or worms?

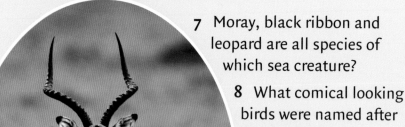

Question 5

293 Animal Habitats

Can you match the animals listed with the habitats shown?

(a) Carp (b) Sun bear (c) Manta ray (d) Oyster catcher (e) Puma
(f) Cheetah (g) Squirrel (h) Polar bear (i) Kangaroo rat (j) Alligator

294 Total Trivia

1 Who started Cubism and is considered its most famous modern painter?

2 What was another name for the plague?

3 Which nutritional food group are milk, meat, eggs, fish and nuts rich in?

4 Which U.S. city is famous for gambling?

5 Who wrote *Treasure Island*?

6 Which sea mammal looks like a seal, but has fur on its body, and, unlike the seal, has ears?

7 What is the opposite of legal?

8 The Cavaliers and Roundheads were opponents In which war?

9 What country's flag shows a red maple leaf?

10 Name the two Baltic states that begin with the letter L.

Question 4

295 Music Mania

1 A-Ha, who recorded the theme to *The Living Daylights*, are from which country?

2 Members of which pop group starred in the 1999 British crime movie *Honest*?

3 *A Fistful of Dollars* launched the movie career of what composer?

4 The 1997 movie *Space Jam* featured which massive-selling hit by R. Kelly?

5 Which classic 60s movie was graced by Simon and Garfunkel's "Mrs Robinson"?

6 What singer starred as May Day in the Bond movie *A View to a Kill*?

7 Which two singers co-starred in *A Star is Born* (1976)?

8 Who contributed five songs to the soundtrack of *The Lion King*?

9 Who recorded the soundtrack to the Tim Burton directed *Batman* movie?

10 Who sang the theme tune to the Bond movie *Licence to Kill*?

Question 1

296 Lights, Camera, Action!

1 Who directed the movies *Jackie Brown* and *Reservoir Dogs*?

2 Scott Joplin's "The Entertainer" featured as the theme music for which Oscar-winning movie?

3 In which movie did Bruce Willis first play the streetwise cop John McClane?

4 What actor was reincarnated as Bobby Ewing in a Southfork shower?

5 In which movie did Tim Allen play a character who accidentally killed Santa?

6 Who played Jesus in the 1965 movie *The Greatest Story Ever Told*?

7 Who played seven different characters in the movie *The Man in the Santa Claus Suit*?

8 In which series of movies does Christopher Lloyd play Dr. Emmett Brown?

9 Who stars as Muhammad Ali in the 2002 movie *Ali*?

10 Who did Tim Curry play in *Muppet Treasure Island*?

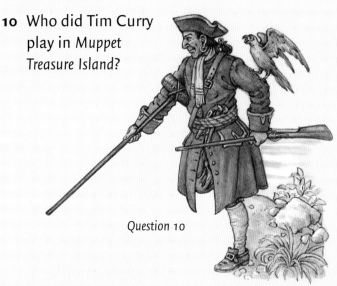

Question 10

297 Great and Famous

1 Who had a hit with "The Sun Ain't Gonna Shine Anymore"?

2 *West Side Story* is based on which play by Shakespeare?

3 Who plays the U.S. president in the movie *Primary Colors*?

4 In what year did Michael Jackson start his solo career: 1966, 1970 or 1979?

5 What was Nikolay Rimsky-Korsakov famous for?

Question 5

6 "Strange Fruits" and "Lover Man" are best-known records by which singer?

7 The American architect, Frank Lloyd Wright, designed which famous building in New York?

8 Whose real name is Steveland Morris?

9 Which character did Harrison Ford play in the *Star Wars* movies?

10 Chester Carlson is responsible for the invention of which useful machine?

★ BACKGROUND BONUS ★
In 1868, C.L. Scholes patented the first modern what?

298   Sporting Chance

1 Which basketball legend was nicknamed "The Georgia Peach"?

2 In which year did synchronized swimming make its Olympic debut?

3 What name is given to the practice of training hawks?

4 How did the boxer Rocky Marciano die?

5 How many members are there in a women's lacrosse team?

6 Who married Tatum O'Neal in 1986?

7 Which British gold medal-winner carried the Union Jack in the opening ceremony of the 2000 Sydney Olympics?

8 What card game is also the name of a floating bridge?

9 Which British driver won the Formula One World Championship in 1976?

10 What sport was originally called kitten ball?

Question 3

299   Scientifically Speaking

1 Which device for seeing distant objects has a name that means for both eyes?

2 What is the common name for your trachea?

3 What day is known as Midsummer's Day?

4 What is another name for a shooting star?

5 What is "dry ice"?

6 What does a barometer measure?

7 What is the lightest gas?

8 Which type of animals are described as "ovine"?

9 What covers more than two-thirds of the world's surface?

10 Which device for measuring time uses running sand?

Question 10

300   Global Matters

1 The Cascade mountain range extends into which two countries?

2 Which two countries have a coastline on the Dead Sea?

3 The Boeing aerospace company is based in which city on the West coast of the United States?

4 What is the capital of Croatia?

5 A covering of ice on an area of land is known by what name?

6 Sparta was an ancient city In which country?

7 If you were in Quito paying for goods in sucres, what country would you be in?

8 Which Baltic state begins with the letter E?

9 A hanging spike of clear ice is known by what name?

10 What continent produces more dairy products (cheese, milk and butter) than any other?

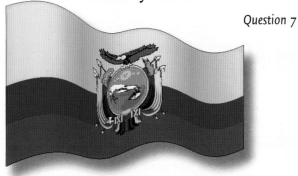

Question 7

> ★ BACKGROUND BONUS ★
> Which strange rock formation can be found in Arches National Park, Utah?

301   Total Trivia

1 What city lies in the middle of Australia?

2 Who had a magic lamp?

3 What is a migraine?

4 What is silent acting called?

5 The Missouri is a tributary of what river?

6 Which U.S. spacecraft made its first flight in 1981?

7 What is the capital of Pakistan?

8 What is the name of an automatic device for controlling temperature?

9 According to the language of flowers, what does the foxglove signify?

10 Which warrior caste of Japan followed a strict code of conduct?

Question 10

302 Written Word: The Bible

1 What is the name of the Virgin Mary's mother?

2 Which was the only miracle performed by Jesus that is mentioned in all four gospels?

3 What star led the Three Wise Men to Jesus?

4 What was the original name of St. Peter?

5 What religion did Mary and Joseph follow?

6 Is the Book of Revelation about the end or the beginning of the world?

7 Jesus grew up in Nazareth. In which modern-day country is Nazareth?

8 In which garden did Judas betray Jesus?

9 Who played Jesus in the 1970s TV series *Jesus of Nazareth*?

10 What was written on two stone tablets and is also known as The Decalogue?

Question 5

303 Lights, Camera, Action!

1 What is the name of the The Grinch's canine sidekick?

2 Who won Oscars for her performances in the movies *Norma Rae* and *Places in the Heart*?

3 What was the title of the 1992 Superhero sequel that starred Michelle Pfeiffer?

4 Who played Jonathan in TV's *Hart to Hart*?

5 Who played Scrooge in the 1951 movie directed by Brian Hurst?

6 In which TV game show do eliminated contestants take the walk of shame?

7 What actor arrested a gang of drug dealers at a Christmas tree stand in the movie *Lethal Weapon*?

8 Which song from the movie *High Society* lent its name to a worldwide TV quiz show?

9 In which movie did Bing Crosby play the character of Bob Wallace?

10 Which was the third *Star Wars* movie to be made?

Question 9

304 Scientifically Speaking

1 What kind of watch is used to time a race?

2 Where is bile stored in the human body?

3 What is the term for a parallelogram with four equal sides?

4 What process causes sounds to be recorded on tape, such as cassettes?

5 What is the name for the science that studies the history of the Earth's crust?

6 The initials WWF are the short name of which international organization that protects animals?

7 If someone asked you to send a hard copy, what would you need to do?

8 What do you call a piece of land that juts out when three of its four sides border water?

9 Which parts of the body does an ENT specialist treat?

10 What part of the body does Alzheimer's disease affect?

Question 10

★ **BACKGROUND BONUS** ★
What is the primary cause of smog in today's modern cities?

305 Sporting Chance: Soccer

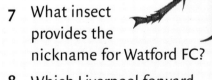

1 Which pop star cried at Wembley in 1984 after Everton beat Watford in the FA Cup?

2 Mark Hughes and Gary Lineker both played for which Spanish soccer club?

3 Which fellow Swede became Sven Goran Eriksson's assistant manager for the England team?

4 What is the name of Glasgow Rangers' ground?

5 At the 1966 soccer World Cup, what nation entered the tournament as defending world champions?

6 For which country did Hristo Stoichtkov play?

Question 7

7 What insect provides the nickname for Watford FC?

8 Which Liverpool forward joined West Ham in 2000?

9 Who was the first player ever to score a hat-trick in a World Cup final?

10 Which Columbian player was murdered after the 1994 World Cup finals?

306   Natural Selection

1. Which European bird of prey hovers over its hunting ground?

2. Are coral animals plant-eaters or meat-eaters?

3. How does the ox-pecker bird help buffalo?

4. Which is the oldest breed of domesticated horse?

5. Why do some plants pack closely together to form cushions?

6. The bladderwort is a meat-eating water plant: true or false?

7. Which sea turtle eats jellyfish as a major part of its diet?

8. How does the cave-racer snake catch bats: by chasing them or hanging by its tail from rocks?

9. Which North American cat preys mainly on cottontail rabbits?

10. Where do snipe nest: in ice fields, grassy meadows or wetlands?

Question 1

★ **BACKGROUND BONUS** ★
What is the largest frog in North America?

307   Total Trivia

1. Manila is the and capital of what country?

2. Which bird has the Latin name *Indicator Indicator*?

3. Which Dutch painter produced about 60 self-portraits and painted *The Night Watch*?

4. Which is the largest member of the cat family?

5. Who wrote *Waverley*, *Rob Roy* and *Heart of Midlothian*?

6. What is the capital of Finland?

7. What kind of boat skims across the surface of the water on underwater wings?

8. The trunk of what tree swells in wet weather and shrinks in dry weather?

9. How is two-thirds written as a decimal?

10. What kind of stone did early people use to make tools and weapons?

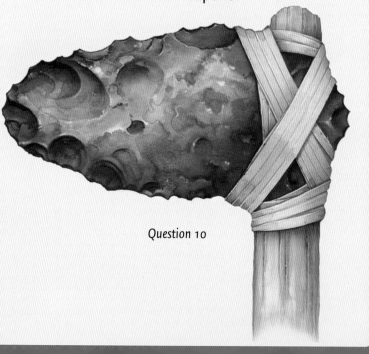

Question 10

308 Music Mania

Name the album:

1 "Breathe", "Firestarter", "Diesel Power".

2 "All I Really Want", "Ironic", "Not the Doctor".

3 "Made of Stone", "Waterfall", "She Bangs the Drums".

4 "Eleanor Rigby", "Yellow Submarine", "Tomorrow Never Knows".

5 "Life in the Fast Lane", "Victim of Love", "Pretty Maids All in a Row".

6 "Never Going Back Again", "The Chain", "Dreams".

7 "Paradise by the Dashboard Light", "Heaven Can Wait", "Two Out of Three Ain't Bad".

8 "The Sound of the Crowd", "Love Action", "I am the Law".

9 "Praise You", "Gangster Tripping", "Acid 8000".

10 "Don't Panic", "High Speed", "Trouble".

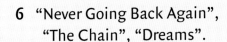

Question 7

309 Making History

1 Who was assassinated in 1968 by James Earl Ray?

2 Who wrote the piano music *Clare de Lune*?

3 Which part of Germany was ruled by Frederick the Great?

4 By what name is East Pakistan now known?

5 Which royal house did Edward I and Richard II belong to?

6 Which 17th- century scientist proved that blood circulates through the body?

7 In what century did Marco Polo visit China?

8 Which important document was signed at Runnymede in the 13th century?

9 In what century was the very first photograph taken?

10 Who flew the Atlantic in the *Spirit of St Louis*?

Question 8

310 Lights, Camera, Action!

1 In which 1992 movie did Tom Cruise mix Pina Coladas and Harvey Wallbangers?

2 Which silent movie actor's real name was Rodolfo d'Antonguolla?

3 In a Christmas special, what did Mr. Bean buy his teddy bear as a Christmas present?

4 Who played the British wife of Ross in *Friends*?

5 In the title of the 1945 movie, Sydney Greenstreet and Barbara Stanwyck spend Christmas where?

6 In which park does Yogi Bear live?

7 The opening words of which movie are spoken by the main character, Benjamin Braddock?

8 Which actor, better known for his Bond roles, played Professor Henry Jones in the 1989 movie?

9 Who played Scrooge in the 1988 movie *Scrooged*?

10 Which actress played Dr. Ellie Satler in *Jurassic Park*?

Question 3

★ **BACKGROUND BONUS** ★
Which movie for kids, starring Gene Wilder, has a delicious sounding title?

311 Natural Selection

1 Which group of predatory fish grow and replace thousands of teeth in a lifetime?

2 Does the hairy frog use the hair-like projections on its skin to absorb oxygen or to attract a mate?

3 Barbary, bighorn and mountain are types of what?

4 In Australia, which snake's bite causes more deaths: the common brownsnake, the taipan or the tiger snake?

5 What plant yields the painkiller codeine?

6 How does the limpet eat?

7 Which large American rodent lives in riverbank burrows and has webbed feet?

8 Which member of the crow family builds a nest with a domed roof: the rook, the jay or the magpie?

9 Which dolphin has made the most contact with humans?

10 How does the edelweiss flower protect itself from extreme cold?

Question 9

312   Sporting Chance

1 Which Italian opera singer sang at the 2000 Sydney Olympics?

2 What connects the Summer Olympic venues of 1904, 1932, 1984 and 1996?

3 Who was disqualified from the 1995 Wimbledon men's singles for hitting a ball against a ball girl?

4 What do the initials FDC mean to a stamp collector?

5 The King George V Cup is contested at Hickstead in what sport?

Question 6

6 What caused Rome to withdraw its application to host the 1908 Summer Olympics?

7 Who beat Carl Lewis to win the long jump at the 1991 World Championships?

8 How many points are awarded to a driver who wins a Formula One Grand Prix race?

9 Who was the last female European winner of the Wimbledon singles in the 20th century?

10 In which sport was a Lonsdale Belt first awarded in 1909?

313   Music Mania

1 What crooner had a hit in 1976 with "When a Child is Born"?

2 Which hit record for Buddy Holly was also the title of a movie starring David Essex?

3 Which type of instrument is Vanessa Mae most commonly associated with?

4 Which 1981 hit for the Pointer Sisters is also the nickname of Eric Clapton?

5 Which hit for Wham contained the line: "Don't leave me hangin' on like a yo-yo"?

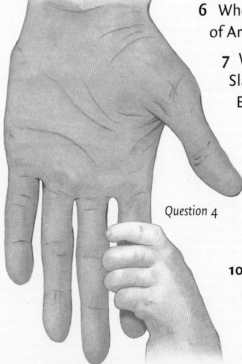

Question 4

6 Who was the singing partner of Art Garfunkel?

7 Who sang lead vocals for Slade on "Merry Xmas Everybody"?

8 Which singer who had a hit with "Jealous Mind" was born Bernard Jewry?

9 In 1956, who wiggled his pelvis whilst singing "Hound Dog"?

10 What song was a posthumous No. 1 for Elvis Presley in 1977?

314 Total Trivia

1 How do pythons and anacondas kill their prey?

2 What part of the body does a chiropodist treat?

3 In which city is the Kremlin?

4 Did dinosaurs lay eggs?

5 Who was the first European to explore the coasts of Australia and New Zealand?

6 What is the name for all the bodies that orbit the Sun and the Sun itself?

7 What is the name of a word made by re-arranging the letters of another word?

8 What is the name for the stone at the top of an arch that locks the whole arch together?

9 Who wrote *The Ugly Duckling*?

10 Where are the Northwest Territories?

Question 6

315 Lights, Camera, Action!

1 Who played the boss of Julia Roberts in the movie *Erin Brockovich*?

2 The Palme d'Or is the top award at which movie festival?

3 Who played the role of Professor Xavier in the movie *X Men*?

4 Which Alan Parker movie was set in Dublin and featured the song "Mustang Sally"?

5 Who played Count Dracula for the last time in the movie *The Satanic Rites of Dracula*?

6 Which heavyweight boxing champion had a cameo role in the 2001 movie *Ocean's Eleven*?

7 Who played the title role in the movie *Edward Scissorhands*?

8 In which movie did Richard Attenborough play a millionaire called John Hammond?

9 Which movie star is the daughter of Tippi Hedren and the ex-wife of Don Johnson?

10 What song was performed by the cast at the beginning of the movie *Grease*?

Question 8

316 Making History

1   From which city did Marco Polo start his Chinese journey?

2   Which famous newspaper was published for the first time in 1785?

3   Who were the first settlers to explore the Rockies?

4   What stone gave the code to hieroglyphic writing?

5   What country did Bernardo O'Higgins help to liberate in 1818?

6   What city was the Praetorian Guard designed to protect?

7   Who found the first northerly route from the Atlantic to the Pacific?

8   How many children were born to Queen Victoria?

9   Which painting by Picasso commemorates the bombing of a Spanish village in 1937?

10 What type of weapon was a Brown Bess?

Question 3

> ★ BACKGROUND BONUS ★
> In which building does U.S. Congress meet?

317 Sporting Chance: Soccer

1   What country does Norberto Solano play for?

2   Which German club did Nottingham Forest beat in the final of the 1980 European Cup?

3   Which Italian soccer striker is nicknamed "The White Feather"?

4   Which club did Manchester United beat with a last-minute goal in the final of the 1999 European Cup?

5   Which goalkeeper went 1,143 minutes without conceding an international goal?

6   Which international side has Alessandro del Piero played for?

7   Who returned to soccer in 1990 as manager of France's national team?

8   What goalkeeper played his 1000th Football League game, whilst playing for Leyton Orient?

9   Which England hero was accused of stealing a bracelet in 1970?

10 Who did Liverpool beat in the final of the 2001 UEFA Cup?

Question 1

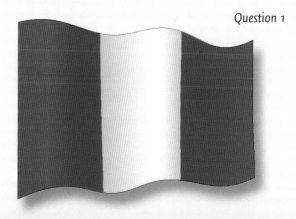

318 Total Trivia

1   What kind of heavenly body is made of very hot gas and gives out heat and light?

2   What is the name for a creature that eats both plants and animals?

3   How many pairs of wings does a fly have?

4   In which country is McGill University?

5   Which Indian city produces more movies than Hollywood?

6   Where does the jaguar live?

7   In which country would you find a kibbutz?

8   What country is Beirut the capital of?

9   Which ancient civilization spilt a drop of blood every morning to please their gods?

10 What is the square of 11?

Question 1

319 Great and Famous

1   Which U.S. actor of the 1940s and 1950s suffered a lip wound in World War I, giving him his distinctive appearance and voice?

2   In 1983, which English pop star was paid the highest sum ever to appear in a concert in California?

3   Which French inventor devised a reading system for blind people?

4   Who wrote *Paradise Lost*?

5   Which fashion designer introduced the "New Look" in 1947?

6   *The Scream* and *The Dance of Life* were amongst which artist's paintings?

7   Who was the daughter of William Godwin and Mary Woolstencraft?

8   Whose plays include *Uncle Vanya* and *The Three Sisters*?

9   What writer created the character of Jeeves?

10 Who was the second president of the United States?

Question 1

★ **BACKGROUND BONUS** ★
Which actress played the part of Sharon Stone in the 1994 move *The Flintstones*?

320 Flying the Flag

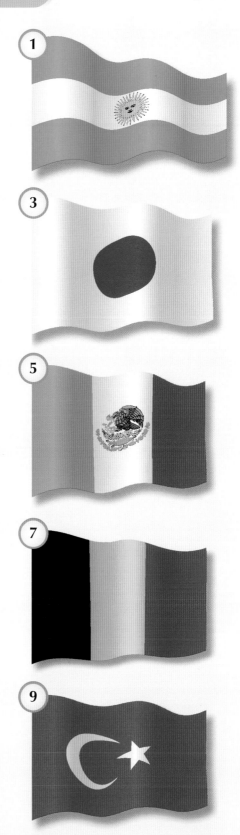

Can you match the flags to the following countries?

(a) Brazil (b) Turkey (c) Mexico (d) Japan (e) Zambia (f) Argentina (g) Australia (h) Denmark (i) Belgium (j) Greece

321 Scientifically Speaking

1. What is the name for a three-dimensional photographic image that is created using laser lights?
2. What is the more common name for calcium oxide?
3. What is the world's hardest substance?
4. When water reaches its boiling point, what does it become?
5. What itchy condition, caused by a fungus, usually affects the area between the toes?
6. Which navigational device uses a magnet suspended or floated in a liquid?
7. What does a dermatologist study?
8. What gas makes up most of the air we breathe?
9. What is 20 percent of 20?
10. In which ocean does the Gulf Stream flow?

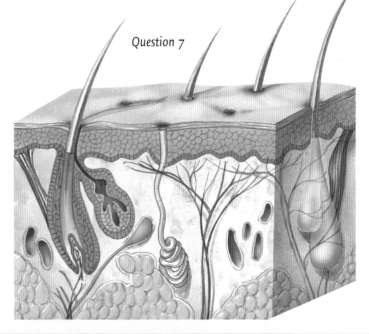

Question 7

322 Sporting Chance

1. How many players are in a handball team?
2. What is Frankie short for in the name of the jockey Frankie Dettori?
3. Which female athlete broke the world record at the 2003 London marathon?
4. What type of sporting contest includes calf roping and bull riding events?
5. Which athlete was stripped of the 100 m gold medal at the 1988 Olympics?
6. Which ice skater allegedly knew about the baton attack on her rival Nancy Kerrigan?
7. What city hosted the 1948 Summer Olympics?
8. In which sport do competitors make the Liffey Descent?
9. Mills Lane is a referee In which sport?
10. Which sports company took their name from an African gazelle?

Question 10

323 Global Matters

1 In which country are the headquarters of the International Olympic Committee?

2 What is the most common mineral found in rocks?

3 What Polish city used to be known as Danzig?

4 In which country would you find Cape Guardafui?

5 A vehicle with the international registration ET comes from what country?

6 What sort of army is found in Xi'an, China?

7 Over what fish did Britain and Iceland battle in the 1970s?

8 What is the former name for Taiwan?

9 Which city is known as "the eternal city"?

10 Which four U.S. states begin and end with the same letter?

Question 4

★ BACKGROUND BONUS ★
Which ancient Roman ruin once held crowds of 50,000 people?

324 Natural Selection

1 Why do South Africans call the brown hyena the beach wolf?

2 Does a polar bear's fur change from white to brown in summer?

3 What tree produces a substance that is vital to the automobile industry?

4 How does the basilisk lizard cross water?

5 Which flightless bird moves on rocks in a series of two-footed jumps?

6 What is the biggest beetle?

7 What does the spitting spider spit?

8 Do sloths live in forests or swamps?

9 What is another name for the manatee?

10 Which fast-moving bird hardly ever lands, and can sleep while flying?

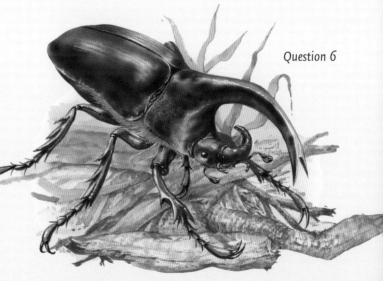

Question 6

325 Natural Selection

1 Do common dolphins live alone or together?

2 Why do fruit bats lick themselves all over?

3 What liquid does the horned lizard squirt from its eyes to deter predators?

4 What is a vinegaroon?

5 What sort of habitat does the tapir live in?

6 What spider catches moths with a sticky ball on a long thread?

7 What crab has a shield like body, covering five pairs of walking legs and a long tail spike?

8 Which snakelike fish did the ancient Romans keep as pets and decorate with jewels?

9 Which desert plant and moth share the same name?

10 Why do some owls bob their heads up and down?

Question 8

326 Scientifically Speaking

1 What do you call a scientist who studies volcanoes?

2 How many wisdom teeth can an adult grow?

3 How many cards are there in each suit of a deck of playing cards?

4 What do you do when you expectorate?

5 What part of a fraction is the dividend?

6 "Rheumatoid" is a type of which bone ailment?

7 Russian blue, Abyssinian and Maine coon are examples of what?

8 What word is used to describe the amount of matter in an object?

9 What is the frequency of sound measured in?

10 What type of medical professional removes plaque?

Question 7

327 Sporting Chance

1 Which golfer won the Masters in 2001 and 2002?

2 Which country hosted the 2002 World Equestrian Games?

3 What is the name of the village in Berkshire where Queen Anne established a famous horseracing course?

4 Which female gymnast won three gold medals at the 1972 Olympics?

5 In which city would you find teams called the Knicks, Giants and Yankees?

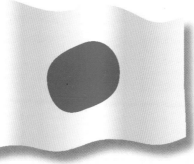

Question 6

6 In which country did karate originate?

7 What does the word Olympiad mean?

8 What name is given to the skiing event where competitors have to swerve in and out to avoid flags?

9 Which athlete first broke the 4-minute mile in 1954?

10 What do the initials PU signify in the form guide of a racehorse?

> ★ **BACKGROUND BONUS** ★
> What sport is Paradorn Srichaphan known for?

328 Total Trivia

1 How many moons has Mars?

2 What lies under the ice at the North Pole?

3 Where is the Cape of Good Hope?

4 Who wrote *Pilgrim's Progress*?

5 What is laver bread made from?

6 Who starred as Sugar Kane Kowalczyk in the 1958 movie *Some Like it Hot*?

7 According to Shakespeare, how many ages of man are there?

8 Doric, Ionic and Corinthian are all orders of what?

9 What Hollywood superstar narrated the movie *Armageddon*?

10 Who is king of the fairies?

Question 6

329 Lights, Camera, Action!

1   In which 1984 movie did Zach Galligan play a teenager who received a mogwai for Christmas?

2   In which TV show does a teenage witch live with her aunts and a talking cat?

3   In the movie *Great Balls of Fire!*, which rock and roller was played by Dennis Quaid?

4   Who won a Best Supporting Actress Oscar for her role in the movie *Ghost*?

5   Which movie, made in 2000, features Nicholas Cage as a car thief?

6   Who won a Best Director Oscar for the movie *Titanic*?

7   In which classic Christmas movie did James Stewart attempt to commit suicide?

8   Who played the Bond girl, Pussy Galore and the Avenger, Cathy Gale?

9   Who played the role of Clark Griswold in the movie *National Lampoon's Christmas Vacation*?

10 In which movie did Anthony Hopkins say, "I'm having an old friend for dinner"?

Question 5

330 Total Trivia

1   Which sea creatures swim by squirting out water through a tube?

2   In which sport was the phrase "hat trick" first used?

3   Who wrote a book about Jemima Puddleduck?

4   What is the name for an area of space that sucks everything into itself, even light?

5   How many wings has a dragonfly?

6   Did the Egyptian god, Anubis, have the head of a cobra, jackal or falcon?

7   Who is the U.S. state of Virginia named after?

8   A sky with altocumulus clouds shares its name with what type of fish?

9   What was the name of the fairy in *Peter Pan*?

10 What is the only food consumed by vampire bats?

Question 6

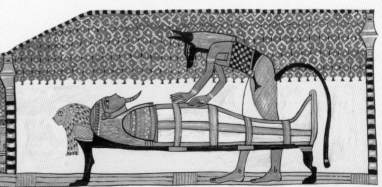

331 Scientifically Speaking

1 Where would you find the rudder of an aircraft?

2 What material was used to produce LP records?

3 How many hours are there in five days?

4 What part of a fish aids buoyancy?

5 A fulcrum is an important part of what type of simple machine?

6 A fuel cell is a type of what?

7 What does a seismologist study?

8 What would a serial or parallel cable be used for?

9 What type of scientist would study quasars, pulsars and asteroids?

10 You would find a cuticle at the base of what parts of the body?

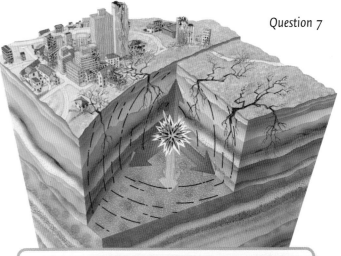

Question 7

> ★ BACKGROUND BONUS ★
> What is another name for a synoptic chart?

332 Making History

1 What composer wrote comic operas with W.S. Gilbert?

2 What country won the first ever soccer World Cup in 1930?

3 In what year was the Hubble Space telescope launched?

4 What king was the first British settlement in United States named after?

5 Which Scots leader defeated the English at Stirling Bridge?

6 Which Italian family ruled Florence from the 15th century to the 18th century?

7 From what ship was the first SOS message broadcast?

8 What was the nickname of U.S. General Norman Schwarzkopf during the Gulf War?

9 Who was known as the "Sun King"?

10 In which World War I battle, lasting 141 days, did the British and French lose 600,000 men?

Question 7

333 Great and Famous

1 Who was known as "The Maid of Orleans"?

2 In the 2001 movie *Miss Congeniality*, which actress plays the undercover cop in a beauty contest?

3 Whose compositions include the operas *Tosca*, *Madame Butterfly* and *Turandot*?

4 What Marquis gave his name to the rules that govern the sport of boxing?

5 Which English explorer was imprisoned in the Tower of London and beheaded in 1618?

6 Which U.S. president introduced the New Deal?

7 Which British impresario was noted for his productions of Gilbert and Sullivan operettas?

8 Who became prime minister of India on its independence in 1947?

9 Who wrote *Don Quixote*?

10 Which astronomer first put forward the theory that the Earth and the planets revolve around the Sun?

Question 5

334 Music Mania

1 What was Soul II Soul's only U.K. No. 1?

2 Whose U.K. chart debut "End of the Road" reached No. 1 in 1992?

3 Which enduring female artist was born in 1950 in St. Kitts in the West Indies?

4 "What Have You Done For Me Lately" was which singer's breakthrough in 1986?

5 "Papa Was A Rollin' Stone" was a hit in 1973 and 1987 for which soul combo?

6 Which former Doobie Brother recorded "Yah Mo B There" with James Ingram?

7 Which producer of Sheena Easton recorded the classic "Forget Me Nots"?

8 Which singer hit No. 1 in the U.S. with "Kiss From a Rose"?

9 Which diva scored a hit with "You Might Need Somebody" in 1997?

10 Who sang a duet with Marvin Gaye on "It Takes Two"?

Question 8

★ **BACKGROUND BONUS** ★
Which musical instrument produces a sound called a "skirl"?

335 Total Trivia

1. In which type of object would you find a rampart above an escapement?

2. Who slept in the teapot at the Mad Hatter's tea party?

3. What is phlebitis the inflammation of?

4. In the 1950s, what war did the Treaty of Panmunjon end?

5. Which Alfred Hitchcock thriller was set mainly at Bodega Bay?

6. What was the infamous London address of the murderer John Christie?

7. What is the more common name for magnesium silicate?

8. What is a female fox called?

9. What type of passenger plane made its maiden flight in February 1969?

10. Who was Roman emperor when Jesus was crucified?

Question 5

336 Lights, Camera, Action!

1. In which movie does Tom Hanks play a prison guard called Paul Edgecomb?

2. Who has played the Prince of Wales, Charlie Chan and Hercule Poirot?

3. In which capital city was the actor Russell Crowe born?

4. Which heart-throb actor plays the father of the spy kids in the movie of the same name?

5. Who played the title role in the epic movie *Spartacus*?

6. What was Billy Crystal's profession in the comedy movie *Analyze This*?

7. Who played Morpheus in the futuristic thriller *The Matrix*?

8. What is the title of the third in the series of *Austin Powers* movies?

9. Which 1964 movie tells the story of an 1879 battle fought in Africa?

10. Which medieval author was portrayed by Paul Bettany in the movie *The Knight's Tale*?

Question 1

337 Making History

1 By what name is the religious group "The Society of Friends" better known?

2 What revolt did Wat Tyler lead in 1381?

3 Which famous pop star was shot dead in New York in 1980?

4 Which English king was defeated at Bosworth in 1485?

5 What country offered Albert Einstein its presidency in 1948?

6 By what name is the Mongol ruler Timur the Lame better known?

7 Where was Napoleon exiled after Waterloo?

8 Who won the Six Day War in 1967?

9 What instrument did Beethoven write his *Emperor Concerto* for?

10 What was Shakespeare's last play?

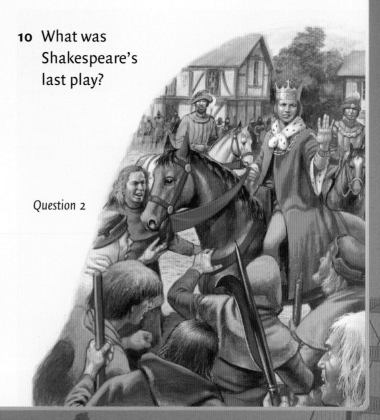

Question 2

338 Scientifically Speaking

Question 3

1 What word describes the horizontal and vertical lines on a graph?

2 What is classified by the letters A, B, AB and O?

3 What kind of plane was a Lancaster?

4 Does an electron have a positive, negative or neutral charge?

5 What is the process whereby yeast acts on sugar to produce alcohol and carbon dioxide?

6 Alfred Nobel, who founded the Nobel Prizes, invented what in 1866?

7 What system do submarines use to "hear" underwater?

8 What is the scientific name for rusting?

9 The Austrian monk Gregor Mendel is associated with what science?

10 What is the normal body temperature of a healthy person?

339 Music Mania

1 Blond Ambition and Drowned World were two of which U.S. megastar's tours?

2 Is Don Alfonso a leading character in *Aida*, *Così Fan Tutte* or *The Barber of Seville*?

3 Which instrument did jazz muscian Miles Davis play?

4 What is the lowest female singing voice?

5 Was the classical composer, Béla Bartók, German, Hungarian or Polish?

6 Born in 1942, who acquired the nickname of The Queen of Soul Music?

7 By what name is U2 front man Paul Hewson better known?

8 Which reggae star sang with The Wailers and had a hit with "No Woman, No Cry"?

9 Sid Vicious replaced Glen Matlock in which controversial punk rock group?

10 Sky Masterson, Miss Adelaide and Nathan Detroit are characters In which musical?

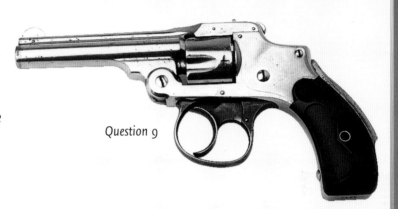

Question 9

340 Global Matters

1 What is abrasion?

2 In which of the world's oceans would you find Kangaroo Island?

3 Which Australian town is further north: Cairns or Townsville?

4 In which continent would you find the Saltilla River?

5 The process of the continents moving apart over thousands of years is known by what name?

6 Which African country is now the only home of the oryx?

7 What is the state capital of Utah?

8 Cameroon was a colony of what country before becoming independent?

9 In which city can you find Michelangelo's famous sculpture called *David*?

10 What is the largest big cat in South America?

Question 10

★ BACKGROUND BONUS ★
Which manmade structure, designed by Joseph B. Strauss, was completed in 1937?

341 Total Trivia

1 Which U.S. actress was married to Frank Sinatra, Artie Shaw and Micky Rooney?

2 What flower was named after the Roman goddess of the rainbow?

3 If a dish is described as chantilly, what is it garnished with?

4 What sea creature is made up of 95% water and has no heart, brain, bones, eyes, gills or blood?

5 In which movie does Denzel Washington play boxer Rubin Carter?

6 Is cynophobia the fear of cats, dogs or mice?

7 Who wrote the play *The Odd Couple*?

8 Where in the body is the tarsal joint?

9 In which city was John F. Kennedy assassinated?

10 Who invented the dynamo?

Question 2

342 Natural Selection

1 What is the smallest land mammal?

2 What tree provided the main wood for English naval ships in the 18th century?

3 Which is the largest member of the dolphin family?

4 How does the chuckwalla lizard avoid predators?

5 How does the female Indian python help her eggs to hatch?

6 How does the frigate bird steal food?

7 Up to how many years can a lobster live: 50 years, 100 years or 150 years?

8 What does the perch fish eat?

9 What is a pond slider?

10 Which apes swing on long arms through the forests of Southeast Asia?

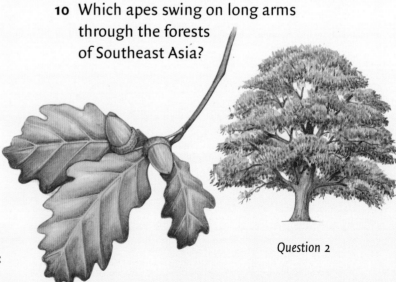

Question 2

> ★ **BACKGROUND BONUS** ★
> Which type of elephant is biggest:
> the African or Asian?

343   Lights, Camera, Action!

1   In which 1990 movie did Robert DeNiro play the patient of Robin Williams?

2   Which film blockbuster was promoted with the publicity blurb, "Protecting the Earth from the scum of the Universe"?

3   Who starred in *Breakfast at Tiffany's* and later played the leader of the *A-Team* on TV?

4   In which movie did James Bond come out of retirement to fight the evil SMERSH?

5   Who played the vigilante Paul Kersey in the *Death Wish* movies?

6   Which 1995 movies earned Susan Sarandon an Oscar for her role as a nun?

7   In which decade did Disney release *Snow White and the Seven Dwarfs?*

8   Which TV police drama was adapted into a 1987 comedy movie co-starring Dan Aykroyd and Tom Hanks?

9   The movie *The Charge of the Light Brigade* was set during which war?

10   In which 1991 movie did Andrew Strong sing "Mustang Sally"?

Question 9

344   Making History

1   In which country would you find the medieval Alhambra palace?

2   Where did a *Viking* land in 1976?

3   Of which African country was Jomo Kenyatta the first president?

4   In what country was the Easter Rising of 1916?

5   What was the spacecraft that made the first Moon landing?

6   Which U.S. president was known as "Ike"?

7   In what city was the first set of traffic lights set up in 1868?

8   What natural wonder is named after aviator James Angel?

9   A velocipede was an early name for what type of vehicle?

10   Who became president of France first in 1945 and later in 1968?

Question 5

345 Making History

1. Which English poet died in 1824 helping Greece in her revolt against the Turks?
2. Which European country was ruled by Tito from 1945 to 1980?
3. What, in ancient Greece, was an amphora?
4. Who captained HMS *Victory* at the Battle of Trafalgar?
5. What was the term given to the dividing line between the West and the Communist bloc?
6. Which Italian city was once ruled by a doge?
7. What did early sailors call the islands where cinnamon, cloves and nutmeg were grown?
8. Which country was known to explorers as "The Roof of the World"?
9. In which U.S. town did the "Gunfight at the OK Corral" take place?
10. What shipboard disease did Captain Cook prevent by taking fresh fruit and fruit juice?

Question 1

346 Lights, Camera, Action!

1. Who played Garth in *Wayne's World*?
2. Which was the first movie set during the Vietnam War to win a Best Movie Oscar?
3. Which 1962 movie told the life story of T.E. Lawrence?
4. Susan Sarandon and Geena Davis play best friends in which 1991 movie?
5. What was the title of the movie in which Barbra Streisand was disguised as a man?
6. Who played Cornelius in the 1968 movie *Planet of the Apes*?
7. In which movie did Julie Walters play a dancing teacher called Mrs. Wilkinson?
8. In which 1995 movie did James Cromwell play Farmer Arthur Hoggett?
9. Who played the title role in the movie *Captain Corelli's Mandolin*?
10. In which 1976 horror movie did Piper Laurie play Sissy Spacek's mother?

Question 8

★ BACKGROUND BONUS ★
Which 1996 movie starring Glenn Close has become a canine classic?

347 Name that Place

Can you identify these natural landmarks?

348 Natural Selection

1 Which native North American mammal can weigh up to 1,000 kg (100 tons)?

2 Why do members of the weasel family have short legs and long bodies?

3 What is the osprey's main food?

4 How does the Surinam toad carry its young?

5 Which forest spider lives in huge communities?

6 How does a snake swallow prey bigger than its own head?

Question 7

7 Why are some birds known as anvil birds?

8 Which insect larva takes up to 15 years to become an adult with a noisy chirp?

9 Does the ostrich use its wings for courtship displays, shading its eggs or both?

10 Which two creatures have the most legs in the animal kingdom?

349 Music Mania

1 A Northern Soul was the precursor to which huge-selling 90s album?

2 Dexy's Midnight Runners were searching for what in 1980?

3 How many studio albums did Kate Bush make in the period 1987 to 2000?

4 No. 1 in the U.K. and U.S., Hysteria was a huge seller for which British rock band?

5 Released the year before he died, what was the title of Otis Redding's magnum opus?

6 Whose debut album was entitled Welcome to the Pleasuredome?

7 Who had a 1983 No. 1 album called Colour by Numbers?

8 Which progressive rock band was Selling England by the Pound in 1973?

9 Whose debut album was called Tuesday Night Music Club?

10 The 2000 album of which songstress was called Rise?

Question 9

350 Global Matters

Question 10

1 What fraction of the Earth's surface does the Pacific Ocean cover?

2 Is jute, cotton or silk Bangladesh's most important export?

3 Where do pilgrims circle the Kaaba Stone?

4 What is the abbreviation EU short for?

5 What is Mauna Loa?

6 What sea does the Orinoco River flow into?

7 Which large sea separates mainland Southeast Asia from the Philippine Islands?

8 A petrified forest is one that has been turned into what?

9 In which county is the English town of Preston?

10 Which large Japanese city was historically called Edo?

★ **BACKGROUND BONUS** ★
Which natural habitat covers just two percent of Earth's surface?

351 Total Trivia

1 Which Australian bird is also called the laughing jackass?

2 What is the only creature that can turn its head in almost a complete circle?

3 What is the name of the famous statue of the goddess Venus in the Louvre Museum in Paris?

4 Gandhi was given the name Mahatma. What does Mahatma mean?

5 What is an ampersand?

6 What is ebony?

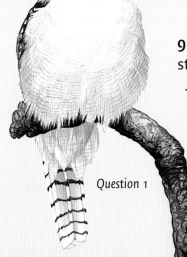

Question 1

7 What method of healing involves inserting needles into the body at certain points?

8 They jumped quickly through the hoop. Which is the adverb in that sentence?

9 What does the acronym NASA stand for?

10 What did William Wallace and Robert the Bruce fight for about 700 years ago?

352   Sporting Chance

1   Which Belgian city hosted the 1920 Summer Olympics?

2   What city hosted the first Summer Olympics held outside Europe?

3   On a golf green, what is "the borrow"?

4   Hicham El Guerrouj won three successive world athletics titles at what event?

5   Lawrence Taylor was named MVP when the New York Giants won the Superbowl in which year?

Question 10

6   On the Olympic flag, which of the five rings represents Europe?

7   Donovan Bailey won the Olympic 100 m gold medal in which year?

8   Which team defeated the Green Bay Packers to win Superbowl XXXII in 1998?

9   Which tennis star had a cameo appearance in the Jim Carrey movie *Me, Myself, and Irene*?

10   Which Australian won the men's Wimbledon Tennis Championships in 1987?

> ★ **BACKGROUND BONUS** ★
> In which sport did Sir Steve Redgrave win five consecutive Olympic gold medals?

353   Total Trivia

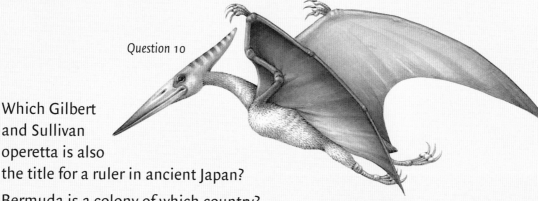

Question 10

1   Which Gilbert and Sullivan operetta is also the title for a ruler in ancient Japan?

2   Bermuda is a colony of which country?

3   What musical instrument literally means "softloud" when translated from Italian?

4   Cagliari is the capital of which Mediterranean island?

5   What is the nearest capital city in the world to the Equator?

6   Pewter is an alloy of which two metals?

7   What is the name for the wearing away of land by running water, weather, ice and wind?

8   The musical *The Boys From Syracuse* was based on which Shakespeare play?

9   Red pinocchio and Floradora are varieties of what flower?

10   What is a pterodactyl?

354   Global Matters

1   The Great St. Bernard's Pass links which two European countries?

2   Damask is a type of woven fabric that took its name from which city?

3   Accra is the capital city of which African country?

4   What is the most highly populated city in China?

5   What is the name given to the deepest part of the ocean floor?

6   In which Asian city would you shop in an area called the Ginza?

7   What is the capital of Libya?

8   The Khyber Pass links which two Asian countries?

9   In which European river would you find the Lorelei Rocks?

10 In which South American country is the city of Recife?

Question 4

355   Great and Famous

1   In 1301, who led the Peasants' Revolt?

2   For what is Australian Nellie Melba famous?

3   What nationality was Nicolas Copernicus?

4   With what social reform is Elizabeth Fry associated?

5   Who composed the opera *Carmen*?

6   Which U.S. actor directed and starred in *Citizen Kane*?

7   John Macdonald became the first prime minister of which country in 1867?

8   Which admiral commanded the British fleet at the Battle of Jutland?

9   Who established the Presbyterian Church of Scotland in 1560?

10 Which French artist is renowned for his paintings of ballet dancers?

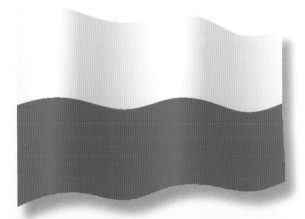

Question 3

356 Total Trivia

1 What is the highest mountain in Africa?

2 Which singing voice comes between soprano and contralto?

3 Which U.S. artist was nicknamed Jack the Dripper?

4 From which chemical compound are mothballs made?

5 What do you get if you mix zinc and copper?

6 What is the capital of Cambodia?

7 What do Frederick Ashton, Marie Rambert and Margot Fonteyn have in common?

8 Tom Selleck, Elliot Gould and Sarah Ferguson have all appeared in which TV show?

9 What kind of creature is a gila monster?

10 Where is the Rift Valley?

Question 3

357 Music Mania

1 "Complicated" and "Anything but Ordinary" featured on which singer's debut album?

2 Cat Stevens comes from which country?

3 Drummer Dave Grohl formed which band after the break-up of Nirvana?

4 *Play* and 18 are both album titles from which artist?

5 B-Real, Sen Dog, DJ Muggs are members of which band?

6 Who climbed a *White Ladder* to fame in 2000?

7 Which band's debut album was called *Pablo Honey*?

8 Whose only U.K. No.1 single was "My Ding-A-Ling" in 1972?

9 Who achieved the first ever million-selling single in the U.K.?

10 Monika Danneman found the dead body of which musical genius in 1970?

Question 9

358 Scientifically Speaking

1. Was the first electronic calculator manufactured in 1953, 1963 or 1973?

2. Brimstone is the old name for what element?

3. How many minutes are there in three and a third hours?

4. What letter represents 1,000 in Roman numerals?

5. The Eustachian tube links the throat to which organ?

6. How are chlorofluorocarbon emissions more commonly known?

7. James Watson and Francis Crick discovered the structure of which substance?

8. Which branch of mathematics is concerned with sines and cosines?

9. Which planet has two moons called Deimos and Phobos?

10. What is removed from dehydrated food?

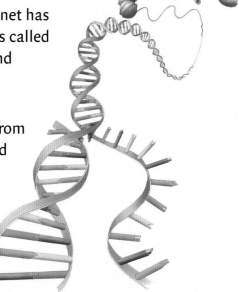

Question 7

359 Making History

1. In which country was Emiliano Zapata a freedom fighter?

2. Of which country was Jan Smuts the prime minister in 1919?

3. Which language, spoken by white South Africans, is derived from Dutch?

4. What was the popular nickname for James Hickock?

5. Which African warriors fought in groups called *impis*?

6. In which year was the modern state of Israel founded?

7. What instrument did Django Reinhardt play?

8. In which war was the Battle of Antietam (1862)?

9. Which European country conquered Brazil?

10. Who built the first nuclear reactor in a squash court in Chicago?

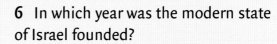

Question 5

★ **BACKGROUND BONUS** ★
Which megalithic wonder was built in three stages over 1,000 years?

360 Scientifically Speaking

1 Joules and calories are measurements of what?

2 What is the name for the tissue that connects bones?

3 A Maglev train travels by using what type of technology?

4 What does an audiologist study?

5 What are igneous rocks formed from?

6 The word "Mach", used for measuring speed, refers to what?

7 What is the body's largest gland?

8 Multiply 32 by the product of 2 and 4.

9 What does LCD stand for?

10 What is the main ingredient of paper?

Question 5

★ **BACKGROUND BONUS** ★
What is the fifth planet from the Sun?

361 Sporting Chance

1 Which Wimbledon tennis champion was called up for military service in 2001?

2 Who ran the fastest 100 m of the 20th century?

3 Who was named Female Athlete of the Century by the International Athletic Federation?

4 Which U.S. tennis player won the women's singles gold medal at the 1996 Olympics?

5 In which country is the Flemington Park racecourse?

6 Which U.S. jockey was nicknamed "The Kentucky Kid" and became champion jockey in the U.K. in 1987?

7 In the Olympic rings, which country is represented by green?

8 Which female tennis star wrote a novel called *Total Zone*?

9 What nation's national anthem is played at the closing ceremony of the Olympic Games?

10 How many times did John McEnroe win the U.S. Open?

Question 7

362   Great and Famous

1. In which country was Adolf Hitler born?
2. Which famous car was designed by Alec Issigonis in 1959?
3. Who wrote the original novel, *Les Misérables*?
4. Winston Churchill was half American: true or false?
5. What nationality was Abel Tasman, discoverer of New Zealand?
6. Who was Queen Elizabeth II's father?
7. Which of the Marx Brothers wore a painted false moustache?
8. What was David Livingstone's job?
9. In which country was the first national park set up in 1872?
10. How did African explorer H.M. Stanley earn his living?

Question 2

363   Music Mania

1. "Breakfast In America" launched which U.K. band into the big league?
2. "Hello I Love You" was a U.S. No. 1 for what band in 1968?
3. Whose "Celebration" hit the Top Ten in both the U.S. and U.K.?
4. Who had the original 1971 hit with "Let's Stay Together"?
5. The Eurythmics were born from the ashes of which late-70s band?
6. Which act released *Manifesto* in 1979, four years after their apparent final album?
7. Who charted with "Don't Leave Me This Way", long before The Communards?
8. In 1972, who charted after a nine-year gap with "Breakin' Up Is Hard To Do"?
9. Whose *Electric Warrior* was one of the best-selling U.K. albums of 1971?
10. Whose first chart hit was "Sylvia's Mother"?

Question 1

364 Total Trivia

1 What was the three-letter surname of the presiding judge in the O.J. Simpson murder trial?

2 In the United States, what was banned from 1917 to 1933 by the 18th Amendment?

3 Who was the first singer to have a U.K. No. 1 hit with the song "Unchained Melody"?

4 Which U.S. city is named after a British prime minister?

Question 9

5 What does the medical condition DVT stand for?

6 What is the only marsupial native to North America?

7 Who was Robert Burns?

8 Would you weigh more or less on the Moon?

9 To what area of medicine does geriatrics refer?

10 What carries satellites into space?

365 Scientifically Speaking

1 The biggest spiders are members of which arachnid family?

2 What type of object can be either a red giant, a white dwarf or a black dwarf?

3 Smoking tobacco harms two major organs of the body; one is the lungs, what is the other?

4 What chemical element has the symbol Kr?

5 What is the boiling point of water on the Celsius scale?

6 What part of the body does arthritis affect?

7 What feature links penguins, rheas, ostriches and kiwis?

8 Which English scientist developed the first modern theory about how gravity works?

9 Where could you find a stigma, carpels and sepals?

10 What planets, apart from Saturn, have rings?

Question 1

366   Natural Selection

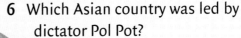

1. How does the bee orchid attract bees to pollinate it?

2. How many compartments does a cow have in its stomach?

3. Which large Swiss dog was used for mountain rescue?

4. Which small, fierce freshwater fish hunts in shoals of thousands?

5. Why do eucalyptus trees have white bark and leaves?

6. Which large sea bird can glide for a day without flapping its wings?

7. In which species of fish does the male incubate the young?

8. What is an ungulate?

9. What kind of animal is the whip-poor-will?

10. Which egg-laying mammal has venomous spurs on its hind legs?

Question 10

★ **BACKGROUND BONUS** ★
What bird is the largest of North America's waterfowl?

367   Making History

1. What was the first make of car to be produced on an assembly line?

2. In what year was Nelson Mandela released from prison?

3. Who became famous for the fabulous Easter eggs he made for the Russian royal family?

4. In which country did the Maya people build pyramids?

5. What was boxer Muhammad Ali's original name?

6. Which Asian country was led by dictator Pol Pot?

7. In which year did the "Jack the Ripper" murders take place in London?

8. Which 18th-century Austrian composer had the Christian names, Wolfgang Amadeus?

9. What weapon did Samson use to defeat the Philistines?

10. What kind of bomber was a World War II *Stuka*?

Question 3

368 Lights, Camera, Action!

1. Who did Kurt Russell play in the movie *Tombstone*?

2. The phrase "Book 'em, Danno" was associated with what TV show?

3. The actress Holly Hunter won an Oscar for her role in which 1993 movie?

4. In which movie did Russell Crowe play Maximus Decimus Meridus?

Question 4

5. In which 1997 movie did Harrison Ford play President James Marshall?

6. Who directed the 2001 movie *Gosford Park*?

7. Marion Morrison was the real name of which U.S. film star?

8. Which cult TV show was created by Gene Roddenberry?

9. What is the name of Roseanne's sister in the TV series *Roseanne*?

10. What was the name of the character played by George Clooney in TV's *ER*?

> ★ **BACKGROUND BONUS** ★
> Which 1999 movie starred
> Leonardo DiCaprio and Virginie Ledoyen?

369 Total Trivia

1. Who was shipwrecked in a land of tiny people?

2. What type of jellyfish has a name relating to a country?

3. Why does the Moon shine?

4. Who was the Italian Fascist leader during World War II?

5. What does a barometer measure?

6. In which war were tanks first used?

7. What is fog?

8. In which sport did teams compete for the Jules Rimet trophy?

9. What is the past tense of "strike"?

10. What planet is nearest to the Sun?

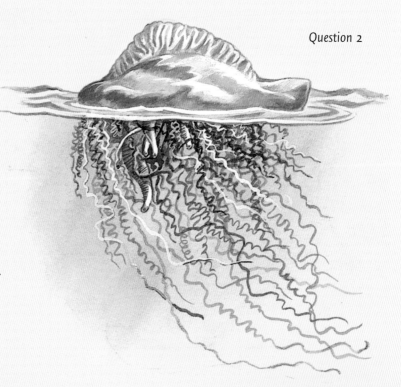

Question 2

370 Scientifically Speaking

1 To what planet does the moon Titan belong?

2 Where would you find a flying jib?

3 What does a horticulturist study?

4 What would a doctor use a sphygmomanometer to measure: height, blood pressure or weight?

5 What reddish-brown metal is formed into thin wires that conduct electricity?

6 What are Saturn's rings made of?

7 In 1938, what did German physicists Otto Hahn and Fritz Strassman achieve?

8 What is the name for the body's liquid waste?

9 What is 0.125 as a fraction?

10 A toy car travels 30 cm (12 in) with six wheel turns. How far would it go with four turns?

Question 6

371 Natural Selection

1 What animal makes a shallow, grassy nest called a form?

2 What insect has a wingspan of up to 14 cm (5.5 in) and lays its eggs on or near water?

3 What is a mudpuppy?

4 What is a mandrake?

5 What mammal needs to drink 70–90 l (18–24 gal) of water a day?

6 Which type of grass grows the tallest and thickest?

7 Why is the tokay gecko lizard so named?

8 What does the bulldog bat do with its long foot claws as it swoops over water?

9 What does a mussel use its "beard" for?

10 What common weed spreads its seeds by feathery-looking parachutes?

Question 3

372 Making History

1 Who danced the "dance of the seven veils"?

2 What started in California in 1848?

3 In which country was the TGV train introduced in 1967?

4 What instrument did jazz legend Louis Armstrong play?

5 What style were the piano compositions of Scott Joplin: ragtime, classical or jazz?

6 What Roman general landed in Britain in 55BC?

7 What river was Jesus baptized in?

8 In which war was the Battle of Verdun fought?

9 Where would a medieval knight have worn a cuirass?

10 For what invention are the Montgolfier brothers remembered?

Question 1

> ★ BACKGROUND BONUS ★
> Which beautiful tomb, built in the 17th century, stands at Agra in northern India?

373 Lights, Camera, Action!

1 In which movie did Tom Hanks play a boy trapped in a 32-year-old man's body?

2 In the title of a 1999 movie, what animal is crouching when a dragon is hidden?

3 When Olivia de Havilland played Maid Marian, who played Robin Hood?

4 What was Frank Sinatra's nickname?

5 What movie star is the daughter of the film director John Huston?

6 In which 1990 movie did Julia Roberts and Keifer Sutherland play medical students?

7 In which 1968 movie did Sally Anne Howes play Truly Scrumptious?

8 In which 1997 movie did Gaz, Gerald, Guy and Dave shed their clothes?

9 Which Scottish comedian played an auctioneer in the movie *Indecent Proposal*?

10 In a 1993 version of *The Three Musketeers*, who played the character D'Artagnan?

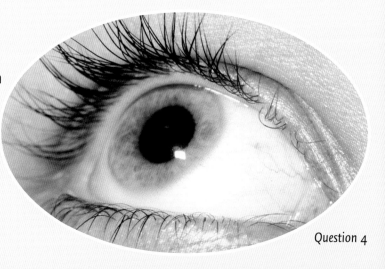

Question 4

374 Country Outlines

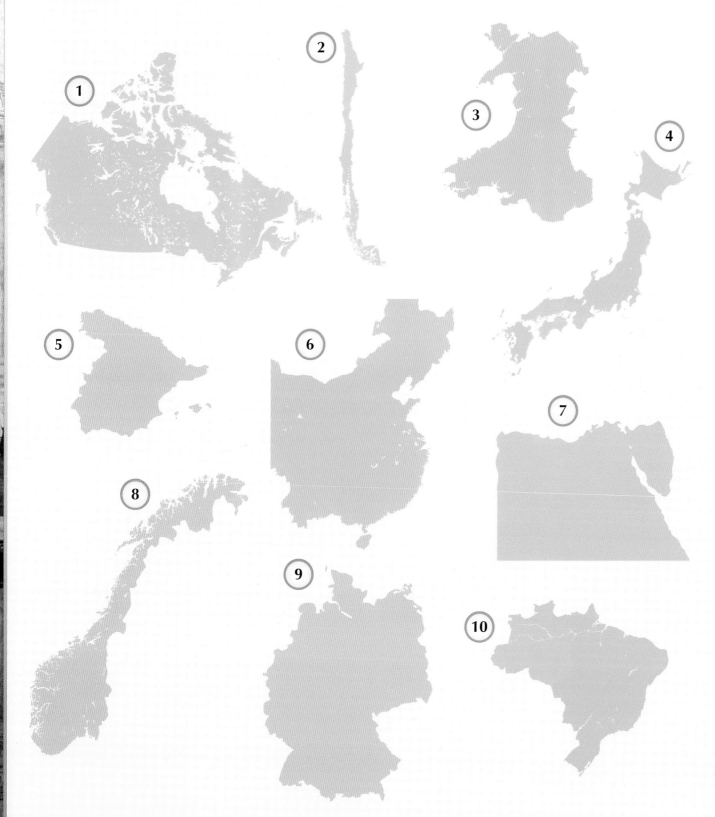

Study the country outlines and match them to the countries listed below.

(a) Brazil (b) Canada (c) Spain (d) Egypt (e) Wales (f) Japan (g) China (h) Germany

(i) Norway (j) Chile

375   Great and Famous

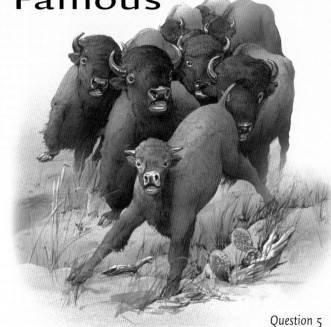

1. Who wrote the poem *The Tyger*?
2. Which tennis player was known as "Little Mo"?
3. Whose operatic compositions include *The Barber of Seville* and *William Tell*?
4. Mrs. Sirimavo Bandarnaike was the first female prime minister of which country?
5. How is William Frederick Cody better known?
6. Who wrote *The Rights of Man*?
7. Whose dictionary was published in 1828?
8. Which famous artist painted the ceiling of the Sistine Chapel?
9. Who wrote *Catch 22*?
10. What is Erno Rubik famous for?

Question 5

★ **BACKGROUND BONUS** ★
Vivienne Scarlett is the stepdaughter of which famous *Cluedo* character?

376   Total Trivia

1. What crashed in the Wall Street Crash?
2. From what country does the flamenco dance come?
3. Which Arctic mammal is one of the largest land carnivores?
4. What continents form the New World?
5. Which British explorer did Roald Amundsen beat to the South Pole in 1911?
6. What does a forensic scientist do?
7. What does the Bayeux Tapestry show?
8. Where is Tierra del Fuego?
9. How does a radio telescope see objects that are too dim for an ordinary telescope?
10. What layer of special oxygen in the atmosphere blocks out dangerous radiation from the Sun?

Question 5

377   Making History

1 What pop stars made a movie called A Hard Day's Night?

2 With what invention is Robert Oppenheimer (1904 to 1967) associated?

3 Which Christian saint was sent by the Pope to convert the English in AD597?

4 In what year did Fidel Castro become prime minister of Cuba?

5 Of what country is David the patron saint?

6 In what year were the Olympic Games held in Berlin?

7 Of which country was Henry the Navigator a prince in the 1400s?

8 With what rock group did Mick Jagger find fame?

9 Who composed the William Tell Overture?

10 What is the ancient Japanese art of bonsai?

Question 1

378   Sporting Chance

1 How many gold medals did Jesse Owens win at the 1936 Olympics?

2 At what Olympic Games did Carl Lewis win four gold medals?

3 In tennis, what is the term for a very high lob?

4 What does "judo" mean in Japanese?

5 What racehorse won the 2003 Dubai World Cup?

6 Which baseball star married Marilyn Monroe?

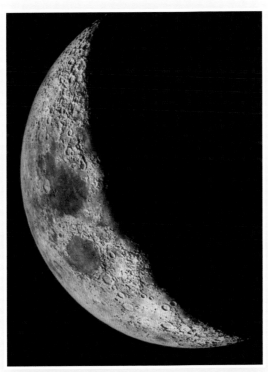

7 In what month is the Kentucky Derby run?

8 The Fastnet Race is contested In which sport?

9 A telltale, a service box and a tin can be found on the court in which racket sport?

10 How is Edson Arantes do Nascimento better known as?

Question 3

379   Total Trivia

1   What does "unique" mean?
2   What is the larval stage of the butterfly and the moth?
3   What is two-fifths of 25?
4   How many carats are there in pure gold?
5   What does an antiseptic do?
6   Who took a force of elephants across the Alps?
7   Which religion follows the teachings of the Qur'an?
8   Which scientist produced the Theory of Relativity?
9   In which war did Florence Nightingale nurse wounded soldiers?

10 What is the term for a narrow inlet of the sea that is surrounded by mountains or hills?

Question 10

380   Global Matters

1   The Maracana Stadium is found in which South American city?
2   What is the abbreviation GNP short for?
3   What country is Kampala the capital of?
4   Into which body of water does the River Niagara flow?
5   What is jet a hard, solid form of?
6   What is the currency of Cuba?
7   What is the capital of Jamaica?
8   What do Arica in Chile and Death Valley in the U.S. have in common?
9   In which country is the Camargue horse?
10 The Nurburgring Racing Circuit is found in which European country?

Question 3

> ★ **BACKGROUND BONUS** ★
> Mount Kilimanjaro can be found in which African country?

381 Sporting Chance: Soccer

1. What country did Peter Schmeichel represent at international level?

2. In what year was the first World Cup organized?

3. Eusebio played for what country?

4. Which European club plays at the Stadio Delle Alpi?

5. Which French club won their seventh league title in 2000?

6. Which Italian club did Asprilla and Zola play for?

7. Who won the 1970 FA Cup final?

8. From which Scottish club did Leeds United buy striker Mark Viduka?

9. Who was the first person to have managed both England's and Australia's national teams?

10. What club is generally accepted as being the oldest in England?

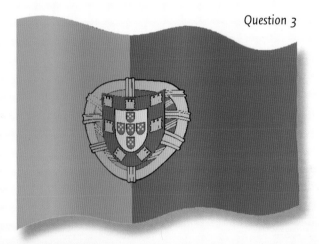

Question 3

382 Written Word

1. Who wrote *For Whom the Bell Tolls*?

2. What name is given to a line on a map that connects points of the same height?

3. *West Side Story* is based on what play by Shakespeare?

4. What is the name of Dorothy's dog in *The Wizard of Oz*?

5. What is the only letter that is worth five points in Scrabble: J, K or V?

6. Who wrote the novel *Bridget Jones's Diary*?

7. What is studied by an ichthyologist?

8. Where is Armistead Maupin's *Tales of the City* series set?

9. In the James Bond novels, who is his boss?

10. What was the name of the captain in pursuit of Moby Dick?

Question 8

383　Written Word

1　In which U.S. city is the headquarters of the Coca-Cola Company?

2　Which Swiss lake is sometimes referred to as The Lake of the Four Cantons?

3　A picture of what building is depicted on the flag of Cambodia?

4　What river flows through the city of Florence?

5　What is the official state bird of Louisiana?

6　Which capital city is served by Orly Airport?

7　Is Lusaka the capital of Zimbabwe, Zaire or Zambia?

8　What is the most northerly of the Channel Islands?

9　Which New Zealand city is nicknamed The Garden City?

10　What country lies immediately south of Egypt?

Question 1

384　Lights, Camera, Action!

1　In which movie did Kirk Douglas play a Norse warrior called Einar?

2　Which 1959 movie saw Charlton Heston competing in a chariot race?

3　Of which biblical epic did Cecil B. De Mille direct two movies, a silent version in 1923 and a sound version in 1956?

4　Which goddess did Honor Blackman play in *Jason and the Argonauts*?

5　Who played Samson in the 1950 movie epic *Samson and Delilah*?

6　Which 1960 movie tells the story of a Roman slave who led a slaves' revolt?

7　What Emperor was played by Peter Ustinov in *Quo Vadis*?

8　Which movie epic of the 1930s was billed as "Margaret Mitchell's Story of the Old South"?

9　On whose novel was the 1984 movie *A Passage to India* based?

10　Who plays Count Almasy in the 1996 movie *The English Patient*?

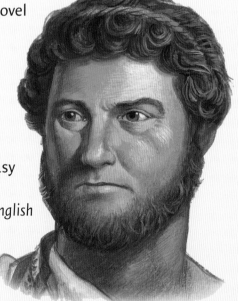

Question 7

385 Natural Selection

1 How does the shrewlike desman hunt?

2 How do flying fish "fly"?

3 Which very tall bird has a communal nest for the eggs of several females?

4 What sort of animal is an ocelot?

5 What plant was once used as a comb for new wool?

6 How did the kangaroo rat get its name?

7 What fish hitches a ride on larger fish such as sharks?

8 What turtle is the heaviest reptile and also one of the fastest?

9 When translated, what dinosaur name means "three-horned face"?

10 Which fast-running beetle is named after a big cat and is a fierce hunter?

Question 9

★ BACKGROUND BONUS ★
What is the largest mammal in North America?

386 Making History

1 What did Native Americans do with pemmican?

2 Of which country were Brian Mulroney and Pierre Trudeau prime ministers?

3 Why did Joseph Lister use carbolic acid in operating rooms?

4 Stephen Crane wrote *The Red Badge of Courage* about what war?

5 Which French ruler was reported to be afraid of cats?

6 What did sailors use hammocks for?

7 Which unit of power, invented by James Watt, measures the output of an engine?

8 In what year was the first "test-tube" baby born?

9 Who disappeared in a flight across the Pacific in 1937?

10 What composer wrote *The Young Person's Guide to the Orchestra*?

Question 2

387 Total Trivia

1 What would you do to a pavane, a polonaise and a polka?

2 Which of these goods were not rationed in Britain during World War II: potatoes, sugar or eggs?

3 In which sport would you play a chukka?

4 What planet has 15 moons named after Shakespearean characters?

5 What is the word for the study of plants and animals in relation to their surroundings?

6 Which English settlers founded Plymouth Colony in America in 1620?

7 Which very large island is a self-governing part of Denmark?

8 Who wrote *The Secret Garden*?

9 What does an anemometer measure?

10 What is the name for the temperature at which a liquid changes to a solid?

Question 10

> ★ **BACKGROUND BONUS** ★
> Which space station was launched by the Soviet Union in 1986?

388 Natural Selection

1 What does the Australian aboriginal name "koala" mean?

2 Which large male ape pushes over dead trees to impress other males?

3 What is the world's smallest bird?

4 What is a pug?

5 Where does spermaceti oil come from?

6 How does the secretary bird kill snakes?

7 Spider, squirrel and howler are types of what?

8 Bees kill more people than any insect apart from the mosquito: true or false?

9 What is the world's rarest snake?

10 Which tall desert plant can live 200 years but may grow only 1 cm (0.4 in) a year?

Question 10

389 Scientifically Speaking

1 What is pinchbeck?

2 How many multiples of 3 are there below 20?

3 The word "cardiac" refers to what part of the body?

4 Llamas and alpacas of South America are related to what animals of Africa and Asia?

5 What is the main source of raw material for plastic?

6 Human beings are bipeds. What does that mean?

7 A body in space travels what kind of path?

8 Which U.S. inventor counts electric light and sound recording among his inventions?

9 What skin ailment is commonly found among people who suffer from asthma?

10 Uluru is the Aboriginal name for which huge rock outcrop in Australia?

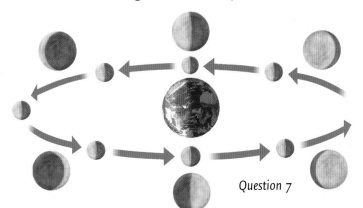

Question 7

390 Sporting Chance

1 Which British horse racing course is the largest in the world?

2 In golf, an eagle is how many holes under par?

3 What city hosted the 1972 Olympic Games?

4 What is the perfect score in tenpin bowling?

5 Which is the only British city to have hosted the Summer Olympics in the 20th century?

6 In which sport would you do a *Harai goshi*?

7 What was the first country beginning with the letter M to host the Summer Olympics?

8 In chess, when can a pawn move diagonally?

9 In which sport would you use a shot called a "boast"?

10 *Petanque* originated in which country?

Question 7

391   Total Trivia

1   What is the capital city of Switzerland?
2   What is the name for the group of nations that were once part of the British Empire?
3   Who first climbed Mount Everest?
4   What is water made up of?
5   What do edentulous mammals lack?
6   An ivory wedding anniversary celebrates how many years of marriage?
7   Canton is the former name for which Chinese city?
8   What is the most powerful chess piece?
9   What is the longest snake?
10 Which English queen ruled only for nine days?

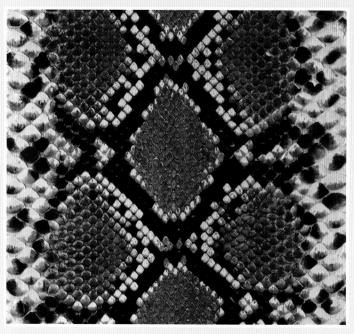

Question 9

392   Scientifically Speaking

1   What constellation is known as The Swan?
2   What kind of waves are used in a remote control?
3   What is the name of the sharp knife used by surgeons during operations?
4   What is amber?
5   Where is the Ross Ice Shelf?
6   What is the square root of 225?
7   Which explosive gas was once used to inflate airships?
8   What does AC stand for in electricity?
9   What do we call the boundary between two air masses?
10 What does a chronometer measure?

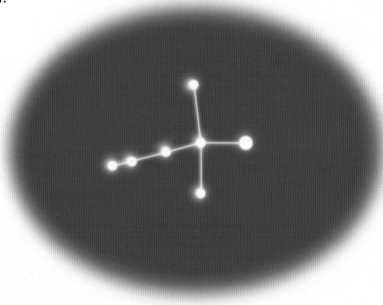

Question 1

393 Global Matters

1 The lyrebird comes from what country?

2 What name is given to the place where a river begins to flow?

3 What was the nationality of the first person to discover chlorine?

4 To what country does India export more of its goods than any other?

5 Where would you find a groyne?

6 Where is the Bridge of Sighs?

7 What is the highest peak in England?

8 Barajas is Spain's largest airport, but In which city is it found?

9 Where can the Golden Temple be found?

10 What is the largest gulf in the world?

Question 6

394 Sporting Chance

Question 6

1 In tennis, what is the name of the stadium in Paris where the French Open is contested?

2 How long is a quarter in water polo?

3 Which Spanish city hosted the 1999 World Athletics Championships?

4 In which country is Calgary, the venue for the 1988 Winter Olympics?

5 What nationality is tennis player Gabriella Sabatini?

6 What connects the Olympic Games of 1896 and 2004?

7 In which country was Martina Hingis born?

8 How many attempts is a pole-vaulter allowed to take at each height?

9 What was the venue of the only Summer Olympics of the 20th century to be held in Belgium?

10 What nationality is the racing driver Emerson Fittipaldi?

> ★ **BACKGROUND BONUS** ★
> The L.A. Kings compete In which sport?

395 Lights, Camera, Action!

1 Who played the title role of Harry Lime in the movie *The Third Man*?

2 How many musical items were included in the movie *Fantasia*?

3 Reckless was the name of which TV family's pet dog?

4 What sport featured in the 1985 movie *American Flyers*?

5 What profession is represented by the TV series *NYPD Blue*?

6 Who played Captain John Miller in the movie *Saving Private Ryan*?

7 In which 1967 movie did Paul Newman eat 50 eggs in one hour?

8 Who starred in the movie *Chinatown*?

9 Which 1953 movie opens with Doris Day singing "The Deadwood Stage"?

10 In which city is *Cagney and Lacey* set?

Question 10

396 Music Mania

1 What was Spandau Ballet's only U.K. No. 1 hit?

2 In 1987, which movie theme became the first Spanish-sung song to top the U.K. charts?

3 Norman Cook (aka Fatboy Slim) played guitar in which influential 1980s band?

Question 3

4 The Bangles were fronted by what singer?

5 Who sang the opening line on the Band Aid single?

6 "Orinoco Flow" was a surprise No. 1 for which singer?

7 Who recorded the title song to the 1981 Bond movie *For Your Eyes Only*?

8 *From Langley Park to Memphis* was a hit album for what band?

9 From where did pop act The Thompson Twins get their name?

10 In which year did "Karma Chameleon" reach No. 1 for Culture Club?

> ★ BACKGROUND BONUS ★
> Which band fronted by Don Henley had a hit with "Take it to the Limit"?

397   Natural Selection

1 What is the common name for the wild cat known as an ounce?

2 The adjective "cervine" refers to which of the following animals: deer, cats or beavers?

3 Other than a walrus, what is the only sea creature that possesses an ivory tusk?

4 Which slow-moving, winged insect has varieties called Chinese and Carolina?

5 Which London park houses London Zoo?

6 How many feet do snails have?

7 From what animal is nutria fur obtained?

8 What is the collective noun for a group of turkeys?

9 What mammals native to Madagascar have species called ring-tailed and Indri?

10 What bird lays the smallest eggs?

Question 9

398   Total Trivia

1 What liqueur may be called "egg brandy"?

2 Which rap artist's real name is Robert van Winkle?

3 Who patented the first sewing machine?

4 Who composed *Peer Gynt*?

5 What is measured using a photometer?

6 What is the longest river in Europe?

7 What is the name for a group of kangaroos?

8 In what decade was the first Miss World contest held?

9 How many vowels are there in the Greek alphabet?

10 What do somniloquists do?

Question 10

399 Total Trivia

1   Boston, Napoleon, Pope Joan and Piquet are all the names of what?

2   Which NASA spacecraft flew past Uranus in 1986?

3   What glands in the body make white blood cells?

4   What is the more common name for dyspepsia?

5   Robben Island is in the bay of which African city?

6   Who directed the movie *Cry Freedom*?

7   In Japan, where on the body is a *tobi* worn?

8   The masked hero Zorro took his name from the Spanish word for what animal?

9   What is the literal translation of *Homo sapiens*: ape man, wise man or upright man?

10 What star sign encompasses the end of March and the beginning of April?

Question 5

400 Lights, Camera, Action!

1   On whose novel was the 1968 horror movie *The Devil Rides Out* based?

2   Which movie adaptation of a George Orwell novel marked the farewell screen appearance of Richard Burton?

3   In which movie adaptation of a Dickens' novel did Jean Cadell play Mrs. Micawber?

4   Which war movie co-starring Lee Marvin, Telly Savalas and George Kennedy was based on a novel by E.M. Nathanson?

5   Who wrote the novels from which *Watership Down* and *The Plague Dogs* were adapted?

6   What actor played Fagin in the 1968 musical adaptation of *Oliver Twist*?

7   Which F. Scott Fitzgerald novel was filmed in 1949 starring Alan Ladd and remade in 1974 starring Robert Redford?

8   Which controversial novel by Anthony Burgess was adapted into a movie?

9   What is the title of the novel on which the Oscar-winning movie *Schindler's List* is based?

10 What novel by Robert Louis Stevenson, filmed in 1960, features David Balfour?

Question 8

401 Great and Famous

1. How is the American writer Samuel Clemens better known?
2. To which royal house did Queen Victoria belong?
3. Which family of Quaker manufacturers established the garden village of Bournville?
4. Who founded a medical mission at Lamberene in Gabon, Africa?
5. Who composed the music for the ballet *Coppelia*?
6. What dancer met a tragic end when her scarf caught in the wheel of her car?
7. Who created the fictional detective "Sergeant Cuff"?
8. Which Austrian doctor founded psychoanalysis?
9. Who invented a system of shorthand in 1837?
10. Who was the inventor of the polaroid camera?

Question 6

402 Scientifically Speaking

1. Where in the body would you find the hyoid bone?
2. What is the element that comprises 70 percent of the Sun's mass?
3. Where in the body is the jejunum?
4. Which two metals make bronze?
5. What element makes up the gas ozone?
6. Optometrists, ophthalmologists and opticians are all concerned with what?
7. If the length of a rectangle is three times its 5 cm (2 in) width, what is its perimeter?
8. What word is used to describe anything relating to breathing?
9. The Manhattan Project was a secret operation to develop what during World War II?
10. What vitamin helps fight disease and improves vision in the dark?

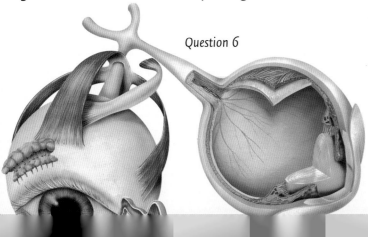

Question 6

★ BACKGROUND BONUS ★
What is the fastest-growing energy source in the world?

403 Lights, Camera, Action!

Question 5

4 Who plays Captain Jonathan Archer in the TV show *Enterprise*?

5 In which city was *Gorky Park* set?

6 Singer Robert Allen Zimmerman is known as who?

1 The phrase "The truth is out there" is associated with which TV show?

2 Louise Lombard played a dress designer in which TV show?

3 What did "Hickory", the Tin Man, want in *The Wizard of Oz*?

7 What character did Linda Gray play in *Dallas*?

8 In which movie did Diana Ross sing "God Bless the Child"?

9 Who wrote the music for *The Lion King* movie?

10 Who hosted the 2002 Oscar ceremony?

404 Total Trivia

1 If a substance is described as stannic, what metal does it contain?

2 How is the year 2000 written in Roman numerals?

3 The year 2000 was the Chinese year of the what?

4 Where in Utah is the headquarters of the Mormon religion?

5 What bird can fly backwards?

6 What literary prize was won by Australian novelist Peter Carey in 2001?

7 In May 1994, the Channel Tunnel was officially opened at which English port?

8 Which pop singer named himself after the composer of the opera *Hansel and Gretel*?

9 Who was the first person to sail single-handed non-stop around the world?

10 Where on a horse would you find the dock?

Question 4

405 Sporting Chance

1 In which sport does play commence with a tip off?

2 What is the alternative name for the hop, step and jump?

3 How old must a horse be to take part in a steeplechase race?

4 Who opened the 1936 Olympic Games?

5 Which is the older in golf: the British Open or the U.S. Open?

6 What is the name of the bars on which female gymnasts compete?

7 What sport is Alberto Tomba known for?

8 On what circuit is the German Grand Prix held?

9 In which sport would you do an "Eskimo roll"?

10 When would you wear a yellow jersey in the Tour de France?

Question 10

> ★ BACKGROUND BONUS ★
> In which sport are the St. Ledger and the Prix de L'Arc de Triomphe contested?

406 Great and Famous

1 Who was the first premier of the Soviet Union?

2 According to Shakespeare, who cried out "A horse! A horse! My kingdom for a horse!"?

3 Whose novels first appeared under the name of Currer Bell?

4 Who invented the miners' safety lamp?

5 Who composed the music for the ballets Swan Lake, The Nutcracker Suite and The Sleeping Beauty?

6 Which landscape painter's works include The Haywain and The Cornfield?

7 Who discovered penicillin?

8 What did Valentina Tereshkova become famous for in 1963?

9 Who led the Protestant Reformation in 16th-century Germany?

10 Who wrote the story of The Ugly Duckling?

Question 3

407 Total Trivia

1 Alphabetically, what is the first book of the Bible?

2 If an object is described as cordate, what part of the body is it shaped like?

3 What is the home state of the literary character Tom Sawyer?

4 A seal is a pinniped. What does this mean?

5 *The Roman Hat Mystery* marked the literary debut of what detective?

6 In which country would you find the Apennine mountain range?

7 What do you call the study of armorial bearings?

8 What is the name given to a long-handled pair of glasses?

9 What is the number represented by the prefix "tetra"?

10 What is apiphobia a fear of?

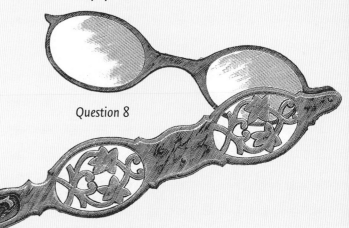

Question 8

408 Lights, Camera, Action!

1 Where did Roger Rabbit live?

2 What is Sean Connery's real first name?

3 Who played the wife of Michael Douglas in *Fatal Attraction*?

4 Who played Ben Hur in the movie of the same name?

5 "If I Were a Rich Man" is a song from what musical?

6 Errol Flynn played Robin Hood in 1938. Who played him in *Robin Hood, Prince of Thieves*?

7 Who played Tony Soprano in the mafia TV drama *The Sopranos*?

8 Who sang the theme to the movie *Goldfinger*?

9 What newspaper did Superman work for?

10 For which TV comedy show was Souza's "Liberty Bell" the theme music?

Question 9

★ **BACKGROUND BONUS** ★
Which 1998 movie starred Robert Redford and Kristin Scott Thomas?

409 Scientifically Speaking

1   Who discovered the neutron?

2   What is measured by the unit known as the coloumb?

3   What fraction of a circle is 120 degrees?

4   Where in the body is the cochlea?

5   Gobi, Sonoran and Namib are all examples of what?

6   What is measured in millibars?

7   What were daguerreotypes?

8   What do we call the small bones that make up the spine?

9   On which type of device might you find a resistor, capacitor, diode and transistor?

10 What is the ohm a measurement of?

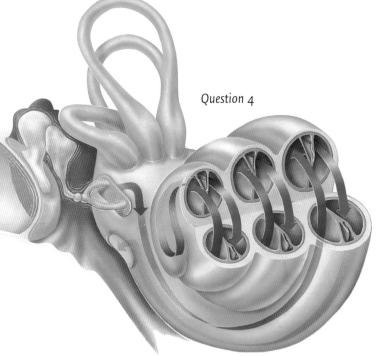
Question 4

410 Sporting Chance

1   What country won four Olympic gold medals in boxing at Sydney 2000?

2   Who came last in the 1988 Winter Olympic ski jump competition for men?

3   Do the Harvard Rules govern baseball or American football?

4   What sport made its debut at the 1998 Winter Olympics?

5   With what sport do you associate the Cresta Run?

6   What does the word "karate" mean in Japanese?

7   In which sport might you catch a crab?

8   What is the official language of the Olympic Games?

9   When was the last Grand Prix held in the United States?

10 At what sport did Fred Perry become world champion in 1929?

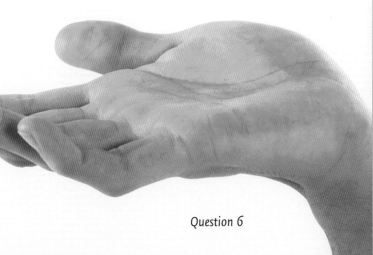
Question 6

411 Making History

1 Ferdinand Marcos was dictator of which country?

2 Who built the first successful helicopter?

3 Peru declared its independence from which country in 1821?

4 Which Israeli prime minster was assassinated in 1995?

5 Which South American country once had Juan Perón as president?

6 Which famous Russian novelist died in November 1910?

7 What kind of engines were pioneered by Robert Goddard and Wernher von Braun?

8 Who wrote the poem *Stopping by Woods on a Snowy Evening*?

9 What are the three types of energy used to power trains?

10 What was Le Corbusier famous as being?

Question 3

412 Total Trivia

1 An *hors d'oeuvre* forms what part of a meal?

2 Who wrote *The African Queen*?

3 What is the name for a group of rhinoceroses?

4 Which domestic animal did the ancient Egyptians worship?

5 Who wrote *Northanger Abbey*?

6 What is the name for microscopic single-celled organisms that can cause disease?

7 Which Australian state is Melbourne the capital city of?

8 What kind of animal has the most number of ribs?

9 Which 18th-century explorer first landed at Botany Bay, Australia?

10 Which capital city can be found on the river Seine?

Question 10

413   Sporting Chance

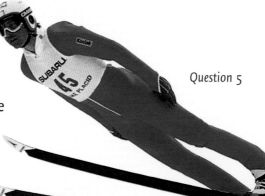

Question 5

1 What is the only sport that represents a letter in the NATO phonetic alphabet?

2 Who won Olympic gold medals for the long jump in 1984, 1988 and 1992?

3 In which country did the card game bridge originate?

4 With what sport do you associate Jesper Parnevik?

5 What form of skiing was the first to be organized competitively?

6 Who added over 55 cm (21.6 in) to the world long jump record in 1968?

7 How many lanes are there in an Olympic-sized swimming pool?

8 How many hulls does a catamaran have?

9 In what country was the tennis star Monica Seles born?

10 What sport featured in the movie *White Men Can't Jump*?

414   Natural Selection

1 What is a detrivorel?

2 Which bird is the largest member of the crow family?

3 Which is the heaviest lizard in the world?

4 Which is the fastest swimming whale?

5 What is the common name for *Atropa Belladonna*?

6 What dinosaur had a name meaning "Earth shaking lizard"?

7 What is bladderwrack?

8 What are the two varieties of artichoke?

9 To what animal is the cacomistle related?

10 During what period in history did the dinosaurs flourish?

Question 6

★ BACKGROUND BONUS ★
What is the third-largest land animal?

415 Written Word

1   What word derives from the Greek, meaning "easy death"?

2   Which famous children's novel was written by Richard Adams?

3   What is the 10th letter of the Greek alphabet?

4   Which nine-letter O word is defined as a female slave in a harem?

5   Which V word is the name given to a farewell speech?

6   Who wrote *The Woman in White*?

7   Sydney Carton is a character in which book by Charles Dickens?

8   In which part of England is the novel *Lorna Doone* based?

9   What does *compos mentis* mean?

10   In which Shakespeare play does Rosalind appear?

Question 2

416 Music Mania

1   What city witnessed the birth and death of the classical composer Schubert?

2   Crispian Mills, the son of Hayley Mills, is the lead singer of which pop group?

3   Who collaborated with Peter Sellers on the 1960 hit "Goodness Gracious Me"?

4   What song did the cast of the movie *There's Something About Mary* sing during the closing credits?

5   In which country was Chopin born?

6   Greta Garbo, Marlon Brando, Grace Kelly, Fred Astaire, Ginger Rogers and Bette Davis are all mentioned in the lyrics of which song?

7   On what is a paradiddle performed?

8   Who is Loretta Lynn's singing sister?

9   How many notes are in a double octave?

10   Which of the Spice Girls was born in Watford in 1972?

Question 4

417 Total Trivia

1 What is a contradiction?
2 How long does it take for the Moon to travel around the Earth?
3 What city is famous for its Temple of Artemis?
4 Who said, "History is more or less bunk"?
5 Where is the Sea of Tranquility?
6 Which great scientist discovered radium?
7 On TV, what was the name of the ranch in *Bonanza*?
8 What makes bread rise?
9 What is the stratosphere?

10 Which warm sea current crosses the Atlantic Ocean and flows up the west coast of Britain?

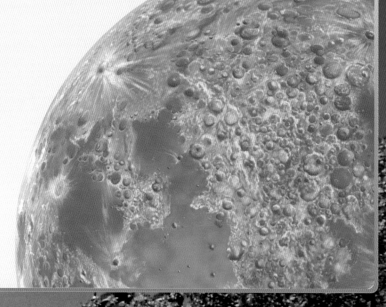

Question 5

418 Global Matters

1 If you were standing in the Cortes, what country's parliament would you be visiting?
2 What letters go at the end of a website address based in Spain?
3 In which city would you find the Tivoli Gardens?
4 Who are Walloons?

Question 9

5 What are hanging valleys formed from?
6 Fish farming is believed to have started in which Asian country?
7 What country forms the eastern coastline of the Persian Gulf?
8 Dacia is the old name for what country?
9 What word describes the rocks and gravel carried along by a glacier?
10 In which city is the Doge's Palace?

★ BACKGROUND BONUS ★
Which famous French landmark was designed by Jean Chalgrin?

419 Natural Selection

1. What part of a flower contains the pollen?
2. What is aformosa?
3. What are all honey bee larvae fed on?
4. On a horse, where is the fetlock?
5. Which equine creature has species called Grevy's, plains and mountain?
6. What species of snake shares its name with a Cuban dance?
7. What type of fish takes its name from the Portuguese meaning "fish with teeth"?
8. Comprising 37 varieties, the toco is the largest species of which long-beaked bird?
9. To what family of birds do canaries belong?
10. If an animal is polled, what is removed?

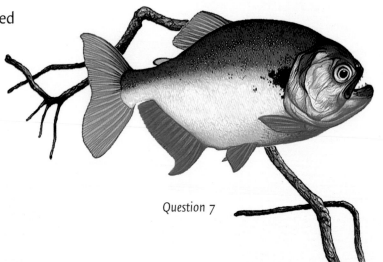

Question 7

420 Making History

1. Between which two cities did the first regular passenger flights start in 1919?
2. Who starred in the movies *The Gold Rush* and *Modern Times*?
3. Which two elements in the air were first named by Lavoisier in 1777?
4. What king led the English at the Battle of Agincourt?
5. In which country was Europe's first motorway built?
6. What conqueror led his army from Greece to western India?
7. In World War II, what were Shermans and Panzers?
8. Who discovered the Pacific Ocean?
9. Who, in Greek mythology, had snakes instead of hair?
10. Balboa was the first European to see what ocean in 1513?

Question 6

421   Music Mania

1   Van Morrison first achieved success with what band?

2   What tenor had a hit with "Canta Della Terra" in 1999?

3   What was C.W. McCall's single hit, popular with truckers?

4   Which classical flautist had a hit with a cover of John Denver's "Annie's Song"?

5   Who had a one-hit No. 1 with "Together We are Beautiful" in 1980?

6   Which Paul Simon song, rejected by Aretha Franklin, was a massive hit?

7   Which huge band astonishingly had only one U.S. No.1 hit with "Need You Tonight"?

8   What was the big Christmas hit for ELP's Greg Lake?

9   Can you name the 1980 disco smash which was Lipps Inc.'s only hit?

10   What band did Kurt Cobain front?

Question 6

★ BACKGROUND BONUS ★
Which early Lennon and McCartney recording had a sweet-sounding title?

422   Sporting Chance

1   What is the lowest boxing weight category?

2   In which sport might you see a "double wake cut"?

3   What is the fastest creature raced in sport?

4   In which sport might you see a "barani"?

5   What nationality is tennis star Thomas Muster?

6   In which U.S. state did surfing originate?

7   In which sport is there a move called a crucifix?

8   In archery, what is a bluffie?

9   What nationality was Rene Lacoste?

10   In which sport is there a series of bouts called a barrage?

Question 1

423   Music Mania

Question 1

1. Carl, Dennis, Brian, Mike and Al are collectively known as what group?

2. In which movie did Elvis Presley sing "Wooden Heart"?

3. The musical *The Boys From Syracuse* is based on which Shakespeare play?

4. Who won eight Grammy Awards for the album *Supernatural*?

5. What movie directed by Mike Leigh chronicled the life story of the composers Gilbert and Sullivan?

6. What is the world's largest opera house?

7. Which Puccini opera heroine leaps to her death from a castle in Rome?

8. What is the nationality of the composer Bela Bartok?

9. The rebec was an early form of what instrument?

10. Catfish Row provides the setting for what opera?

★ BACKGROUND BONUS ★
In 1984, "Caribbean Queen" was a worldwide hit for which soul sensation?

424   Making History

1. What is the name of the official body that elects popes?

2. What was discovered by Robert Ballard in 1985?

3. Which historical figure said, "Put your trust in God and keep your powder dry"?

4. What was founded in 1831 by King Louis Philippe to assist in the control of French colonies?

5. Which capital city was formerly called Krung Threp?

6. What conflict was ended by the Treaty of Panmunjon?

7. Sarnia was the Roman name for what island?

8. What artefact was discovered on the island of Melos in 1822?

9. What state did the United States purchase from France in 1603?

10. What was the first organization to win the Nobel Peace Prize twice?

Question 1

425 Global Matters

1 What city is overlooked by the Blue Mountains and is served by Kingsford Smith International Airport?

2 Which European capital city stands on Faxey Bay?

3 What country is separated from Spain by the Straits of Gibraltar?

4 According to an old saying, which Italian city should you visit before you die?

5 What kind of geographical feature can be rain-shadow, continental or tropical?

6 Which European capital city stands on the River Aare?

7 To what country do the Galapagos Islands belong?

8 What river flows into the world's largest delta?

9 Which capital city was formerly called Christiana?

10 What country is the smallest island of the Greater Antilles?

Question 1

426 Total Trivia

1 What does a phillumenist collect?

2 Which country has the world's oldest national flag?

3 On what river does the Angel Falls stand?

4 To what religion do Sangha monks belong?

5 What is the name given to the Turkish dish that comprises honey and nuts in filo pastry?

6 Who is the Greek god counterpart of the goddess Amphitrite?

7 In 1936, who was voted *Time Magazine* Woman of the Year?

8 What was the surname of the famous painter Rembrandt?

9 What is potamophobia a fear of?

10 In which country was Leon Trotsky assassinated in 1940?

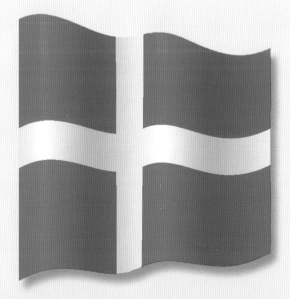

Question 3

427 Written Word

1 The Petkoffs are the central family in which play set in Bulgaria?

2 Which is the shortest of Shakespeare's plays?

3 Which literary character married Angel and murdered Alec?

4 What type of bird did Geoffrey Chaucer refer to as "a prophet of doom"?

5 *Rupert of Hentzau* is the sequel to which adventure novel?

Question 4

6 Which literary sleuth first appeared in a story called *The Nine Tailors*?

7 In which month is *Romeo and Juliet* set?

8 In *The Jungle Book*, what type of creature is Mang?

9 Which classic novel is set in a house called Manderley?

10 Agnes Fleming is the mother of which literary character?

★ **BACKGROUND BONUS** ★
Which Agatha Christie novel was originally written as a three-part play?

428 Scientifically Speaking

1 Where on the body is your occiput?

2 What is the more common name for magnesium sulphate?

3 What is the only chemical element named after an American state?

4 What is studied by an oneirologist?

5 Copper was named after what island?

6 What planet was discovered in 1846?

7 What is coprolite?

8 What is the final stage in the life cycle of a star called?

9 What kind of gas is produced by the Haber-Bosch process?

10 Which class of rocks are formed from the wastage of earlier rocks?

Question 4

429 Natural Selection

1 If an animal is described as succivorous, what does it feed on?

2 In which country did pheasants originate?

3 If an animal is described as oviporous, what does it mean?

4 *Orcinus orca* is the scientific name for what creature?

5 If an object is described as testudinal, what animal is it shaped like?

6 Which bird family does the mynah bird belong to?

7 From what type of creature is the incense onycha obtained?

8 *Galapago* is the Spanish name for what animal?

9 What bird has varieties called Australian brown, American white and spot-billed?

10 The kowhai is the national flower of what country?

Question 3

430 Lights, Camera, Action!

1 Red Connors was the sidekick of which screen cowboy?

2 Who played the grandmother Esther in *The Waltons*?

3 In which movie did Richard Gere play Dr. Plarr?

4 What novel was first filmed in 1926 under the title of *The Sea Beast*?

5 Which movie musical is based on a Frederic Molnar play called *Liliom*?

6 Who played the child bride of Jerry Lee Lewis in the movie *Great Balls of Fire*?

7 Which film studio released *The Jazz Singer*, the first ever talking movie?

8 Which Hollywood legend, born Ruth Galveston, went on to star in the TV soap *Knot's Landing*?

9 In the movie *Gone With The Wind*, what city burns to the ground?

10 Which novel by David Storey was adapted into a 1963 movie starring Richard Harris?

Question 4

431 Great and Famous

1 Which two U.S. presidents received the Nobel Peace Prize in the 20th century?

2 Who won an Oscar playing a character called Loretta Castorini?

3 In which country was the explorer Ferdinand Magellan born?

4 Which U.S. president married Mary Todd?

5 What painter born in 1881 once said, "My curiosity crosses over every frontier of curiosity"?

6 At what battle did Horatio Nelson lose his arm?

7 In 1989, who invented the World Wide Web?

8 Harry Houdini was born In which city?

9 *The Small Woman* is the title of a biography chronicling the life of which missionary?

10 What is the nationality of the man who designed the Sydney Opera House?

Question 8

432 Total Trivia

1 Who was the first U.S. president to visit China?

2 What is the oldest city in Germany?

3 Of which country is Santa Anna the second largest city?

4 The word "slalom" originated In which language?

5 In which sport do competitors negotiate haystacks and eddies?

6 Which historical novel features a jester called Wamba?

Question 8

7 What was Russia's parliament called between 1906 and 1917?

8 Which operatic heroine commits suicide by falling on her father's sword?

9 What city is served by Dum Dum Airport?

10 In 1969, El Salvador was embroiled in a four-day war with what country?

★ **BACKGROUND BONUS** ★
The word *sangha* relates to what religion?

433 Sporting Chance

1   In which sport did childcare expert Dr. Benjamin Spock win an Olympic gold medal in 1924?

2   What city played host to the first Paralympics?

3   After which American tennis doubles champion is the Davis Cup named?

4   In 1845, what team became the first ever organized baseball team?

5   Which was the first city outside of Europe to host the Summer Olympics?

6   What is the alternative name of the Spanish ball game *pelota*?

7   What is a natatorium?

8   In what event did Hilda Johnstone compete in the Olympics at the age of 70?

9   What was the first Olympic Games to be televised?

10   In which American state was the first Ryder Cup contested?

Question 7

434 Written Word: The Bible

1   The Book of Genesis ends with the death of who?

2   How many Books of Kings are there in the Old Testament?

3   What book is addressed to "the seven churches that are in Asia"?

4   Who told Hagar she was to have a baby called Ishmael?

5   What name is often given to the Books of Proverbs, Job and Ecclesiastes?

6   Who tried to buy the Holy Spirit from Peter and John?

7   How long did David rule over Israel?

8   What is the fifth book of the New Testament?

9   Two thousand of what animal drowned in the Sea of Galilee?

10   What was the name of the fourth horseman of the Apocalypse?

Question 4

435 Scientifically Speaking

1 If you suffer from ailurophobia, what is your greatest fear?

2 A substance combines with oxygen to produce heat and light. What name is given to this process?

3 In the human body, what is the more common name for the gastronemius?

4 In 1628, who penned a celebrated work that analysed the circulation of the blood?

5 Where would you find the Maxwell Gap and the Keeler Gap?

6 What is a substance lacking if it is described as anhydrous?

7 On the Beaufort Scale, what comes between a whole gale and a hurricane?

8 Where is the Mound of Mars Positive to be found?

9 In the human body, where is the canthus?

10 What was first achieved by the brothers Daniel and Christopher Smith in 1982?

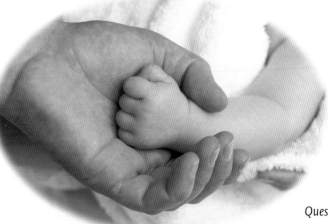

Question 8

436 Making History

1 In which war was the Battle of Jamara River fought?

2 Peter II was the last king of which European country?

3 During what war did the Siege of Ladysmith take place?

4 What was the nationality of the last non-Italian Pope before John Paul II?

5 Who was the first U.S. president to give a speech before the British parliament?

6 Who founded the Philadelphia police force in 1737?

7 Who crowned Napolean as emperor?

8 What conflict was ended by the Treaty of Panmunjon?

9 What saint died in 1226?

10 In which decade did Constantinople change its name to Istanbul?

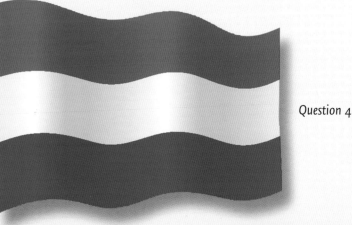

Question 4

437 Global Matters

1 Which European capital city has a name meaning "buildings on marsh"?

2 In which city is the Jacques Cartier Bridge?

3 What is the largest inland sea?

4 The name of Gibraltar derived from what language?

5 In which city is the world's largest palace?

6 On which Mediterranean island did the sweet pea originate?

7 Which is the largest of the Society Islands?

8 Found in the North Sea, what are Beryl and Montrose?

9 Which is the largest of the Dodecanese Islands in the Mediterranean Sea?

10 What is the name of the highest peak in the Rockies?

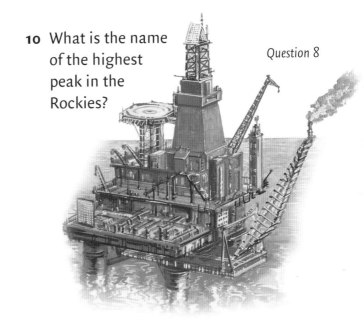

Question 8

★ **BACKGROUND BONUS** ★
Which massive waterfall can be found on the border of Argentina and Brazil?

438 Music Mania

1 What is the occupation of the operatic character Rigoletto?

2 Which singer provided vocals on the Oscar-winning songs "It Goes Like It Goes", "Up Where We Belong" and "I've Had The Time Of My Life"?

3 Who sang the first line on the 1985 U.S.A. For Africa hit "We Are The World"?

4 In 1960, The Beatles failed an audition to become what singer's backing band?

5 Which soul legend was backed by the Famous Flames?

6 What is the name of the villain in The Threepenny Opera?

7 What is Glenn Miller's signature tune?

8 Who recorded the album *Diamond Life*?

9 The musical *Half a Sixpence* was based on a novel by which author?

10 What do the initials RCA stand for with regard to the record label?

Question 10

1
1 They worked in a mine
2 Sheep meat 3 India
4 Red 5 A genie 6 Clouds
7 Cocoa beans
8 Temperature
9 London 10 Stringed

2
1 The death's head hawkmoth
2 In the air 3 A banana tree
4 The tiger 5 An oxlike animal
6 A hummingbird 7 A giant
tortoise 8 Feather-cleaning
9 The king cobra 10 Gosling

BACKGROUND BONUS:
A bird

3
1 Technical Knockout 2 Eight
3 Chicago Cubs 4 American
Football 5 Bowling 6 Two
7 Leopard's spots 8 Cricket
9 Motor racing 10 Serve

4
1 Gladiator games 2 Rommel
3 Thailand 4 Guinea pigs
5 A fossil 6 German
submarines 7 Silver coins
8 Japan 9 Macmillan (British
prime minister not U.S.
president) 10 Saladin

5
1 Queen Victoria 2 Vitamin C
3 The United States
4 Germany 5 A Russian dog
named Laika 6 They were all
Roman emperors 7 Italy
8 A long, spearlike weapon
9 Tasmania 10 Gandhi
BACKGROUND BONUS:
Pyramids

6
1 Grass 2 Ten 3 Table tennis
4 Ice hockey 5 Rollerblades
6 Cycling 7 Square 8 Golf
9 Bishop 10 40–40

7
1 Penguin 2 A drey 3 Camel
4 A dachshund 5 Kelp (it is a
seaweed) 6 A leap 7 Bats
8 An eagle 9 A nanny goat
10 In trees

8
1 A lens 2 Gunpowder 3 40
4 Gravity 5 17 6 Your voice
7 A galaxy 8 Deep red
9 Under the sea 10 Two

9
1 Infectious diseases 2 Metal
3 A jack-in-the-box 4 1,584
5 Upper case 6 North and
South Poles 7 Your hand
8 Africa 9 1/4 10 Decibels (dB)

BACKGROUND BONUS:
Tidal wave

10
1 Spinach 2 The body 3 24
4 The arms 5 The camel
6 Open or public spaces 7 12
8 Tom and Jerry 9 Ten
10 Green

11
1 Badminton 2 Baseball
3 Basketball 4 Pool 5 Ice
skating 6 Table tennis
7 Tenpin bowling 8 American
Football 9 Snowboarding
10 Rollerblading

12
1 Cowardly 2 24 May
3 Vegetable 4 One-eighth
5 Plants and animals 6 Sheep
7 Frog 8 The Pope 9 Five
10 Skiing

BACKGROUND BONUS:
Zebra

13
1 A serpent 2 Kill him as a
sacrifice to God 3 Tablets of
stone 4 Manna 5 Fed 5,000
people 6 Nazareth
7 Zacchaeus 8 His wisdom
9 The Romans 10 Four

14
1 Polish 2 Basketball 3 Peru
4 Baby Spice 5 Elton John
6 Benito Mussolini
7 Undersea 8 Stamps
9 Judy Garland 10 Tina Turner

15
1 A boat 2 A compass
3 The weather 4 Mercury
5 180 6 Elbow 7 Your forehead
8 North 9 Pollen
10 The bottom of your leg

16
1 Holland 2 Europe 3 Lima
4 Alaska 5 District (of
Columbia) 6 Ben Nevis
(Scotland) 7 Greenland
8 Spain 9 Emerald (The
Emerald Isle) 10 North

BACKGROUND BONUS:
A terrace

17
1 A bird 2 Many teeth
3 A climber 4 In trees
5 Lightning 6 It ambushes it
7 The squirrel 8 Their tongue
9 In thick woodlands
10 The tiger

18
1 A clock 2 Frozen food
3 An iceberg 4 It keeps them
clean 5 Nostrils 6 The
atmosphere 7 West 8 Cliffs
9 90 10 37

19
1 Celtic 2 France 3 Paulo di
Canio 4 Kilmarnock 5 Five
6 Birmingham 7 Switzerland
8 Turkey 9 Glasgow
10 Arsenal

20
1 The mackerel 2 They jump
and fly 3 The dolphin 4 Shark
5 The leaves 6 Frog 7 The
thrush 8 A spider 9 Panting
10 In the ocean

21

1 Rome 2 Beethoven
3 Ancient Egyptians 4 He
made four 5 Russia 6 300BC
7 Stonewall 8 1346 9 Macbeth
10 William the Conqueror

22

1 Baseball 2 *Three Men and a
Little Lady* 3 Frankie Muniz
4 Tuppence a bag 5 Pluto
6 Red 7 Killer whale 8 Pickles
9 Glenn Close 10 Toaster

BACKGROUND BONUS:
Hollywood

23

1 Stringed 2 Three 3 It is the
fear of enclosed spaces
4 Bill Clinton 5 At the front
6 The ostrich 7 Coast 112
8 Tulip 9 Libya 10 Italy

24

1 The euro 2 The oak
3 Flowers 4 A microchip or a
silicon chip 5 2,993
6 A brick-shaped bar of gold
7 *Stegosaurus* 8 The Olympic
Games 9 A type of shoe
10 Composers

25

1 The trumpet 2 The accordion
3 "Wannabe" 4 Minogue
5 Jennifer Lopez 6 Motorbike
7 Tom Jones 8 *Shrek* 9 Danny
10 Percussion

BACKGROUND BONUS:
Punk rock

26

1 Three minutes 2 Javelin
3 Water polo 4 Strawberries
5 Table tennis 6 Central Park
7 Japan 8 Tobogganing
9 A home run
10 Black-and-white chequered

27

1 The United States 2 1590
3 Michelangelo 4 1540
5 A bull 6 A lance 7 Raising
water 8 Horse-soldier
9 Alexander the Great
10 Pegasus

28

1 A sow 2 The lion 3 A talon
4 In its pouch 5 Its gills
6 A bird (the heaviest flying
bird) 7 The giant squid
8 An insect 9 The mule
10 In deserts

29

1 The Spanish Armada 2 Daisy
Duck 3 The French horn
4 An oasis 5 Straw or reed
6 A square 7 China 8 Parrot
9 Reptile 10 Pride

30

1 India 2 Neptune 3 The Tiber
4 An early bicycle 5 An early
car 6 The Indian Ocean
7 A centurion 8 France
9 A fighter plane 10 Jupiter

31

1 Two 2 Polo 3 Personal best
4 Bronze 5 Caddy 6 A baton
7 Baseline 8 Ropes 9 60
minutes 10 A gum shield

BACKGROUND BONUS:
Snooker

32

1 Who dares wins 2 Water
lilies 3 Bread 4 Water
5 Romania 6 Second 7 Judo
8 It has flippers 9 Lake
10 Bees

33

1 The seagull 2 To cool off
3 The locust 4 Every year
5 Butterflies 6 A spider (in
Australia) 7 A cob 8 They give
birth to live young 9 The
African elephant 10 Moose

BACKGROUND BONUS:
Giraffe

34

1 Chrysanthemums 2 Poppies
3 Tulips 4 Roses 5 Crocuses
6 Marigolds 7 Daisies
8 Primroses 9 Pansies
10 Snowdrops

35

1 Spain 2 Badminton 3 Mice
4 14th 5 Australia 6 A dam
7 Jumbo jet 8 In your mouth
(they are teeth) 9 Six 10 Ate

36

1 Julia Roberts 2 The Yellow
Brick Road 3 Springfield
4 *Anastasia* 5 Indiana 6 Donald
Duck 7 Jet fighter pilots
8 Paris 9 Artificial
10 Fox

BACKGROUND BONUS:
Venice

37

1 An eaglet 2 *Compsognathus*
3 A bull 4 Five 5 Whale shark
6 Tropical forests 7 The toad
8 Yes, it "walks" on its spines
9 Very loud 10 On vines

38

1 The Romans 2 The American
Civil War 3 Queen Victoria
4 World War I 5 *The Hunchback
of Notre Dame* 6 Abacus 7 Two
million 8 A bolt 9 Australia
10 A jet plane

39

1 The Scorpion King 2 *Deep
Blue Sea* 3 Hobbits 4 Lord
Farquaad 5 "Beautiful
Stranger" 6 Rocky
7 A volcanic eruption 8 Paris
9 Brain 10 *Mrs. Doubtfire*

40

1 The ferret 2 A drone
3 It collects it 4 Mud 5 Sour
6 An oyster 7 Six weeks
8 To find new nesting sites
9 The gorilla 10 Sand

41

1 Pull it out 2 A metal 3 0.3
4 A pulley 5 A crescent
6 Sleep 7 A gas 8 Partly burnt
wood 9 A polygon 10 Up

42

1 Two 2 National League
3 Touchdown 4 Figure skating
5 A basketball court 6 Three
shots 7 Five 8 Baseball
9 The horse 10 Frankie Dettori

43

1 A black panther 2 Neon
3 Blue 4 Never, Never Land
5 The cat 6 A frog
7 Hogwart's Express 8 Rome
9 Dr. Seuss 10 *Harry Potter and
the Order of the Phoenix*

44

1 Babe 2 Donkey 3 *The Grinch*
4 Mr. Burns 5 Jamie Lee Curtis
6 Scud 7 *Chicken Run*
8 Grasshoppers 9 *Ice Age*
10 Baloo

BACKGROUND BONUS:
The eye

45

1 For eggs and goats' milk
2 Animals 3 A famous flier
4 Acting (all three became
famous actors) 5 Jonah
6 John Milton 7 Asia
8 Edmund Spenser 9 Ballet
dancing 10 Archimedes
BACKGROUND BONUS:
Pirates

46

1 One 2 A computer
3 Jupiter 4 12 5 Ribs
6 Mercury 7 Lead 8 Papier-
mâché 9 30 minutes
10 Under the water

47

1 Serena Williams 2 China
3 A dolphin 4 The Powerpuff
Girls 5 Baseball 6 Boxing
7 February 8 Snowy owl
9 Maine and Massachusetts
10 The hare

48

1 Asia and Africa 2 Arizona
3 11.3 km (7 mi)
4 A strawberry tart
5 Mediterranean 6 The beaver
7 Florida 8 A mountain
(second highest) 9 Bangkok
10 Cuba

49

1 Cormorant 2 Stand out
brightly 3 Honey
4 A sheepdog 5 Yellow
6 In trees 7 A mammal
8 Three 9 Give birth to baby
rattlers 10 South America

50

1 Chelsea 2 Scottish
3 Aston Villa 4 45 minutes
5 Own goal 6 Clyde
7 Ipswich Town 8 France
9 Queen's Park Rangers
10 Three

BACKGROUND BONUS:
Studs

51

1 Both 2 The letter P
3 Cunning (descriptive word)
4 Two (o and e) 5 Shot
6 Key 7 Macbeth 8 Peach
9 Molar 10 Arson

52

1 The eagle 2 Mamba
3 Tentacles 4 White 5 Soar in
circles 6 Foxgloves 7 The
chameleon 8 Spiders
9 The elephant 10 Underwater

BACKGROUND BONUS:
Flamingoes

53

1 A sundial 2 Sweat 3 Hail
4 23:45 5 The Milky Way
6 A gramophone 7 Your heart
8 Volume 9 180 10 Eight

54

1 Wasp 2 His nose 3 The fear
of bees 4 Pepper
5 Hammerhead shark
6 Chow chow 7 Saturn
8 Mars 9 Eve 10 A lizard

55

1 Summer Bay 2 Harry Potter
3 *The Land Before Time*
4 Brad Pitt 5 Woody
6 Elvis Presley 7 Snake
8 Cameron Diaz 9 Keanu
Reeves 10 The Batmobile

56

1 35 2 A very heavy rainstorm
3 An equilateral triangle
4 Your mouth and nose
5 Purple 6 Patterns of stars in
the sky 7 16:00 8 Sunrise and
sunset 9 65 10 A cork

57

1 Snake 2 Chile 3 The Beatles
4 Nine months
5 Octopus 6 A beetle
7 A flattened circle
8 An unmanned aircraft
9 Saxophone 10 They are all
square numbers
BACKGROUND BONUS:
Goose

58

1 The hands 2 Monaco
3 Five 4 Basketball 5 Boston
Celtics 6 Chyna 7 Bullseye
8 An eagle 9 Hangman
10 Kareem Abdul-Jabbar
(38,387 points)

59

1 A swift 2 True 3 A snake
4 Mountains 5 The pumpkin
6 The vulture 7 A snake
8 Camouflage
9 Huskies 10 False

60

1 A helicopter 2 One fold gives
two identical halves
3 China (the others are
continents) 4 The koala
5 Knives 6 The sparrow
7 A fawn 8 William the
Conqueror 9 France
10 All of them

61

1 32 2 Saturn 3 Five 4 Spring
5 Your ear 6 The mosquito
7 The radius 8 A barge
9 Faster 10 Move fast back
and forth

BACKGROUND BONUS:
On the Sun

62

1 In case the engines broke
down or ran out of fuel
2 Thatch (straw) 3 Boudicca
4 18th century 5 The
Americans, when the British
surrendered 6 Sophocles
7 Captain William Bligh
8 Gustav Holst 9 Pharaoh
10 Pluto, in 1930

63

1 New York Yankees
2 Madonna 3 Green Bay
Packers 4 Four points
5 The purse 6 Kane 7 Golf
8 Darts 9 Jerry Lawler
10 Baseball

64

1 Friday 2 Paris 3 Careful with
money 4 Flag 5 Pen 6 Three
7 Horse 8 Wizard 9 Calf 10 U

65

1 True 2 1,000 3 Grapes
4 Aladdin 5 Iowa 6 North
7 They give up their throne
8 France 9 The Mediterranean
10 Your aunt

66

1 True 2 A chihuahua
3 A millipede 4 Give birth to
babies 5 Evergreens 6 Hiding
on a flower 7 To the squid
8 A marsupial 9 On rocky
shores 10 A lizard

67

1 The Alps 2 Ship 3 It is a cold
ocean current off the coast of
South America 4 William Penn
5 A boy who carried
gunpowder 6 150,000BC 7 A
mechanical harvester 8 Buried
in a tomb 9 Small 10 Sailors
BACKGROUND BONUS:
Hadrian's Wall

68

1 Camouflage 2 The night sky
3 False 4 Four 5 In your eye
6 Green 7 Sunday 8 Digging
9 Four 10 All natural things

69

1 Light 2 The sons of Noah
3 His birthright (the rights as
the eldest) 4 She was a judge
5 Methuselah 6 A story with a
deeper meaning 7 The road
from Jerusalem to Jericho
8 A dove 9 A sycamore tree
10 He was crucified

70

1 The magpie 2 Like its head
3 The nectar of flowers
4 The eagle 5 A lizard
6 Rabbits 7 Scorpions
8 A Shetland pony 9 Maize
10 In trees

71

1 Hard 2 The apple
3 Mothers-in-law 4 Eight
5 Bart Simpson 6 Sagittarius
7 The blue whale
8 Seasickness 9 The German
air force 10 Coral

72

1 U.S.S.R. and U.S.A. 2 Sir
Walter Raleigh 3 An old type
of gun 4 Amy Johnson 5 Thor
6 French 7 Louis Pasteur
8 The Huns 9 They crossed
from Asia on exposed land
10 Japan

73

1 250 2 5/8 3 90° 4 The eye
5 A rainbow 6 Increase in size
7 Electrical current (Amp)
8 21 (12 + 9) 9 In the engine
10 Oxygen

74

1 China 2 Spiders
3 *Tyrannosaurus rex*
4 *A Knight's Tale* 5 Two (Sleepy
and Sneezy) 6 Spirit
7 Margalo 8 Hercules
9 Islands of Lost Dreams
10 Barney Rubble
BACKGROUND BONUS:
Moulin Rouge

75

1 The Chinese 2 The Qur'an
3 Japan 4 Christopher
Columbus 5 Latin 6 An apple
(making him think about
gravity) 7 World War II (1939
to 1945) 8 The Nile
9 A wooden horse
10 18th (1700s)

76

1 Sol Campbell 2 Newcastle
United 3 Brazil 4 Germany
5 French 6 1998 7 David
Beckham 8 Republic of
Ireland 9 Blue 10 Germany

77

1 Southwest 2 Sweden
3 Denmark 4 Europe
5 Golden Gate Bridge 6 Dutch
7 Yangtzee (Chang Jiang) River
in China 8 West coast 9 Eiffel
Tower 10 Hungary

BACKGROUND BONUS:
Florence

78

1 The basking shark 2 On land
3 Hawkmoths 4 By staying in
the water 5 A type of lizard
6 To filter small animals, on
which they feed, from the
water 7 A small rat 8 No, all
live in communities 9 True
10 In the sea

79

1 The United States 2 San
Francisco 49ers 3 The Grand
National 4 One 5 9.78
seconds 6 Puck 7 Throwing a
punch 8 The beam 9 Grid
10 Butterfly

BACKGROUND BONUS:
Greyhound

80

1 Kitten 2 Swimming strokes
3 Early German airships
4 Your lungs 5 In the Tower of
London 6 Holland 7 Six
square sides 8 Four 9 An
iceberg 10 The elephant

81

1 One 2 Sea snake, the others are fish 3 Peregrine falcon 4 A horse 5 Reptiles 6 Mainly scavengers 7 Beans 8 A joey 9 Its feet 10 Zebra

82

1 Blue 2 Jedi 3 Kevin 4 Squirrel 5 Scooby Doo 6 Hamm 7 *The Emperor's New Groove* 8 Kron 9 Snowbell 10 *Space Jam*

83

1 Birds of prey 2 The newt 3 Arachnid (it has eight legs) 4 The mouse 5 Very heavy 6 A canary 7 Four legs 8 Rhinoceros beetles 9 In sandy seabeds 10 At sea

BACKGROUND BONUS:
Clover

84

1 Sicily 2 Soldiers who fight on foot 3 True 4 The ancient Egyptians 5 A dragon 6 Berlin 7 Join 8 Waylon Smithers 9 It is a tube shaped like a can of beans 10 Seaweed

85

1 Leopard 2 Owl 3 Tortoise 4 Cat 5 Frog 6 Seal 7 Flamingo 8 Crocodile 9 Dog 10 Hippo

86

1 Squash 2 China 3 Wheat 4 Warren 5 A square 6 Antarctica 7 Japan 8 Hang 9 The cat 10 The Equator

BACKGROUND BONUS:
The hula

87

1 Flamingo 2 A parrot 3 Drink nectar 4 True 5 Insects 6 A collie or sheepdog 7 The iris 8 It lays eggs 9 Damp conditions 10 The badger

88

1 Robert Louis Stevenson 2 A famous murderer 3 Florence Nightingale 4 One 5 The Ford Model-T 6 The printing press 7 Four 8 The Vikings 9 Tchaikovsky 10 China

89

1 "Away In A Manger" 2 Beach Boys 3 Bon Jovi 4 "Imagine" 5 Christina Aguilera 6 Oasis 7 Kate Winslett in *A Christmas Carol* 8 *Top Gun* 9 Irving Berlin 10 Anastacia

90

1 Hens 2 *Little Women* 3 Blush 4 Mary Shelley 5 Percy Shelley 6 Hercule Poirot 7 Jane Austen 8 A troupe 9 *Little Lord Fauntleroy* 10 Enid Blyton

BACKGROUND BONUS:
Ode to Autumn

91

1 No, they were pushed along 2 Italy 3 The feudal system 4 A Roman warship 5 1215 6 Benjamin Franklin 7 Essex 8 Soldiers 9 Easter Island 10 Near Florence, Italy

92

1 Bob Geldof 2 Norah Jones 3 A pear tree 4 *Chain Reaction* 5 Musical notes 6 Belinda Carlisle 7 Eminem 8 Beethoven 9 "Mary's Boy Child" 10 *Invincible*

93

1 A year 2 Italy 3 Swedish 4 Hands 5 Kentucky and Kansas 6 Reindeer 7 Japan 8 Sphinx 9 Europe 10 Antarctica

94

1 The poppy 2 Start or commence 3 206 4 New Zealand 5 A flock 6 Lochs 7 The supply of water for crops 8 William Shakespeare 9 *The Wind in the Willows* 10 In South America (mainly in Brazil)

95

1 Metal 2 Stars 3 24 4 Triplets 5 It freezes 6 A runway 7 7 8 They catch fire 9 48 10 Light

BACKGROUND BONUS:
Test tube

96

1 *The Mummy* 2 Sandra Bullock 3 *Hook* 4 *Minority Report* 5 *The Goonies* 6 *Aladdin* 7 Boo 8 *Shrek* 9 New York 10 Walt Disney

97

1 Ice 2 Boxing 3 By the coast 4 Tennis 5 Green 6 Conkers 7 Croquet 8 Volley 9 Montreal Canadiens 10 A jib

98

1 16 2 Your ear 3 A tugboat 4 The hovercraft 5 Molten rock 6 An oil tanker 7 Your lungs 8 The nucleus 9 18 10 Natural

99

1 A person, place or thing 2 The trombone 3 Belfast 4 A crater 5 Have a short sleep 6 A stone in a sling 7 To clear something from your nose 8 *Brachiosaurus* 9 The owl 10 A kind of whip

100

1 A hobbit 2 Sherlock Holmes 3 Hercule Poirot 4 Dickens 5 Uncle Remus 6 One 7 Peter Pan 8 *The Hobbit* 9 Ted Hughes 10 *Dracula*

101

1 A skunk 2 Berlin 3 A warthog
4 *My Fair Lady*
5 David Duchovny 6 *Moulin Rouge* 7 *Cats and Dogs*
8 An elephant 9 *Evita* 10 *Fame*

102

1 The male peacock
2 Australia 3 A dog 4 Yes, fruit bats 5 A pine tree
6 The heron 7 A kite 8 A fly
9 The zebra 10 Open meadows

103

1 1930s (1939 to 1945)
2 New Zealand 3 The Stone Age 4 Six 5 Roundheads
6 The Matterhorn
7 Telephone 8 John F. Kennedy
9 Scribes 10 Queen Victoria

BACKGROUND BONUS:
The Parthenon

104

1 Touchdown 2 Two
3 Pretending to pass the ball
4 Sumo wrestling 5 Hurling
6 Houston and St. Louis 7 Tee
8 Baseball 9 High jump
10 Fencing

105

1 Glasgow 2 Spain 3 The Grand Canyon 4 St. Paul's Cathedral 5 Victoria 6 Venice
7 South Pole 8 Italy 9 The euro 10 Brazil

106

1 A basketball team 2 Six
3 50 minutes 4 Die 5 Prince of Wales 6 It blows from the west
7 Neptune 8 Road
9 The snake 10 Four

107

1 France 2 *The Mayflower*
3 The Suffragettes 4 Hawaii
5 Queen Elizabeth I 6 16th century 7 Richard Nixon
8 Leonardo da Vinci 9 Three
10 Amelia Bloomer

108

1 Bobsleigh 2 Javelin 3 Tiger Woods 4 Los Angeles Lakers
5 Olympic torch 6 Detroit Red Wings 7 Seven 8 Buffalo Bills
9 Hurling 10 Triple jump

BACKGROUND BONUS:
American football

109

1 All Saints 2 Kylie Minogue
3 Flute 4 Sydney Opera House
5 The evening 6 Geri Halliwell
7 Meatloaf 8 Luciano Pavarotti
9 Triangle 10 The Police

110

1 Snowflake 2 It spins
3 Constellations 4 Three days
5 The steam engine
6 A fishing boat 7 Two
8 Brass 9 Humidity
10 Carbon dioxide

BACKGROUND BONUS:
Lightning

111

1 The Australian rugby union team 2 Ireland 3 Greenwich Mean Time 4 6 5 The Cheshire Cat 6 A pearl
7 Swimming 8 A British prime minister 9 A butterfly
10 Martin Luther King

112

1 Ché Guevara 2 Louis Armstrong 3 Judy Garland
4 Queen Elizabeth I 5 Alfred Hitchcock 6 William Shakespeare 7 Frank Sinatra
8 Samuel L. Jackson 9 Nicole Kidman 10 Salman Rushdie

113

1 Whitehall 2 Madison Avenue
3 Vienna 4 Pennsylvania
5 Thistle 6 Mississippi
7 Dundee 8 High-speed (Train à Grande Vitesse) 9 Malta
10 Jamaica

BACKGROUND BONUS:
Desert

114

1 The spinal cord 2 The sextant
3 600 4 Electricity
5 Movement energy
6 The clutch pedal
7 The atmosphere
8 A mixture 9 Asleep 10 Car

115

1 *Gladiator* 2 Bruce Willis
3 The 1950s 4 Charlton Heston 5 *Men in Black*
6 *The Matrix* 7 *Star Wars*
8 *The Fugitive* 9 Susan Sarandon and Geena Davis
10 *Terminator II*

116

1 Canadian 2 Seoul
3 Boxing 4 Jonathan Edwards
5 Soccer's World Cup 6 The 19th century 7 Shergar
8 Basketball 9. Squash 10 14

117

1 China 2 Gertrude Ederle
3 Turkey 4 The straits that are now named after him 5 It could be loaded more quickly
6 Cuba 7 He was the knight's servant 8 John F. Kennedy
9 St. Andrew 10 Paddle wheels
BACKGROUND BONUS:
Easter Island

118

1 Types of knot 2 Madagascar
3 Meteorites 4 Cabbage
5 Peter Pan 6 Dutch settlers in South Africa 7 Because it is pulled by gravity 8 France
9 Oranges, lemons, limes grapefruits 10 A cockerel

119

1 Bedrock 2 Russell Crowe
3 Gillian Anderson 4 Ross
5 Frasier 6 The Penguin
7 Chicago 8 Whitney Houston
9 Tom Hanks 10 Casper

120

1 Tenpin bowling ball 2 San Francisco 49ers 3 Mike Powell
4 Boston Celtics 5 Croquet
6 Lleyton Hewitt 7 Tiger Woods 8 Five 9 Marbles
10 A baseball bat

121

1 Eric Cantona 2 Michael Owen 3 Liverpool 4 Roger Milla 5 Sunderland 6 Italy 7 Inter Milan 8 Bobby Moore 9 Italy 10 Brazil

122

1 *The Taming of the Shrew* 2 *Shine* 3 *Jurassic Park* 4 *Barbarella* 5 Dorothy Lamour 6 Alan Arkin 7 Tchaikovsky 8 *Steamboat Willie* 9 *The Robe* 10 *Braveheart*

123

1 Dodo 2 Butterfly 3 Deer 4 Blubber 5 Four 6 Ostrich 7 Fat 8 Hexagonal 9 Mulberry 10 Boar

BACKGROUND BONUS:
The cheetah

124

1 1975 2 Richard Nixon 3 Blackbeard 4 Charlotte Brontë 5 Steam engine 6 The Great Pyramid 7 Three 8 Canada 9 Kublai Khan 10 Mao Tse-tung

125

1 A microscope 2 Cabbage 3 Winter 4 They push apart 5 An astrologer 6 11 and 2 7 Larger 8 Green plants 9 Obtuse 10 20:45

126

1 Mule 2 Monkey 3 A kind of fungus 4 Colt 5 Stamen 6 Daddy-longlegs 7 Pup 8 Kiwi 9 A tail 10 Poppies

127

1 Palm trees 2 Mozart 3 Italy (on the island of Sicily) 4 Chess 5 The octopus and squid 6 Transistors 7 The walrus 8 Rice 9 Twice 10 1914

128

1 Bandy 2 A dog 3 Oval 4 Swim the English Channel 5 The first to climb Mount Everest 6 6–6 7 Right side 8 Dressage 9 High jump 10 Norwegian

BACKGROUND BONUS:
Boxing

129

1 Strings 2 The pineapple 3 To the stern (the back) 4 Billie Holiday 5 The sari 6 The eye 7 Peru 8 Motor racing 9 Richard I 10 Red Square

130

1 The giant salamander 2 Thin, damp skin 3 Plant nectar 4 Fish 5 They are all different 6 In abandoned prairie dog burrows 7 It is a tadpole at first 8 Buffalo 9 Orchid family 10 The root

131

1 Male side 2 Dead men 3 Absence 4 Very High Frequency 5 Curator 6 Compass 7 Hyphen 8 A postage stamp 9 500 10 Pod

132

1 Sir Alec Guinness 2 Elizabeth Taylor 3 Mickey Mouse 4 Florence 5 Wednesday Addams 6 Cadfael 7 A tiger 8 John Travolta 9 *Men in Black* 10 Calista Flockhart
BACKGROUND BONUS:
Four Weddings and a Funeral

133

1 A giant crossbow 2 Thomas Edison 3 Pluto 4 Rabbis 5 The Taj Mahal 6 Douglas Bader 7 Pennsylvania 8 Marc Anthony 9 To support a wall 10 2,000 years ago

134

1 North America 2 South Africa 3 Brussels 4 Hawaii 5 Edinburgh 6 Italy 7 Canadian dollars 8 The Gateway Arch 9 Portugal 10 Argentina and Chile

135

1 J 2 Michael Jackson 3 Scott Joplin 4 Cor Anglais 5 Erasure 6 *Fame* 7 The Coconuts 8 Boyzone 9 Bass 10 Blur

BACKGROUND BONUS:
The clarinet

136

1 Charles II 2 Rumpelstiltskin 3 17 4 A synagogue 5 Maize 6 The fly, with his little eye 7 Blue 8 Hot and wet 9 The Middle Ages 10 The salmon

137

1 Jeff Goldblum 2 Cher 3 Golden Gate Bridge 4 JFK 5 Sugar 6 *Indiana Jones and the Last Crusade* 7 Cary Grant 8 Joan Crawford 9 *City Slickers* 10 *Bugsy Malone*

138

1 Mia Farrow 2 Charles Schulz 3 Mikhail Gorbachev 4 She was a pirate 5 Playwright 6 Cyprus 7 Portuguese 8 Salman Rushdie 9 A bouncing bomb 10 1981
BACKGROUND BONUS:
Antarctica

139

1 From the sound of its call 2 Tails 3 Leaves 4 The red squirrel 5 By birds 6 Feathers 7 True 8 They all feed on blood 9 In the Arctic tundra 10 Beaks

140

1 Claude Monet 2 James Watt 3 Josef Stalin 4 Leonardo da Vinci 5 Ned Kelly 6 The American Civil War 7 Ravens 8 Winston Churchill 9 Anne Boleyn 10 Krakatoa

141

1 British 2 Nicotine
3 A barrier fitted to a gateway
4 A woman (Mary Ann Evans)
5 A blade on a rifle 6 AD1000
7 Two 8 The jet engine
9 Thomas Hardy 10 Napoleon
BACKGROUND BONUS:
Cathedral of St. Peter and
St. Paul

142

1 Bruce Willis 2 Ursula
Andress 3 The American Civil
War 4 Gladiator 5 Insomnia
6 Monty Python and the Holy
Grail 7 Bill and Ted's Bogus
Journey 8 Zeppo 9 Me, Myself,
and Irene 10 The Kray twins

143

1 F. Scott Fitzgerald 2 Mary
Magdalene 3 Scott Joplin
4 Andy Warhol 5 Walt Disney
6 Peter Ustinov 7 Sam Spade
8 Georges Braque 9 Graham
Greene 10 John McEnroe

144

1 Moses 2 Hieroglyphic script
3 Pasteurization 4 Yeast
5 Five 6 The hyena 7 The
Mongol Empire 8 Deer
9 One-fifth 10 20

145

1 In the Himalaya Mountains
2 Polar bear 3 The Pyrenees
4 Tutankhamun 5 Six and
the goalkeeper 6 A château
7 A fish 8 The piano
9 Sherlock Holmes
10 The trout

146

1 San Francisco 49ers
2 Miami Dolphins 3 Kareem
Abdul-Jabbar 4 Hurling
5 Venus Williams
6 Denver Broncos and
Minnesota Vikings 7 A cricket
bat 8 Japan 9 French 10 10

147

1 Back 2 3 3 An empty space
4 Geometry 5 Eight
6 He introduced antiseptic
7 Printing 8 Your head
9 In your ear 10 Rocks and
how Earth was formed

BACKGROUND BONUS:
Circuit board

148

1 Guglielmo Marconi
2 A keyboard instrument
3 The Spanish 4 To give
warning of dangerous gases
5 A dive-bomber 6 The camel
7 Alice Through the Looking Glass
8 France 9 One made for
carrying coal 10 The first
lifebelt

149

1 168 2 To check if something
is level 3 A hydrofoil 4 Pierre
and Marie Curie 5 6° 6 The
Earth 7 A cone 8 A transplant
9 A straight line 10 Land

150

1 Flags 2 Citizen's Band
3 At the end 4 Dance
5 Intensive Care Unit 6 Head
7 The letter i 8 Antidote
9 Very cold 10 Prisoner (of
War)

151

1 Matt le Blanc (Joey in
Friends) 2 The Little Vampire
3 Doc 4 Snakes 5 Lions
6 The Aristocats 7 Homeward
Bound: The Incredible Journey
8 Free Willy 9 The Snowman
10 Gotham City
BACKGROUND BONUS:
Antz

152

1 The Chinese 2 Snakes
3 The letter s 4 Spain and
Portugal 5 China 6 The
toucan 7 Ankara 8 In your
kidneys 9 The Indian Ocean
10 Gander

153

1 Paris 2 The rat 3 Reptiles
4 Sandstone 5 The sheep
6 Faster than the speed of
sound 7 Muscles in your arms
8 Dancing 9 Six 10 The Great
Pyramid, Egypt

154

1 Darth Maul 2 Garlic
3 Santa Claus the Movie
4 Harry Potter 5 Cinderella
6 Tom Cruise 7 Will Smith
8 Harrison Ford 9 Rowan
Atkinson 10 Lawyer

155

1 Mosquito 2 Live young
3 Botany 4 Gum tree 5 Filly
6 Pig 7 A toad 8 Python
9 St. Bernard 10 Penguins

BACKGROUND BONUS:
Snake

156

1 Table salt 2 Plastic
3 A number less than zero
4 A loom 5 Birds 6 It sounds
deeper 7 Information
8 Eyelids 9 Tetrahedron
10 A comet

157

1 Emperor Zurg 2 Aerosmith
3 A Christmas Carol 4 Lisa
Kudrow 5 Eddie Murphy
6 The Genie 7 The Joker
8 Alien 9 Britney Spears
10 Frodo

158

1 Japan 2 2,000 3 Hawaii
4 Greece 5 Prague 6 Bulgaria
7 Knoll 8 Aztec 9 Tuareg
10 Peru

159

1 Sputnik 2 Waterproof
material 3 In your bones
4 A switch 5 Smaller 6 A hang
glider 7 Four 8 To frown
9 Fruit and vegetables
10 Rapid Eye Movement

BACKGROUND BONUS:
Neon

160

1 Jack Charlton 2 Japan
3 Jamaica 4 Roberto di
Maggio 5 Leeds United
6 Bobby Robson 7 Dixie Dean
8 Sweden 9 Alan Shearer
10 Nottingham Forest

161
1 Ceylon 2 A maple leaf
3 Notre Dame 4 Bangkok
5 Copenhagen 6 Africa
7 Menai Straits 8 Jaffa
9 Subtropical coastal areas
10 Peacock

BACKGROUND BONUS:
Farming

162
1 An official count of the
population 2 It is a boat with
two hulls 3 The mussel
4 Jerusalem 5 A leopard
6 Hypnosis 7 Gemini
8 Atlantic 9 Its cathedral
10 Sweden

163
1 Swimming 2 100 3 Mike
Tyson 4 Melbourne 5 A flic
flac 6 Soccer 7 Hong Kong
8 Puck 9 A Mini 10 A mallett

164
1 Above ground in tall grass
(and other plants)
2 To threaten enemies
3 Capybara 4 Cactus
5 The red fox 6 The banana
7 They all lay their eggs on
land 8 The albatross
9 Over half 10 Birds

165
1 Cain and Abel 2 An architect
3 Swiss 4 A sculptor
5 Abraham Lincoln
6 Bill Gates 7 North Pole
8 Argentina 9 Pontius Pilate
10 H.G. Wells

166
1 "From the Middle Ages"
2 Oxygen 3 Igor Stravinsky
4 His land or property
5 Australia 6 Tiananmen
Square 7 The potato 8 *The Jazz
Singer* 9 The Eiffel Tower in
Paris 10 The Dalai Lama

167
1 On the water 2 They are all
parts of a horse 3 Oxygen
4 At night 5 A shellfish
6 Upstream 7 Back legs
8 In rainforest trees 9 Ten
10 An owl

168
1 Silicon 2 Things that are
farther away 3 Albert Einstein
4 0.75 5 Slows them down
6 A cone 7 Windpipe 8 On the
ocean floor 9 Friction
10 The knee cap

BACKGROUND BONUS:
Clouds

169
1 *Lady and the Tramp*
2 *G.I. Jane* 3 Fluffy 4 Geese
5 *Edward Scissorhands*
6 Cameron Diaz 7 *E.T. the
Extra-Terrestrial* 8 1950s (1952)
9 Hulk Hogan 10 *Pocahontas*

170
1 Beirut 2 Mustard 3 Cardiff
4 Sunflower State 5 Geneva
6 Peking 7 20th century
8 Brighton Royal Pavilion
9 Alaska 10 The Statue of
Liberty

171
1 Saliva 2 M 3 Evaporation
4 He was the first man in space
5 A submarine 6 Orbit 7 The
ear 8 The thin wire called a
filament 9 The tongue 10 210

172
1 To filter food from water
2 The water buffalo 3 A mare
4 7 m (23 ft) 5 Tomato, the
rest are herbs 6 Shrimps
7 Bamboo 8 Palm trees
9 A herbivore, only eating
plants 10 A rocky beach
BACKGROUND BONUS:
Giant panda

173
1 The didgeridoo 2 A plum
3 The Romans 4 Gunpowder
5 The puffin 6 Sinuses
7 Soprano 8 To stop
something before it begins
9 Christianity 10 It is an exit

174
1 Lara Croft 2 Courtney Cox
3 Superman 4 Sandy
5 Baseball 6 Penguin
7 Olive Oyl 8 *Star Wars*
9 Austria 10 *The Parent Trap*

175
1 Spinning wool thread on a
spindle 2 Uranus 3 Polish
4 H.G. Wells 5 Swiss army
knife 6 Everest 7 Artists
8 1979 9 Florence
10 The Senate

BACKGROUND BONUS:
A Renaissance wall painting

176
1 Aspirin 2 0.001 3 It splits
into red, orange, yellow,
green, blue, indigo and violet
4 Geysers 5 A meteorologist
6 Breathing in 7 Wind speed
8 In your jaw 9 A probe
10 Prime numbers

177
1 Switzerland 2 Foxy Loxy
3 Rice 4 The lungs 5 At the
back of the nose and throat
6 2 7 A watermelon 8 The
United Nations 9 Berlin
10 The owl and the pussycat

178
1 Tennessee Titans
2 The Netherlands 3 Hank
Aaron (755) 4 Steve Backley
5 World Boxing Organization
6 Cycling 7 Nolan Ryan
8 Tenpin bowling 9 Damon
Hill 10 Ravel's Bolero
BACKGROUND BONUS:
Rally

179
1 Nepal 2 More than half
3 Six million 4 Wind
5 Malaysia 6 Spain 7 Iceland
8 2.5 cm (1 in) 9 Spain
10 Australia

180
1 The Mediterranean Sea and
the Indian Ocean 2 Woodrow
Wilson 3 Al Capone 4 The
Jews 5 A Saturn rocket 6 Junks
7 Alfred the Great 8 Because
it seemed to be peaceful
9 Rudolph Valentino
10 Jerusalem

181

1 Trampolining 2 Pin spotter 3 Three 4 Wrestling 5 Fencing 6 Evander Holyfield 7 Billiards 8 Two years old 9 Salt Lake City 10 Chris Eubank

182

1 Velociraptors 2 *Sleeping Beauty* 3 A cricket called Jiminy Cricket 4 *Osmosis Jones* 5 *Lady and the Tramp* 6 *Spirited Away* 7 *Tarzan* 8 *Honey I Shrunk the Kids* 9 India 10 Miss Piggy
BACKGROUND BONUS:
Elizabeth Taylor

183

1 Iran 2 Narnia 3 Roman 4 Vasco da Gama 5 Hirohito 6 The American War of Independence 7 Constantine 8 Edward Kennedy Ellington 9 Russia 10 The volcano Vesuvius erupted

184

1 The ray 2 New Zealand 3 The sea anemone 4 The mongoose 5 Ants or termites 6 Elephants 7 Crocodile 8 Bird of prey 9 False 10 Pink

185

1 *Atlantis* 2 Bicycle 3 M 4 *The Jungle Book* 5 Dogs 6 West 7 Hundred Acre Wood 8 Catherine Zeta Jones 9 *American Pie* 10 World War II

186

1 Switzerland 2 Guyana 3 Platinum 4 By pretending to be dead 5 20 6 The hummingbird 7 Portugal 8 Italian dumplings 9 30 10 France

187

1 An owlet 2 The otter 3 With their antennae 4 The Persian cat 5 Oats 6 The woodpecker 7 The snake 8 False (apart from large gorillas) 9 Cabbage 10 A snail

188

1 Bananarama 2 Queen 3 "No Diggity" 4 "Careless Whisper" 5 A Eurovision Song Contest win 6 Ian Dury and the Blockheads 7 "I'll Be Missing You" 8 The Beatles 9 "Albatross" 10 "Like a Virgin"
BACKGROUND BONUS:
Red Hot Chili Peppers

189

1 Siamese twins 2 Collects and stores urine 3 A swarm 4 France 5 A kind of whale 6 Gymnastic exercises for men 7 Dandruff 8 Two 9 Scales 10 Iraq

190

1 25 2 Yes 3 10° 4 It doesn't rust 5 Above 6 Protractor 7 The computer's screen 8 Small 9 24 hours 10 The propeller

BACKGROUND BONUS:
A star

191

1 Stonehenge 2 Angkor Wat 3 Pyramids at Giza 4 Sydney Opera House 5 Taj Mahal 6 Notre Dame 7 Machu Picchu 8 Agia Sophia 9 The Great Wall of China 10 Golden Gate Bridge

192

1 Cycling 2 Judo 3 Zola Budd 4 Wayne Gretsky 5 Pittsburgh Steelers 6 Joe DiMaggio 7 Celluloid 8 Gymnastics 9 1.8 m (6 ft) 10 Featherweight

193

1 *Harry Potter and the Chamber of Secrets* 2 Oddball 3 Hyenas 4 *Pokémon: The Movie 2002* 5 40 6 *The Aristocats* 7 *The Little Mermaid* 8 George of the Jungle 9 Milk 10 William Shakespeare

194

1 Nirvana 2 Destiny's Child 3 The Who 4 REM 5 The Rolling Stones 6 No Doubt 7 Backstreet Boys 8 Coldplay 9 Status Quo 10 T Rex

195

1 Frances Hodgson Burnett 2 Terry Pratchett 3 Charles Darwin 4 Discourage 5 An adverb 6 Achilles 7 Terry Deary 8 A state of great confusion or unrest 9 Prince Charles 10 Hamlet
BACKGROUND BONUS:
Pasta

196

1 Gold 2 7 3 Smaller 4 A washing machine 5 10.8 6 15 7 A plane 8 Your ribs 9 Energy from the Sun 10 Acid rain

197

1 A dog 2 The Native Americans 3 In the Pacific Ocean 4 The United States 5 Jane Austen 6 The person owes the bank 7 Calf 8 Thursday 9 60 10 Rice

198

1 Pope John Paul II 2 *The Elephant Man* 3 Theodore Roosevelt 4 Amy Johnson 5 His right ear 6 Steven Spielberg 7 Katharine Hepburn 8 Ethelred 9 Russia 10 Sir Robert Baden-Powell
BACKGROUND BONUS:
Buddha

199

1 Ash 2 George Foreman 3 Ronald Reagan 4 Ice hockey 5 Primo Carnera 6 Jesse Owens 7 Houston Rockets 8 Steve Fossett 9 New York Islanders 10 Yamaha

200

1 Indian Ocean 2 South America 3 Stalactites 4 Malmo 5 Dormant 6 Mountain 7 Indonesia 8 South America 9 Pork 10 North America

201
1 Seals 2 Aaron 3 David Livingstone 4 The sunflower 5 True 6 Brazil 7 Bridges 8 The St. Lawrence River 9 A butterfly 10 Bethlehem

202
1 Eight 2 Stratford-upon-Avon 3 The Congo 4 *The Great Britain* 5 Iran 6 Nicholas II 7 Istanbul 8 The machine gun 9 Lenin 10 The Hanging Gardens

BACKGROUND BONUS:
London

203
1 A fish 2 Its back legs 3 Cacao tree 4 A bivalve 5 The stinging nettle 6 Grit 7 The marine turtle 8 Crabs 9 The penguin 10 The zebra

204
1 East 2 Serpent or snake 3 Candlemas 4 The Ten Commandments 5 A feeding trough for animals 6 39 7 Arrival or coming 8 Jerusalem 9 Herodias 10 Goliath

205
1 Goldie Hawn 2 Sergeant Bilko 3 Glen Campbell 4 *The Washington Post* 5 *The Mask of Zorro* 6 James Herriot 7 *The Good, the Bad and the Ugly* 8 Angela Lansbury 9 Kermit the Frog 10 Liam Neeson

206
1 Table tennis 2 Kentucky Derby 3 Steve Redgrave 4 Australian 5 John Curry 6 Butterfly 7 Maureen Connolly 8 Basketball 9 Davy Jones 10 Thailand

207
1 World Emperor 2 Charles Sturt 3 Mexico and Guatemala 4 The Globe 5 Egypt 6 House of Plantagenet 7 Italy 8 13th century 9 The Bahamas 10 Ming

BACKGROUND BONUS:
Sunflowers

208
1 The Salvation Army 2 The seahorse 3 The shamrock 4 Portuguese 5 Africa 6 The gorilla 7 A bull 8 The Colosseum 9 Ottawa 10 Autobiography

209
1 Argentinian cowboys 2 Gondolas 3 Autumn or fall 4 Maya ruins 5 Malta 6 Alps 7 Oranges 8 Russia 9 Florida 10 Its atmosphere and weather

210
1 A smelly spray 2 To scare enemies 3 In cells in the hive 4 The Virginia opossum 5 True 6 The pike 7 Attached to tree trunks 8 Warm-blooded 9 Pollen-bearing flowers 10 On land
BACKGROUND BONUS:
Blossom

211
1 The 1990 World Cup 2 False, he supported Everton 3 Monaco 4 Nigerian 5 Alan Smith 6 Watford 7 Howard Wilkinson 8 Leeds United 9 Sheffield Wednesday 10 Sunderland

212
1 A reptile 2 Dew (it lives in the desert) 3 The eel is the only fish 4 The guinea pig 5 The peanut 6 The baby mouse opossum 7 Because it sings during storms 8 The scorpion 9 By curling into a ball and rolling away 10 More than 400

213
1 The porcupine 2 Libretto 3 Table tennis 4 A planetarium 5 On the feast of St. Stephen 6 Guglielmo Marconi 7 Queen Mary I 8 The Strait of Gibraltar 9 Dinosaurs 10 Mt. Elbrus (in the Russian Federation)

214
1 Blood 2 The eye 3 Litmus paper 4 100 5 Muscle 6 Electricity 7 Head, thorax, abdomen 8 Solid, liquid, gas 9 The radius 10 Its climate

215
1 Cliff Richard 2 Moby 3 Dolly Parton 4 Cockles and mussels 5 Frank and Nancy Sinatra 6 Gloria Estefan 7 "Blue Christmas" 8 Wings 9 "For Your Eyes Only" 10 Wilcox

BACKGROUND BONUS:
Drumming for Bon Jovi

216
1 Ireland 2 Trebuchet 3 Pluto 4 Japan 5 The transistor 6 Stalin 7 Measuring the depth of the river Nile 8 1946 9 The Hippocratic oath (after Hippocrates) 10 Eight

217
1 Crocodiles 2 The trapdoor spider 3 The bison 4 The chimpanzee 5 The manta ray 6 Fish 7 By squirting venom 8 The lion 9 Australia 10 A type of lizard

BACKGROUND BONUS:
Orb-web spider

218
1 *Flubber* 2 Sam Neill 3 *My Left Foot* 4 The Beatles 5 Billy the Kid 6 Crete 7 Cate Blanchett 8 Jack Wild 9 *West Side Story* 10 Ariel, the Little Mermaid

219
1 Lava 2 German measles 3 260 4 The skin 5 Three-quarters 6 The backbone 7 A compass 8 A gas 9 The retina 10 Sand

220
1 Canada 2 366 days 3 Tirana 4 The leaves 5 Fire 6 Facsimile 7 Hinduism 8 Texas 9 Donna 10 Getting old

221

1 Danish 2 California
3 Peanuts 4 Lead and tin
5 *The War of the Worlds*
6 Cambodia 7 Margaret
Thatcher 8 1492 9 Canada
10 Ziggurats

222

1 HMS *Pinafore* 2 Havana
3 Lani Hall 4 Mark Knopfler
5 Bernie Taupin, "Candle in
the Wind" 6 Kenny Jones
7 22 8 Victor Hugo 9 Crete
10 Saxophone

223

1 1929 2 Cambodia or
Kampuchea 3 Victor 4 Twin
brothers 5 *Brewster's Millions*
6 *Face/Off* 7 *Bedknobs and
Broomsticks* 8 Chico
9 *Dangerous Minds* 10 Bruce Lee

BACKGROUND BONUS:
Moose

224

1 A Siamese cat 2 Cairo
3 Costa Rica 4 Charles
Dickens 5 Amethyst
6 Minnie Mouse 7 The Seine
8 Lloyd George 9 Butterfly
10 A kaleidoscope

225

1 The knee 2 95 percent
3 In your leg 4 Sound and how
it travels 5 Vitamin K 6 Mars
7 Water 8 Rocks 9 The feeling
that you need to be sick
10 Food and diet

BACKGROUND BONUS:
Petri dish

226

1 Carl Lewis 2 Yugoslavia
3 Babe Ruth 4 Rex Williams
5 Moscow 6 Tim Henman
7 Yew 8 Bandy 9 Gary Player
10 "Thorpedo"

227

1 The Commodores
2 *The Exorcist* 3 Austria
4 *Reservoir Dogs* 5 *Trainspotting*
6 George Michael 7 Wings
8 *Back to the Future* 9 The Sex
Pistols 10 Madonna

228

1 Killer Whale 2 Nicaragua
3 New York 4 Mikhail
Gorbachev 5 Black mamba
6 J.S. Bach 7 Japan
8 Austria 9 Sudan 10 1980

229

1 In a tree 2 Flatfish 3 Mussel
4 Southern hemisphere 5 True
6 A fruit 7 Certain snakes
8 Saffron 9 A troop
10 The sweet chestnut

BACKGROUND BONUS: It has
the most feathers of any bird

230

1 A bat 2 It helps digest food
3 Termites 4 Venus 5 Four
6 Gibraltar 7 In the wrist
(it's a bone) 8 8 9 Diabetes
10 Teeth and bones

231

1 Anthony Quinn starred in
them 2 Jane in the *Tarzan*
movies 3 John Travolta
4 The Three Stooges
5 Walter Matthau 6 Chess
7 Vivien Leigh 8 Danny Glover
9 Joy Adamson 10 Stephen Fry

232

1 Castanets 2 18 3 Grapes
4 The brothers Grimm
5 Copenhagen 6 *Chicago*
7 A private detective 8 A foal
9 Cartilage 10 Savings

233

1 A winning point 2 A free
shot 3 Bullfighting 4 Hasim
Rahman 5 Javelin 6 A yacht
7 Badminton 8 Surfing
9 International Skating Union
10 A short sprint race

BACKGROUND BONUS:
Women's basketball

234

1 A stone on which it smashes
snails 2 It looks like a dead
leaf 3 It dies 4 The giraffe
5 To protect its brain as it
pecks trees 6 Palm tree
7 A pit in loose sand
8 A legless amphibian
9 The sloth 10 Siberia

235

1 Mary Magdalene 2 Eve
3 Egypt 4 Thou shalt not
commit adultery 5 Salome
6 27 7 The Angel Gabriel
8 Luke 9 Cologne Cathedral
10 St. Matthew

236

1 1947 2 The first coast-to-
coast railroad 3 Handel 4
150,000 years ago 5 Samuel
Taylor Coleridge 6 The French,
led by Napoleon 7 President
Hoover 8 The Rockies 9 A
movie dance team 10 Apollo

237

1 Paris 2 Paul McCartney
3 A herb 4 Bow-shaped
5 The Mediterranean
6 Daniel Defoe 7 Jerusalem
8 A detonator 9 Oliver
Cromwell 10 The Russian
Federation

238

1 The snow goose 2 Up to 3.22
km/h (2 mph) over short
distances 3 South America
4 The chipmunk 5 Broad-
leaved trees 6 To keep clean
when feeding 7 For moving
through sand 8 Marine worm
9 Tuna is the only fish 10 5 kg
(11 lb)

239

1 United Kingdom 2 Brazil
3 Cyprus 4 Crust 5 Turkey
6 United States and United
Kingdom 7 The Cedar of
Lebanon 8 Vancouver
9 Venezuela 10 Germany

BACKGROUND BONUS:
The Wailing Wall

240

1 Microscope 2 Muscles
3 A dentist 4 ECG
(electrocardiogram) 5 Zinc
6 The Moon 7 The ballpoint
pen 8 Zebra 9 3,600
10 The lungs

BACKGROUND BONUS:
Tulip

241
1 Memphis 2 200 3 Let
4 Athletics 5 Featherweight
6 Seven 7 Ice skating
8 Chess 9 Persia
10 Ché Guevara

242
1 Troilus and Cressida 2 Arthur
Conan Doyle 3 The Great Gatsby
4 Pangram 5 Enid Bagnold
6 Robert Burns 7 Shirley
8 Lolita 9 Herbert Ernest
10 Puddleby on Marsh

243
1 The Seventh Cavalry 2 Sir
Thomas More 3 The Nile
4 Tower Bridge 5 Bangladesh
6 Wall paintings 7 The Pacific
Ocean 8 An early submarine
9 France 10 The Philippines

244
1 Julius Caesar 2 Fester
3 Jackie 4 James Doohan
5 Tommy Lee Jones 6 Jean-
Claude Van Damme
7 Helicopter 8 Ruth Ellis
9 Dennis Potter 10 Jennifer
Aniston

245
1 Up to 25,000 2 Cuba 3 It
cleans up wounds on fish
4 The grizzly bear 5 It needs
sunlight to live 6 The cattle
egret 7 In the father's throat
8 The giant spider crab
9 The llama 10 The vulture
BACKGROUND BONUS:
The dromedary camel

246
1 Japan 2 A greyhound 3 11
4 Racketball 5 Silver 6 A bear
7 Virginia Wade 8 La Paz Golf
Club, Bolivia 9 Discus
10 Alfa Romeo

247
1 Saturn 2 The Montgolfier
brothers 3 Burning 4 Cancer
5 Water 6 The Tropic of
Capricorn 7 Revolutions per
Minute 8 Bicep and tricep
9 The revolver 10 Pulleys

248
1 African elephants 2 On the
Moon 3 To catch their prey
4 Norway, Sweden and
Denmark 5 The Moon hides
the Sun from the Earth
6 To admit defeat 7 Roald
Dahl 8 Golf 9 D-Day
10 Cutlery

249
1 Napoleon 2 Queen Victoria
3 New Amsterdam
4 Galapagos Islands
5 Socrates 6 On Venus
7 Ancient Egypt
8 The Apostles 9 Robert
Menzies 10 The Western
(Wailing) Wall

250
1 Stephen King 2 Piglet
3 Limp 4 Fox 5 A round
domed building 6 Ballot
7 D.H. Lawrence 8 A boat
9 In the year of our Lord
10 Trees

BACKGROUND BONUS:
Driving Miss Daisy

251
1 Old Trafford had been
bombed 2.They refused to
wear boots 3 David O'Leary
4 Crown Paints 5 Gianluca
Vialli 6 Arsenal 7 Gerd Muller
8 Barcelona 9 Liberian
10 Alan Ball

252
1 Schilling 2 Chile 3 Darwin
4 Portugal 5 South Korea
6 American 7 Reservoir
8 China 9 Mali 10 Sri Lanka

253
1 Hulk 2 Audie Murphy
3 Kathleen Turner 4 Dirty
Dancing 5 Tomorrow Never Dies
6 Teenage Mutant Ninja Turtles
7 Tootsie 8 Archibald Leach
9 Tommy 10 Joe Pesci

BACKGROUND BONUS:
Sinbad and the Eye of the Tiger

254
1 Elton John 2 Jimi Hendrix
3 Jay Kay (Jamiroquai)
4 Nat King Cole 5 Missy Elliott
6 Justin Timberlake
7 Prince 8 Pink 9 Gloria
Estefan 10 Tina Turner

255
1 Sioux 2 R.F. Scott 3 Trafalgar
4 The Chinese 5 Hirohito of
Japan 6 William Golding
7 The Alamo 8 Champagne
9 Victoria Falls 10 John Alcock
and Arthur Brown

256
1 Jaws 2 The Elbe 3 Goldie
Hawn 4 A vein 5 Salvation
Army 6 Juniper berries
7 The fugu fish 8 A bird
9 Brazil 10 Samuel Beckett

257
1 12 2 Women's Tennis
Association 3 Virginia Wade
4 Snowboarding 5 Show
jumping 6 San Francisco
49ers 7 Crown green bowling
8 Budgerigars 9 Marbles
10 Ferrari
BACKGROUND BONUS:
Catcher

258
1 Black Beauty 2 Gerald Durrell
3 Twelfth Night 4 I forbid
5 Newspeak 6 Seraphim
7 Kephalonia 8 Far From the
Madding Crowd 9 All the vowels
appear in order 10 A toasted
ham and cheese sandwich

259
1 The tongue 2 Mace 3 Atoll
4 Frets 5 The Edge of Reason
6 Richard III 7 Selective
breeding 8 In secret 9 Dante
10 Verona

260
1 Egg yolk 2 The
hippopotamus 3 3,600
4 A chronometer 5 Peru
6 Wolfgang Amadeus Mozart
7 Budapest 8 Aphrodite 9 An
Arab sailing ship 10 A square

261

1 Wile E. Coyote 2 Eucalyptus
3 Jenny 4 Scorpion (Scorpio)
5 Fly 6 Rhesus monkey
7 A venomous tree snake
8 Badger 9 Ferret 10 Five

BACKGROUND BONUS:
Daffodil

262

1 An ulcer 2 90 (it is one
quarter of a circle) 3 A grain
grown in warm climates
4 The same 5 Photography
6 In your brain 7 Vocal cords
8 Iron 9 Cell division
10 Static electricity

263

1 Belgium 2 Lobster
3 The Indian Ocean 4 Brussels
5 A bird 6 Iraq 7 Jambalaya
8 A wind gauge 9 Mexico City
10 Fleece

264

1 Augustus Caesar
2 Elephants 3 15th century
4 Venice 5 1990 6 They all
abdicated 7 The Channel
Tunnel 8 The 8th century
9 China 10 Baines

265

1 Loss of memory 2 Jupiter,
Uranus and Neptune
3 One-fifth 4 In a flower
5 Read-Only Memory
6 A hearing test 7 The joints
8 1,000 9 Imperial 10 Kidney

BACKGROUND BONUS:
The space shuttle

266

1 Digital monsters 2 Jodie
Foster 3 Robbie Coltrane
4 Jurassic Park 5 Humphrey
Bogart 6 Russia 7 Eygpt
8 Wall Street 9 Woody Allen
10 A woodpecker

267

1 Wolfgang Amadeus Mozart
2 Cambodia 3 Abraham
4 Alfred 5 Giant 6 Iguana
7 Michael 8 Jack Lemmon
9 Kathy Bates 10 The banjo

268

1 Athens 2 Austin 3 Turkey
4 Lotus 5 Uganda 6 Arizona
7 Sudan 8 Honshu
9 Copenhagen 10 Bath

BACKGROUND BONUS:
Mosque

269

1 Italy 2 Columbus
3 Two minutes 4 Australian
Aboriginals 5 Arthur Miller
6 She was executed by
guillotine 7 Jefferson 8 Chile
9 Canterbury Cathedral
10 Beijing

270

1 The elf owl 2 The gourd fruit
3 The octopus 4 The Arctic fox
5 The spine-tailed swift, timed
at 160 km/h (99 mph) 6 Two
point forward and two back on
each foot 7 Badger 8 Octopus
9 The pika 10 It reaches 100 m
(328 ft) tall

271

1 Mercury 2 In a joint
3 Germany (about 80 million
people) 4 The Danube
5 Napoleon, in 1821 6 0.333
7 Dragonfly 8 Sierra Leone
9 Tears 10 Eire

272

1 Sri Lanka 2 Bolivia
3 Australia 4 Tourism
5 Fortress 6 Mexico
7 Wyoming 8 Port au Prince
9 Oslo 10 Prague, the rest are
German cities

273

1 The Smurfs 2 Lionel Richie
3 Lenny Kravitz 4 Prince
5 Paul McCartney 6 Leo Sayer
7 Madness 8 Aretha Franklin
9 LL Cool J 10 New Kids on
the Block

BACKGROUND BONUS:
Violin

274

1 Javelin 2 Camel
3 Gymnasium 4 The king
5 12th dan (white)
6 Pete Sampras 7 Grass court
8 Curling 9 Three
10 Czechoslovakia

275

1 1920s (1928) 2 Squash
3 Fancier 4 Running 5 Turin
6 Kurt Angle 7 Golf 8 Oliver
McCall 9 Eric Liddell
10 Lindsay Davenport

276

1 New Zealand 2 Ted Danson
3 Twiggy 4 Beau Bridges
5 Morgan Freeman
6 Madonna 7 Pizza 8 Casino
Royale 9 Julia Roberts
10 Drew Barrymore

BACKGROUND BONUS:
Greta Garbo

277

1 The telescope 2 Egypt
3 World War I 4 The Amazons
(Greek women warriors)
5 Portugal 6 Conquistadors
7 Nelson Mandela 8 Russia
9 Eisenhower 10 Finnish

278

1 Oxygen 2 Boot 3 Mars
4 The blades 5 SOS 6 Five
7 49 8 A marine biologist
9 One-ninth 10 Heart disease

279

1 The Periodic Table of
Elements 2 Zero 3 The mouse
4 Arteries 5 Bones and teeth
6 The battery 7 Pluto
8 The Mesozoic 9 Salty
10 200 billion

280

1 Host 2 Little Women 3 They
read the same forward and
backward 4 John Steinbeck
5 Samuel Pepys 6 Kathakali
7 Roofs 8 A homonym
9 Hasty 10 John Milton

BACKGROUND BONUS:
Cloud

281
1 The Tower of London 2 Peru
3 Cactus 4 The Indian Ocean
5 Genoa 6 Morocco 7 Norway
8 Holland 9 Switzerland
10 Quebec

282
1 Greece 2 Chairman Mao
3 Alternating current or AC
4 About 4.5 billion years old
5 Iceland 6 The statue of
Christ 7 The Victory 8 One
9 Perseus 10 Persia

283
1 Freddie Mercury
2 Trombone 3 1981
4 "Red, Red Wine" 5 Bill
Wyman 6 Edward Elgar
7 India 8 Saxophone 9 Moulin
Rouge 10 Fleetwood Mac

284
1 Nomads 2 New Zealand
3 A snail 4 The pointed teeth
or eye teeth 5 Istanbul
6 They are all poultry
7 Postpone 8 Radiation
9 Libya 10 The War of the
Roses

285
1 Simón Bolívar 2 Count
3 55BC 4 The kidney
5 Belgium 6 Geronimo
7 Joan of Arc 8 Six
9 Cowboys 10 Royal Air Force

BACKGROUND BONUS:
Big Ben

286
1 Rocky Marciano 2 12
3 Cuban 4 The yips
5 The vertical rows 6 The
Olympic flag 7 International
Cricket Conference
8 Heptathlon 9 Polo
10 Pam Shriver

287
1 A boar 2 Moths 3 Cartilage
4 Elephants (tusks are large
incisors) 5 Gannet 6 Whelp
7 Sperm whale 8 Marlin
9 The Amazon 10 Carp

BACKGROUND BONUS:
The lotus

288
1 Abyssinia 2 Hong Kong
3 The Atlantic Ocean 4 Sitting
Bull 5 Saint Cuthbert
6 Saudi Arabia 7 A rifle
8 Oscar Wilde 9 England
and France 10 Parliament

289
1 Royal tombs 2 Rodents
3 An arc 4 An English painter
5 Judaism 6 St. Petersburg
7 Portuguese 8 Flax
9 Please turn over
10 Roman poets

290
1 Dr. Evil 2 Jim Morrison
3 Jumping Jack Flash
4 Betty Rubble 5 Conspiracy
Theory 6 Annie Get Your Gun
7 Friday the 13th 8 Dave
9 Groundhog Day 10 Blade

291
1 Bjorn Borg 2 Massachusetts
3 Payne Stewart 4 Lost a shoe
5 The bar 6 Target practice
7 Scotland (St. Andrews)
8 Standard Scratch Score
9 Houston 10 Fishing

BACKGROUND BONUS:
110 m hurdles

292
1 The tomb bat 2 Giraffe
3 Madagascar 4 Aardvark
5 African antelopes 6 Murder
7 Eel 8 Boobies 9 Turkey
10 Worms

293
1 (d) 2 (i) 3 (j) 4 (c) 5 (b)
6 (h) 7 (e) 8 (g) 9 (f) 10 (a)

294
1 Pablo Picasso 2 The Black
Death 3 Protein 4 Las Vegas
5 Robert Louis Stevenson
6 The sea lion 7 Illegal
8 The English Civil War
9 Canada 10 Latvia and
Lithuania

295
1 Norway 2 All Saints 3 Ennio
Morricone 4 "I Believe I Can
Fly" 5 The Graduate 6 Grace
Jones 7 Kris Kristofferson and
Barbra Streisand 8 Elton John
9 Prince 10 Gladys Knight

296
1 Quentin Tarantino
2 The Sting 3 Die Hard
4 Patrick Duffy 5 The Santa
Clause 6 Max Von Sydow
7 Fred Astaire 8 Back to the
Future 9 Will Smith
10 Long John Silver

297
1 Walker Brothers 2 Romeo and
Juliet 3 John Travolta 4 1970
5 Composer 6 Billie Holiday
7 Frank Lloyd Wright 8 Stevie
Wonder 9 Hans Solo
10 Photocopier machine

BACKGROUND BONUS:
Typewriter

298
1 Ty Cobb 2 1984 3 Falconry
4 In a plane crash 5 Twelve
(ten in a men's) 6 John
McEnroe 7 Steve Redgrave
8 Pontoon 9 James Hunt
10 Softball

299
1 Binoculars 2 Your windpipe
3 21 June 4 A meteor 5 Solid
carbon dioxide 6 The pressure
of the atmosphere 7 Hydrogen
8 Sheep 9 Water 10 Hour-
glass

300
1 Canada and the United
States 2 Israel and Jordan
3 Seattle 4 Zagreb 5 Ice cap
6 Greece 7 Ecuador
8 Estonia, Latvia and Lithuania
9 Icicle 10 Europe

BACKGROUND BONUS:
Devil's Garden

301

1 Alice Springs 2 Aladdin
3 A severe prolonged headache
4 Mime 5 The Mississippi
6 The shuttle 7 Islamabad
8 A thermostat 9 Insincerity
10 The Samurai

302

1 Anne 2 The feeding of the
five thousand 3 The Star of
Bethlehem 4 Simon
5 Judaism 6 The end 7 Israel
8 The Garden of Gethsemane
9 Robert Powell 10 The Ten
Commandments

303

1 Max 2 Sally Field 3 *Batman
Returns* 4 Robert Wagner
5 Alistair Sim 6 *The Weakest
Link* 7 Mel Gibson 8 "Who
Wants to be a Millionaire"
9 *White Christmas* 10 *Return of
the Jedi*

304

1 A stopwatch 2 The gall
bladder 3 A rhombus
4 Magnetism 5 Geology 6 The
World Wildlife Fund 7 Print
out a computer file on to paper
8 A peninsula 9 Ear, nose and
throat 10 The brain
BACKGROUND BONUS:
Exhaust fumes

305

1 Elton John 2 Barcelona
3 Tord Grip 4 Ibrox Stadium
5 Brazil 6 Bulgaria 7 Hornets
8 Titi Camara 9 Geoff Hurst,
in 1966 10 Andres Escobar

306

1 The kestrel 2 Meat-eaters
3 By cleaning its skin of ticks
4 The Arab 5 To survive the
cold 6 True, it sucks in water
organisms 7 The green turtle
8 It hangs by its tail from rocks
9 Bobcat 10 In wetlands
BACKGROUND BONUS:
The bullfrog

307

1 The Philippines 2 The
greater honey guide
3 Rembrandt 4 The Siberian
tiger 5 Walter Scott
6 Helsinki 7 A hydrofoil
8 The baobab tree 9 0.666
recurring (0.67) 10 Flint

308

1 *The Fat of the Land* 2 *Jagged
Little Pill* 3 *The Stone Roses*
4 *Revolver* 5 *Hotel California*
6 *Rumours* 7 *Bat Out of Hell*
8 *Dare* 9 *You've Come a Long
Way, Baby* 10 *Parachutes*

309

1 Martin Luther King
2 Debussy 3 Prussia
4 Bangladesh 5 House of
Plantagenet 6 William Harvey
7 13th century 8 Magna Carta
9 19th century 10 Charles
Lindbergh

310

1 *Cocktail* 2 Rudulph Valentino
3 A pair of eyes 4 Helen
Baxendale 5 Connecticut
6 Jellystone Park 7 *The Graduate*
8 Sean Connery 9 Bill Murray
10 Laura Dern
BACKGROUND BONUS:
*Willy Wonka and the
Chocolate Factory*

311

1 Sharks 2 To absorb oxygen
from water 3 Sheep 4 The
common brownsnake 5 The
opium poppy 6 It takes algae
from rocks with its tongue
7 The coypu 8 The magpie
9 The bottlenose dolphin
10 It grows hairs on its leaves
and stalk

312

1 Andrea Bocelli 2 All were
venues in the United States
3 Tim Henman 4 First day
cover 5 Show jumping
6 A volcanic eruption 7 Mike
Powell 8 Ten points 9 Jana
Novotna 10 Boxing

313

1 Johnny Mathis 2 "That'll Be
the Day 3 Violin 4 "Slow
Hand" 5 "Wake Me Up Before
You Go-Go" 6 Paul Simon
7 Noddy Holder 8 Alvin
Stardust 9 Elvis Presley
10 "Way Down"

314

1 By squeezing and suffocating
it 2 The feet 3 Moscow
4 Yes, like all reptiles
5 Captain James Cook
6 The Solar System 7 Anagram
8 The keystone 9 Hans
Christian Andersen 10 Canada

315

1 Albert Finney 2 Cannes
3 Patrick Stewart
4 The Commitments
5 Christopher Lee 6 Lennox
Lewis 7 Johnny Depp
8 *Jurassic Park* 9 Melanie
Griffith 10 "Summer Nights"

316

1 Venice 2 *The Times*
3 Trappers 4 The Rosetta
Stone 5 Chile 6 Rome and its
emperor 7 Roald Amundsen
8 Seven 9 *Guernica* 10 A type
of musket

BACKGROUND BONUS:
The Capitol Building

317

1 Peru 2 SV Hamburg
3 Fabrizio Ravanelli 4 Bayern
Munich 5 Dino Zoff 6 Italy
7 Michel Platini 8 Peter
Shilton 9 Bobby Moore
10 Alavés

318

1 A star 2 An omnivore 3 Two
4 Canada 5 Bombay 6 In the
forests of South America
7 Israel 8 Lebanon
9 The Aztecs 10 121

319

1 Humphrey Bogart 2 David
Bowie 3 Louis Braille
4 John Milton 5 Christian Dior
6 Edvard Munch 7 Mary
Shelley 8 Anton Chekhov
9 P.G. Wodehouse
10 John Adams
BACKGROUND BONUS:
Halle Berry

320

1 (f) 2 (a) 3 (d) 4 (g) 5 (c)
6 (h) 7 (i) 8 (j) 9 (b) 10 (e)

321
1 Hologram 2 Quicklime
3 Diamond 4 Steam
5 Athlete's foot 6 A magnetic
compass 7 The skin
8 Nitrogen (78.08%) 9 4
10 The Atlantic

322
1 Seven 2 Lanfranco 3 Paula
Radcliffe 4 Rodeo 5 Ben
Johnson 6 Tonya Harding
7 London 8 Canoeing
9 Boxing 10 Reebok

323
1 Switzerland 2 Quartz
3 Gdansk 4 Somalia 5 Egypt
6 Terracotta army 7 The cod
8 Formosa 9 Rome
10 Alabama, Alaska, Arizona,
Ohio

BACKGROUND BONUS:
Colosseum

324
1 It scavenges along the tide
line 2 No, they are white all
year 3 The rubber tree 4 By
running very fast on its back
legs 5 The rockhopper
penguin 6 Rhinoceros or
goliath beetle 7 A sort of glue
or liquid silk 8 Forests 9 Sea
cow 10 The swift

325
1 In a group 2 To keep cool as
they fan themselves 3 Blood
4 A false scorpion that squirts
vinegar mixture 5 Dense forest
(with streams) 6 The bolas
spider 7 The horseshoe crab
8 The eel 9 The yucca bush
and yucca moth 10 It helps
judge distance

326
1 A vulcanologist 2 Four 3 13
4 Spit 5 The lower half
6 Arthritis 7 Domestic cat
8 Mass 9 Hertz (Hz)
10 A dentist or dental hygienist

327
1 Tiger Woods 2 Spain 3 Ascot
4 Olga Korbut 5 New York
6 Japan 7 Every four years
8 Slalom 9 Roger Bannister
10 Pulled up

BACKGROUND BONUS:
Tennis

328
1 Yes (Two, Deimos and
Phobos) 2 Sea 3 At the
southern tip of Africa 4 John
Bunyan 5 Seaweed 6 Marilyn
Monroe 7 Seven 8 Orders of
architecture 9 Charleton
Heston 10 Oberon

329
1 *Gremlins* 2 *Sabrina the Teenage
Witch* 3 Jerry Lee Lewis
4 Whoopi Goldberg 5 *Gone in
60 Seconds* 6 James Cameron
7 *It's a Wonderful Life* 8 Honor
Blackman 9 Chevy Chase
10 *Silence of the Lambs*

330
1 Squids and octopuses
2 Cricket 3 Beatrix Potter
4 Black hole 5 Four 6 Jackal
7 Queen Elizabeth I, the Virgin
Queen 8 Mackerel
9 Tinkerbell 10 Blood

331
1 On the tail fin 2 Vinyl 3 120
4 Swim bladder 5 Lever
6 Battery 7 Earthquakes
8 Connecting devices to a
computer 9 An astronomer
10 Fingernails and toenails

BACKGROUND BONUS:
Weather map

332
1 Arthur Sullivan 2 Uruguay
3 1990 4 James I (Jamestown)
5 William Wallace
6 The Medici family
7 *The Titanic* 8 Stormin'
Norman 9 Louis XIV
10 The Somme

333
1 Joan of Arc 2 Sandra Bullock
3 Puccini 4 Queensberry 5 Sir
Walter Raleigh 6 Franklin D.
Roosevelt 7 Richard D'Oyly
Carte 8 (Jawaharlal) Nehru
9 Miguel de Cervantes
10 Nicolas Copernicus

334
1 "Back to Life" 2 Boyz II Men
3 Joan Armatrading 4 Janet
Jackson 5 The Temptations
6 Michael McDonald 7 Patrice
Rushen 8 Seal 9 Shola Ama
10 Kim Weston

BACKGROUND BONUS:
Bagpipes

335
1 A clock 2 The dormouse
3 A vein 4 The Korean War
5 *The Birds* 6 10 Rillington
Place 7 Talcum powder
8 Vixen 9 Boeing 747
10 Tiberuis

336
1 *The Green Mile* 2 Peter Ustinov
3 Wellington 4 Antonio
Banderas 5 Kirk Douglas
6 Psychiatrist 7 Laurence
Fishburne 8 Goldmember
9 Zulu 10 Geoffrey Chaucer

337
1 The Quakers 2 The Peasants'
Revolt 3 John Lennon
4 Richard III 5 Israel
6 Tamerlane 7 St. Helena
8 Israel 9 Piano (and
orchestra) 10 *Henry VIII*

338
1 Axis 2 Blood types
3 A bomber 4 Negative
5 Fermentation 6 Dynamite
7 Sonar 8 Oxidation
9 Genetics 10 37°C (98.6°F)

339
1 Madonna 2 Cosi Fan Tutte
3 Trumpet 4 Contralto
5 Hungarian 6 Aretha Franklin
7 Bono 8 Bob Marley 9 The
Sex Pistols 10 *Guys and Dolls*

340
1 The process of wearing away
2 Indian Ocean 3 Cairns
4 North America
5 Continental drift 6 Chad
7 Salt Lake City 8 Germany
9 Florence, Italy 10 The jaguar

BACKGROUND BONUS:
Golden Gate bridge

341
1 Ava Gardner 2 Iris
3 Whipped cream 4 Jellyfish
5 *The Hurricane* 6 Dogs 7 Neil
Simon 8 The ankle 9 Dallas
10 Michael Faraday

342
1 The pygmy white-toothed
shrew 2 The oak 3 The orca
4 It wedges its body in a rocky
crevice 5 By coiling around
them 6 It harasses other birds
7 100 years 8 Meat-eater
9 A turtle 10 Gibbons
BACKGROUND BONUS:
African Elephant

343
1 *Awakenings* 2 *Men In Black*
3 George Peppard 4 *Casino
Royale* 5 Charles Bronson
6 *Dead Man Walking*
7 1930s (1937) 8 *Dragnet*
9 Crimean War
10 *The Commitments*

344
1 Spain 2 Mars 3 Kenya
4 Ireland 5 *Apollo 11* 6 Dwight
Eisenhower 7 London 8 The
Angel Falls 9 Bicycle
10 Charles de Gaulle

345
1 Lord Byron 2 Yugoslavia
3 A big two-handled vase
4 Captain Hardy 5 The Iron
Curtain 6 Venice
7 The Spice Islands 8 Tibet
9 Tombstone, Arizona
10 Scurvy

346
1 Dana Carvey 2 *Platoon*
3 *Lawrence of Arabia*
4 Warren Beatty 5 *Yentl*
6 Roddy McDowall 7 *Billy Elliot*
8 *Babe* 9 Nicholas Cage
10 *Carrie*

BACKGROUND BONUS:
101 Dalmations

347
1 Giant's Causeway 2 Uluru
3 Iguaçu Falls 4 Mount
Kilimanjaro 5 Grand Canyon
6 Rio de Janeiro 7 Guilin
Pinnacles 8 The Rock of
Gibraltar 9 The Great Barrier
Reef 10 Mount Fuji

348
1 The bison 2 So they can
pursue prey into burrows
3 Fish 4 In pockets of skin
in the mother's back
5 The dome-web spider 6 By
unhinging its jaws 7 Their
calls sound like a hammer on
metal 8 The cicada 9 Both
10 Centipedes and millipedes

349
1 *Urban Hymns* (The Verve)
2 *The Young Soul Rebels*
3 Two 4 Def Leppard
5 Otis Blue 6 Frankie Goes
to Hollywood 7 Culture Club
8 Genesis 9 Sheryl Crow
10 Gabrielle

350
1 One-third 2 Jute 3 Mecca
4 European Union 5 Active
volcano 6 Atlantic Ocean
7 South China Sea
8 Fossils 9 Lancashire
10 Tokyo

BACKGROUND BONUS:
Rainforest

351
1 The kookaburra 2 The owl
3 Venus de Milo 4 Great soul
5 The character & 6 A hard
jet-black wood 7 Acupuncture
8 Quickly 9 National
Aeronautics and Space
Administration
10 Scotland's independence

352
1 Antwerp 2 St. Louis (1904)
3 The slope of the green
4 1,500 m 5 1987 6 The blue
ring 7 1996 8 Denver Broncos
9 Anna Kournikova 10 Pat
Cash

BACKGROUND BONUS:
Rowing

353
1 The Mikado 2 Britain
3 Pianoforte 4 Sardinia
5 Quinto, Ecuador 6 Tin and
lead 7 Erosion 8 *A Comedy of
Errors* 9 Rose 10 A prehistoric
flying reptile

354
1 Italy and Switzerland
2 Damascus 3 Ghana
4 Shanghai 5 Abyssal plain
6 Tokyo 7 Tripoli
8 Afghanistan and Pakistan
9 The Rhine river 10 Brazil

355
1 Wat Tyler 2 Opera singing
3 Polish 4 Prison reform
5 Georges Bizet 6 Orson
Welles 7 Canada 8 Admiral
Jellicoe 9 John Knox 10 Edgar
Degas

356
1 Mount Kilimanjaro
2 Mezzo-soprano 3 Jackson
Pollock 4 Naphthalene
5 Brass 6 Phnom Penh
7 Ballet 8 *Friends* 9 A lizard
10 Eastern Africa

357
1 Avril Lavigne 2 England
3 The Foo Fighters 4 Moby
5 Cypress Hill 6 David Gray
7 Radiohead 8 Chuck Berry
9 Bill Haley & the Comets
10 Jimi Hendrix

358
1 1963 2 Sulphur 3 200
4 M 5 The ear 6 CFC gases
7 DNA 8 Trigonometry
9 Mars 10 Water

359
1 Mexico 2 South Africa
3 Afrikaans 4 "Wild Bill"
Hitchcock 5 Zulus 6 1948
7 Guitar 8 The American Civil
War 9 Portugal 10 Enrico
Ferni

BACKGROUND BONUS:
Stonehenge

360
1 Heat energy 2 Ligaments
3 Magnetic levitation
4 Human hearing 5 Lava
6 The speed of sound in the air
7 The liver 8 256 9 Liquid
Crystal Display 10 Wood pulp

BACKGROUND BONUS:
Jupiter

361
1 Goran Ivanisevic 2 Maurice Greene 3 Fanny Blankers-Koen 4 Lindsay Davenport 5 Australia 6 Steve Cauthen 7 Australia 8 Martina Navratilova 9 Greece 10 Four

362
1 Austria 2 The Mini 3 Victor Hugo 4 True 5 Dutch 6 George VI 7 Groucho 8 Missionary 9 United States (Yellowstone) 10 He was a journalist

363
1 Supertramp 2 The Doors 3 Kool and the Gang 4 Al Green 5 The Tourists 6 Roxy Music 7 Harold Melvin and the Bluenotes 8 Neil Sedaka 9 T. Rex 10 Dr. Hook

364
1 Ito 2 Alcohol 3 Jimmy Young 4 Pittsburgh 5 Deep vein thrombosis 6 Opposum 7 A Scottish poet 8 Less 9 Old people 10 Rockets

365
1 Tarantula 2 A star 3 The heart 4 Krypton 5 100 degrees 6 The bones 7 They are all birds that cannot fly 8 Sir Isaac Newton 9 In a flower 10 Jupiter, Uranus and Neptune

366
1 The flower resembles a bee 2 Four 3 The St. Bernard 4 The piranha 5 To reflect sunlight and avoid overheating 6 The albatross 7 Seahorse 8 A hoofed mammal 9 Bird 10 The duck-billed platypus
BACKGROUND BONUS:
Trumpeter swan

367
1 The Ford Model-T 2 1990 3 Carl Fabergé 4 Mexico 5 Cassius Clay 6 Cambodia 7 1888 8 Mozart 9 An ass's jawbone 10 Dive-bomber

368
1 Wyatt Earp 2 *Hawaii 5 0* 3 *The Piano* 4 *Gladiator* 5 *Airforce One* 6 Robert Altman 7 John Wayne 8 *Star Trek* 9 Jackie 10 Dr. Doug Ross

BACKGROUND BONUS:
The Beach

369
1 Gulliver 2 Portuguese man o' war 3 Because it reflects light from the Sun 4 Benito Mussolini 5 Air pressure 6 World War I 7 A cloud that forms close to the ground 8 Soccer 9 Struck 10 Mercury

370
1 Jupiter 2 On a sailing boat (a type of sail) 3 The way plants can be grown for food 4 Blood pressure 5 Copper 6 Rock fragments 7 They split the atom 8 Urine 9 One-eighth 10 20 cm (8 in)

371
1 The hare 2 The dragonfly 3 A salamander 4 A poisonous plant 5 The elephant 6 Bamboo 7 After its call 8 Drags fish from the surface of the water 9 It anchors it to rocks 10 The dandelion

372
1 Salome 2 The Gold Rush 3 France 4 Trumpet 5 Ragtime 6 Julius Caesar 7 The Jordan 8 World War I 9 On his chest and back 10 The first successful hot-air balloon

BACKGROUND BONUS:
Taj Mahal

373
1 *Big* 2 *Tiger* 3 Errol Flynn 4 "Ol' Blue Eyes" 5 Angelica Huston 6 *Flatliners* 7 *Chitty Chitty Bang Bang* 8 *The Full Monty* 9 Billy Connolly 10 Chris O'Donnell

374
1 (b) 2 (j) 3 (e) 4 (f) 5 (c) 6 (g) 7 (d) 8 (i) 9 (h) 10 (a)

375
1 William Blake 2 Maureen Connolly 3 Rossini 4 Ceylon (1960 to 65) 5 Buffalo Bill 6 Thomas Paine 7 Noah Webster 8 Michelangelo 9 Joseph Heller 10 The Rubik Cube
BACKGROUND BONUS:
Mrs. Peacock

376
1 The U.S. Stock Market 2 Spain 3 Polar bear 4 North and South America 5 Robert Scott 6 Gives technical details about a crime 7 The invasion of England in 1066 8 At the southern tip of South America 9 It collects radio waves from space 10 Ozone layer

377
1 The Beatles 2 The atomic bomb 3 Augustine 4 1959 5 Wales 6 1936 7 Portugal 8 The Rolling Stones 9 Rossini 10 Growing miniature trees

378
1 Four 2 1984, Los Angeles 3 Moon ball 4 "The Gentle Way" 5 Moon Ballad 6 Joe DiMaggio 7 May 8 Yachting 9 Squash 10 Pelé

379
1 Only one of its kind 2 The caterpillar 3 10 4 24 5 It kills bacteria 6 Hannibal 7 Islam 8 Albert Einstein 9 The Crimean War 10 A fiord

380
1 Rio de Janiero 2 Gross National Product 3 Uganda 4 Lake Ontario 5 Coal 6 The Cuban Peso 7 Kingston 8 They are two of the world's driest places 9 France 10 Germany
BACKGROUND BONUS:
Kenya

381
1 Denmark 2 1930 3 Portugal
4 Juventus 5 Monaco 6 Parma
7 Chelsea 8 Celtic 9 Terry
Venables 10 Notts County

382
1 Ernest Hemmingway
2 Contour 3 Romeo and Juliet
4 Toto 5 K 6 Helen Fielding
7 Fish 8 San Francisco 9 M
10 Captain Ahab

383
1 Atlanta 2 Lake Lucerne
3 The Temple of Angkor
4 River Arno 5 Pelican
6 Paris 7 Zambia 8 Alderney
9 Christchurch 10 Sudan

384
1 The Vikings 2 Ben Hur
3 The Ten Commandments
4 Hera 5 Victor Mature
6 Spartacus 7 The Emperor
Nero 8 Gone with the Wind
9 E.M. Forster
10 Ralph Fiennes

385
1 It uses its nose as a snorkel
2 They glide on large pectoral
fins 3 The ostrich 4 A wild cat
5 The teasel 6 Because it hops
on its back legs 7 The remora
8 The leatherback turtle
9 *Triceratops* 10 The tiger beetle
BACKGROUND BONUS:
Bison

386
1 They ate it (it was dried
meat) 2 Canada 3 To kill
germs and prevent infection
4 The American Civil War
5 Napoleon 6 They slept in
them 7 Horsepower 8 1978
9 Amelia Earhart
10 Benjamin Britten

387
1 Dance 2 Potatoes 3 Polo
4 Uranus 5 Ecology
6 The Pilgrim Fathers
7 Greenland 8 Frances
Hodgson Burnett
9 The strength of the wind
10 The freezing point
BACKGROUND BONUS:
Mir

388
1 "No drink" 2 The orangutan
3 The bee hummingbird
4 A breed of dog 5 The sperm
whale 6 By stamping on them
and pecking 7 Monkey 8 True
9 The Antiguan racer
10 The saguaro cactus

389
1 An alloy of copper
2 Six (3, 6, 9, 12, 15, 18)
3 The heart 4 Camels
5 Petroleum 6 We walk on
two legs 7 Orbit 8 Thomas
Alva Edison 9 Eczema
10 Ayers Rock

390
1 Newmarket 2 Two
3 Munich 4 300 5 London
6 Judo 7 Mexico
8 When it's taking another
piece 9 Squash 10 France

391
1 Berne 2 The Commonwealth
3 Edmund Hillary and Tensing
Norgay 4 Oxygen and
hydrogen 5 Teeth 6 14
7 Guangzhou 8 The queen
9 The python, up to 10 m
(33 ft) long 10 Lady Jane Grey

392
1 Cygnus 2 Infra-red 3 Scalpel
4 The fossilised sap of conifers
5 Antarctica 6 15 7 Hydrogen
8 Alternating current 9 A front
10 Time

393
1 The Gulf of Mexico
2 Australia 3 Source
4 Swedish 5 U.S.A.
6 On a shoreline 7 Venice
8 Scafell Pike 9 Madrid
10 Amirtsar, India

394
1 Roland Garros 2 Seven
minutes 3 Seville 4 Canada
5 Argentinian 6 Athens
7 Switzerland 8 Three
9 Antwerp 10 Brazilian

BACKGROUND BONUS:
Ice hockey

395
1 Orson Wells 2 Eight
3 The Waltons 4 Cycling
5 U.S. police force
6 Tom Hanks
7 Cool Hand Luke
8 Jack Nicholson
9 Calamity Jane 10 New York

396
1 "True" 2 "La Bamba"
3 The Housemartins
4 Susanna Hoffs 5 Paul Young
6 Enya 7 Sheena Easton
8 Prefab Sprout 9 Herge's
Adventures of Tintin 10 1983

BACKGROUND BONUS:
The Eagles

397
1 Snow leopard 2 Deer
3 Narwhal 4 Praying mantis
5 Regents Park 6 One
7 Coypu 8 Rafter
9 Lemur 10 Hummingbird

398
1 Advocaat 2 Vanilla Ice
3 Elias Howe 4 Edvard Grieg
5 Light intensity 6 The Volga
7 A mole 8 1950s (1951)
9 Seven 10 Talk in their sleep

399
1 Card games 2 *Voyager 2*
3 Lymph glands 4 Indigestion
5 Cape Town 6 Richard
Attenborough 7 On the foot
(it is a sock) 8 Fox 9 Wise
man 10 Aries (the Ram)

400
1 Dennis Wheatley 2 *1984*
3 *David Copperfield* 4 *The Dirty
Dozen* 5 Richard Adams
6 Ron Moody 7 *The Great Gatsby*
8 *A Clockwork Orange*
9 *Schindler's Ark* 10 *Kidnapped*

401
1 Mark Twain 2 Hanover
3 Cadbury 4 Albert Schweitzer
5 Delibes 6 Isadora Duncan
7 Wilkie Collins (in *The
Moonstone*) 8 Sigmund Freud
9 Sir Isaac Pitman
10 Edwin Land

402
1 The throat 2 Hydrogen
3 The small intestine
4 Copper and tin 5 Oxygen
6 Eyes (and vision) 7 40 cm
(16 in) 8 Respiratory 9 The
atomic bomb 10 Vitamin A

BACKGROUND BONUS:
Wind power

403
1 *The X-Files* 2 House of Elliott
3 A heart 4 Scott Bakula
5 Moscow 6 Bob Dylan
7 Linda Gray 8 *Lady sings the
Blues* 9 Sir Elton John and Tim
Rice 10 Whoopi Goldberg

404
1 Tin 2 MM 3 The Dragon
4 Salt Lake City
5 The hummingbird
6 The Booker Prize
7 Folkestone 8 Engelbert
Humperdinck
9 Robin Knox-Johnston
10 The tail

405
1 Basketball 2 The triple jump
3 Four years old 4 Adolf Hitler
5 The British Open 6 The
asymmetric bars 7 Skiing
8 Hockenheim 9 Canoeing
10 When leading the race

BACKGROUND BONUS:
Horse racing

406
1 (Vladimir Ilyich) Lenin
2 Richard III 3 Charlotte
Brontë 4 Sir Humphry Davy
5 Tchaikovsky 6 John
Constable 7 Sir Alexander
Fleming 8 She was the first
woman in space 9 Martin
Luther 10 Hans Christian
Andersen

407
1 Acts 2 A heart 3 Mississippi
4 It has flippers 5 Ellery Queen
6 Italy 7 Heraldry 8 Lorgnette
9 Four 10 Bees

408
1 Toontown 2 Thomas 3 Anne
Archer 4 Charlton Heston
5 *Fiddler on the Roof* 6 Kevin
Costner 7 James Gandolfini
8 Shirley Bassey 9 *The Daily
Planet* 10 *Monty Python's Flying
Circus*

BACKGROUND BONUS:
The Horse Whisperer

409
1 James Chadwick (1932)
2 Electric charge 3 One-third
4 The ear (a liquid-filled tube)
5 Desert 6 Atmospheric
pressure 7 Early types of
photographs 8 Vertebrae
9 A circuit board
10 Electrical resistance

410
1 Cuba 2 Eddie "The Eagle"
Edwards 3 American football
4 Snowboarding 5 Bobsleigh
6 "Empty hand" 7 Rowing
8 French 9 1991
10 Table tennis

411
1 The Philippines 2 Igor
Sikorsky 3 Spain 4 Yitzhak
Rabin 5 Argentina 6 Leo
Tolstoy 7 Rocket engines
8 Robert Frost 9 Steam, diesel,
electricity 10 Architect

412
1 The first course 2 G.S.
Forester 3 A crash 4 The cat
5 Jane Austen 6 Bacteria
7 Victoria 8 The snake
9 Captain James Cook
10 Brussels

413
1 Golf 2 Carl Lewis 3 Turkey
4 Golf 5 Ski jumping 6 Bob
Beamon 7 Eight 8 Two
9 Yugoslavia 10 Basketball

414
1 An animal that feeds on dead
matter 2 The raven 3 The
Komodo dragon 4 The killer
whale 5 Deadly nightshade
6 *Seismosaurus* 7 Seaweed
8 Jerusalem and globe
9 Raccoon 10 Jurassic
BACKGROUND BONUS:
The hippopotamus

415
1 Euthanasia 2 *Watership Down*
3 Kappa 4 Odalisque
5 Valedictory 6 Wilkie Collins
7 *A Tale of Two Cities* 8 Exmoor
9 Sane, of sound mind
10 *As You Like It*

416
1 Vienna 2 Kula Shaker
3 Sophia Loren
4 "Build Me Up Buttercup"
5 Poland 6 "Vogue" by
Madonna 7 Drums 8 Crystal
Gayle 9 15 10 Geri Halliwell

417
1 The opposite of something
else 2 Almost a month (27.33
days) 3 Ephesus 4 Henry Ford
5 On the Moon 6 Marie Curie
7 Ponderosa 8 Yeast
9 A layer in the atmosphere
10 The Gulf Stream

418
1 Spain 2 .es 3 Copenhagen
4 A group of French-speaking
people from Belgium
5 Glaciers 6 China 7 Iran
8 Romania 9 Moraine
10 Venice

BACKGROUND BONUS:
Arc de Triomphe

419
1 The anther 2 A type of wood
3 Royal jelly 4 On the leg
5 Zebra 6 Mamba 7 Piranha
8 Toucan 9 Finch 10 Horns

420
1 Paris and London
2 Charlie Chaplin 3 Oxygen
and nitrogen 4 Henry V
5 Germany 6 Alexander the
Great 7 Tanks 8 Francisco
Pizarro (1513) 9 Medusa
10 Pacific

421
1 Them 2 Andrea Bocelli
3 "Convoy" 4 James Galway
5 Fern Kinney 6 "Bridge over
Troubled Water" 7 INXS
8 "I Believe in Father
Christmas" 9 "Funkytown"
10 Nirvana
BACKGROUND BONUS:
"A Taste of Honey"

422
1 Strawweight 2 Water skiing
3 Pigeons 4 Trampolining
5 Austrian 6 Hawaii
7 Men's gymnastics
8 A practice shot 9 French
10 Fencing

423
1 The Beach Boys 2 G.I. Blues
3 *A Comedy of Errors* 4 Carlos
Santos 5 Topsy Turvy 6 The
Metropolitan Opera House in
New York 7 Tosca
8 Hungarian 9 Violin
10 *Porgy and Bess*
BACKGROUND BONUS:
Billy Ocean

424
1 The Council of Cardinals
2 The wreck of the Titanic
3 Oliver Cromwell
4 The Foreign Legion
5 Bangkok 6 The Korean War
7 Guernsey 8 Venus de Milo
9 Louisiana
10 The International Red Cross

425
1 Sydney 2 Reykjavik
3 Morocco 4 Naples
5 Deserts 6 Berne 7 Ecuador
8 The Ganges 9 Oslo
10 Puerto Rica

426
1 Matchbox labels 2 Denmark
3 Carrao River 4 Buddhist
5 Baklava 6 Poseidon 7 Wallis
Simpson 8 Van Rijn 9 Rivers,
or running water 10 Mexico

427
1 *Arms And The Man* 2 *Macbeth*
3 *Tess Of The D'urbervilles* 4 Barn
owl 5 *The Prisoner Of Zenda*
6 Lord Peter Wimsey 7 July
8 A bat 9 *Rebecca*
10 Oliver Twist

BACKGROUND BONUS:
Black Coffee

428
1 The back of the head
2 Epsom salts 3 Californium
4 Dreams 5 Cyprus
6 Neptune 7 Fossilized
dinosaur dung 8 White dwarf
9 Ammonia 10 Sedimentary

429
1 Sap 2 China 3 It lays eggs
4 Killer whale 5 Tortoise
6 Starling 7 Marine snails
8 Tortoise 9 Pelican
10 New Zealand

430
1 Hopalong Cassidy 2 Ellen
Corby 3 The Honorary Consul
4 *Moby Dick* 5 *Carousel*
6 Winona Ryder 7 Warner
Brothers 8 Ava Gardner
9 Atlanta 10 *This Sporting Life*

431
1 Theodore Roosevelt and
Woodrow Wilson 2 Cher in the
movie *Moonstruck* 3 Portugal
4 Abraham Lincoln 5 Pablo
Picasso 6 The Battle Of Santa
Cruz 7 Tim Berners-Lee
8 Budapest 9 Gladys Aylward
10 Danish, Jorn Utzon

432
1 Ulysses Grant 2 Cologne
3 El Salvador 4 Norwegian
5 Canoeing 6 *Ivanhoe* 7 Duma
8 Madame Butterfly
9 Calcutta 10 Honduras

BACKGROUND BONUS:
Buddhism

433
1 Rowing 2 Rome in 1960
3 Dwight Davis 4 New York
Knickerbockers 5 St. Louis in
the U.S. in 1904 6 Jai Alai
7 A swimming pool
8 Dressage 9 1936 Berlin
Olympics 10 Massachusetts

434
1 Joseph 2 Two 3 The Book of
Revelation 4 An angel
5 The Books of Wisdom
6 Simon the Sorcerer
7 Forty years 8 The Acts of the
Apostles 9 Pigs 10 Death

435
1 Cats 2 Combustion
3 The calf muscle 4 William
Harvey 5 In the rings of Saturn
6 Water 7 Storm 8 On the
palm of the hand 9 The corner
of the eye 10 They were the
first test tube twins

436
1 The Spanish Civil War
2 Yugoslavia 3 The Boer War
4 Dutch 5 Ronald Reagan
6 Benjamin Franklin
7 He crowned himself
8 The Korean War 9 Saint
Francis of Assissi 10 1930

437
1 Brussels 2 Montreal
3 The Caspian Sea 4 Arabic
5 Beijing, Imperial Palace
6 Sicily 7 Tahiti 8 Oil fields
9 Rhodes 10 Mount Elbert

BACKGROUND BONUS:
Iguaçu Falls

438
1 Jester 2 Jennifer Warnes
3 Lionel Richie 4 Billy Fury
5 James Brown 6 Mack the
Knife 7 "Moonlight Serenade"
8 Sade 9 H.G. Wells, the novel
being *Kipps* 10 Radio
Corporation Of America

THE ULTIMATE QUIZ KIT

First published in 2005 by Miles Kelly Publishing Ltd
Bardfield Centre, Great Bardfield, Essex, CM7 4SL

Copyright © Miles Kelly Publishing Ltd 2005

Some material in *The Ultimate Quiz Kit* first appeared in
Quiz Night © 2001 by Miles Kelly Publishing

2 4 6 8 10 9 7 5 3 1

Publishing Director: Anne Marshall

Designer: Tom Slemmings

Concept Cover Design: Warris Kidwai

Reprographics: Anthony Cambray, Mike Coupe, Stephan Davis, Ian Paulyn

The publishers would like to thank the following for their help
in preparing this publication: CYP Ltd, Caroline Kelly, Ian Paulyn,
Ned Miles, Juliet Rees, Chris Rigby

ISBN 1-84236-639-4

Printed in China

British Library Cataloguing-in-Publication Data
A catalogue record for this book is available from the British Library

www.mileskelly.net
info@mileskelly.net